GERMAN

A ROUGH GUIDE DICTIONARY PHRASEBOOK

Credits

Compiled by Lexus with Horst Kopleck
Lexus Series Editor: Sally Davies
Rough Guides Phrase Book Editor: Jonathan Buckley
Rough Guides Series Editor: Mark Ellingham

First edition published in 1995 by Rough Guides Ltd,
62–70 Shorts Gardens, London WC2H 9AB.
Reprinted in 1996, 1997 and 1998.
Revised in 1999.

Distributed by the Penguin Group.

Penguin Books Ltd, 27 Wrights Lane, London W8 5TZ
Penguin Books USA Inc., 375 Hudson Street, New York 10014, USA
Penguin Books Australia Ltd, 487 Maroondah Highway,
PO Box 257, Ringwood, Victoria 3134, Australia
Penguin Books Canada Ltd, Alcorn Avenue,
Toronto, Ontario, Canada M4V 1E4
Penguin Books (NZ) Ltd, 182–190 Wairau Road,
Auckland 10, New Zealand

Typeset in Bembo and Helvetica to an original design by Henry Iles.
Printed in Spain by Graphy Cems.

British Library Cataloguing in Publication Data
A catalogue for this book is available from the British Library.

ISBN 1-85828-610-7

HELP US GET IT RIGHT

Lexus and Rough Guides have made great efforts to be accurate and
informative in this Rough Guide German phrasebook. However, if you feel
we have overlooked a useful word or phrase, or have any other
comments to make about the book, please let us know. All contributors
will be acknowledged and the best letters will be rewarded with a free
Rough Guide phrasebook of your choice. Please write to 'German
Phrasebook Update', at either Shorts Gardens (London) or Hudson Street
(New York) – for full addresses see above. Alternatively you can email us at
mail@roughguides.co.uk

Online information about Rough Guides can be found at our website
www.roughguides.com

CONTENTS

Introduction

The Rough Guide German dictionary phrasebook is a high-ly practical introduction to the contemporary language. Laid out in clear A-Z style, it uses key-word referencing to lead you straight to the words and phrases you want – so if you need to book a room, just look up 'room'. The Rough Guide gets straight to the point in every situation, in bars and shops, on trains and buses, and in hotels and banks.

The main part of the Rough Guide is a double dictionary: English-German then German-English. Before that, there's a page explaining the pronunciation system we've used, then a section called The Basics, which sets out the fundamental rules of the language, with plenty of practical examples. You'll also find here other essentials like numbers, dates and telling the time.

Forming the heart of the guide, the English-German section gives easy-to-use transliterations of the German words wherever pronunciation might be a problem, and to get you involved quickly in two-way communication, the Rough Guide includes dialogues featuring typical responses on key topics – such as renting a car and asking directions. Feature boxes fill you in on cultural pitfalls as well as the simple mechanics of how to make a phone call, what to do in an emergency, where to change money, and more. Throughout this section, cross-references enable you to pinpoint key facts and phrases, while asterisked words indicate where further information can be found in the Basics.

In the German-English dictionary, we've given not just the phrases you're likely to hear, but also all the signs, labels, instructions and other basic words you might come across in print or in public places.

Finally the Rough Guide rounds off with an extensive Menu Reader, giving a run-down of food and drink terms that you'll find indispensable whether you're eating out, stopping for a quick drink, or browsing through a local food market.

Gute Reise!

have a good trip!

Basics

Pronunciation

In this phrase book, the German has been written in a system of imitated pronunciation so that it can be read as though it were English. Bear in mind the notes on pronunciation given below:

ay	as in m**ay**
e	as in g**e**t
g	always hard as in **g**oat
ī	as the 'i' sound in m**i**ght
J	like the 's' sound in plea**s**ure
KH	as in the Scottish way of saying lo**ch**
oo	as in b**oo**k
oo	as in mons**oo**n
œ	like the 'ew' in f**ew** but without any 'y' sound
ow	as in c**ow**
uh	like the 'e' in butt**er**
ur	as in f**ur** but without any 'r' sound

The common German sound 'ei', as in Einstein, is written either with a 'y' or as 'ine'/'ite'/'ile' etc as in f**ine**/k**ite**/wh**ile**.

Abbreviations

acc	accusative		m	masculine
adj	adjective		n	neuter
dat	dative		nom	nominative
f	feminine		pl	plural
gen	genitive		sing	singular

Notes

In the English-German section, when two forms of the verb are given in phrases such as 'can you ...?' **kannst du/können Sie ...?** the first is the familiar form and the second the polite form (see the entry for yo**u**).

An asterisk (★) next to a word means that you should refer to the Basics section for further information.

Nouns

All German nouns begin with a capital letter. They have one of three genders – masculine, feminine or neuter. Usually, the gender of a noun will have to be learnt together with the word itself. Certain noun endings, however, are reliable indicators of gender. For example:

Masculine nouns: ending in **-or**

der Motor	**der Professor**
dair **moh**tohr	dair prof**e**ssohr
the engine	the professor

Feminine nouns: ending in **-ei, -heit, -in, -keit, -ung**

die Polizei	**die Abtei**
dee pohlits-**ī**	dee ap-**ty**
the police	the abbey

die Freiheit	**die Gesundheit**
dee fr**y**-hite	dee gez**oo**nt-hite
freedom	health

die Engländerin	**die Schauspielerin**
dee **e**ng-lenderin	dee sh**ow**-shpeelerin
the Englishwoman	the actress

die Telefonistin	**die Flüssigkeit**
dee telefohn**i**stin	dee fl**oo**ssish-kite
the telephonist	the liquid

die Geschwindigkeit	**die Reservierung**
dee geshv**i**ndish-kite	dee rezairv**ee**roong
the speed	the reservation

die Verbindung
dee fairb**i**ndoong
the connection

Neuter nouns: ending in -chen, -ment

das Mädchen	**das Verkehrszeichen**
dass **may**tshen	dass fairk**air**ss-tsyshen
the girl	the road sign
das Kompliment	**das Medikament**
dass komplim**ent**	dass medikam**ent**
the compliment	the medicine

Plurals

There are a certain number of general rules about the formation of plurals, but the plural of most German nouns, like their gender, will have to be learnt individually.

Many German nouns form their plural by adding **-e**, **-n** or **-en**.

der Berg	die Berge
dair bairk	dee **bair**g-uh
the mountain	the mountains
die Reise	**die Reisen**
dee **rize**-uh	dee **ry**zen
the journey	the journeys
die Mahlzeit	**die Mahlzeiten**
dee **mahl**tsite	dee **mahl**tsyten
the meal	the meals

Many nouns of foreign origin, though not all, form their plural by adding **-s**.

das Auto	**die Autos**
dass **ow**to	dee **ow**tohss
the car	the cars

but:

der Computer	**die Computer**
dair 'computer'	dee 'computer'
the computer	the computers

Some nouns do not change at all in the plural. Others add -er. This is often, but not always, combined with a change of vowel: a number of nouns which contain an **a**, an **o** or a **u** have an umlaut (**ä**, **ö** or **ü**) in their plural form.

der Wagen	**die Wagen**
dair **vah**gen	dee **vah**gen
the car	the cars
der Apfel	**die Äpfel**
dair **a**pfel	dee **e**pfel
the apple	the apples
der Koch	**die Köche**
dair koKH	dee **ku**rsh-uh
the cook	the cooks
das Tuch	**die Tücher**
dass tooKH	dee too sher
the cloth	the cloths

The following list of regular noun endings should prove useful:

noun ending	gender	plural
-ar	m	-are
-är	m	-äre
-chen	n	-chen
-eur	m	-eure
-ich	m	-iche
-heit	f	-heiten
-in	f	-innen
-ium	n	-ien
-keit	f	-keiten
-ling	m	-linge
-ment	n	-mente
-nis	n	-nisse
-or	m	-oren
-schaft	f	-schaften
-ung	f	-ungen

Articles and Cases

German has three genders, masculine (**m**), feminine (**f**) and neuter (**n**). Each gender has its own article.

For masculine nouns, the definite article ('the' in English) is **der** and the indefinite article ('a' in English) **ein**:

der Mann	**ein Mann**
dair man	ine man
the man	a man

For feminine nouns, the definite article is **die** and the indefinite article **eine**:

die Frau	**eine Frau**
dee frow	**ine**-uh frow
the woman	a woman

For neuter nouns, the definite article is **das** and the indefinite article **ein**:

das Kind	**ein Kind**
dass kint	ine kint
the child	a child

The plural form of the definite article, regardless of the gender of a noun, is **die**:

die Männer	**die Frauen**
dee menner	dee frowen
the men	the women

die Kinder
dee kinder
the children

There are four cases: nominative, accusative, genitive and dative. The form of the definite and indefinite articles changes in line with the case being used, as shown in the following tables:

The Definite Article

	m	f	n	pl
nom	der	die	das	die
acc	den	die	das	die
gen	des	der	des	der
dat	dem	der	dem	den

The Indefinite Article

	m	f	n
nom	ein	eine	ein
acc	einen	eine	ein
gen	eines	einer	eines
dat	einem	einer	einem

The nominative is the case used for words when they are the subject of the sentence:

der Wagen fährt schnell
dair **vah**gen fairt shnell
the car goes fast

The accusative is the case used for words when they are the object of the sentence:

ich habe den Wagen gestern gekauft
ish **hah**b-uh dayn **vah**gen ge**st**ern ge**kow**ft
I bought the car yesterday

The genitive is the case used to show possession:

der Preis des Wagens war sehr hoch
dair price dess **vah**genss var zair hohкн
the price of the car was very high

The dative is the case used to show motion towards a person or an object:

er ging dem Wagen entgegen
air ging daym **vah**gen entg**ay**gen
he walked towards the car

Prepositions

Most German prepositions take either the accusative or the dative or both.

The accusative is used after the following prepositions:

bis	biss	until
durch	doorsh	through
für	foor	for
gegen	gaygen	against
ohne	ohn-uh	without
um	oom	around

wir gehen durch die Stadt
veer gayen doorsh dee shtatt
we walk through the town

ohne die Kinder
ohn-uh dee kinder
without the children

The dative is used after the following prepositions:

aus	owss	out of
außer	owsser	except
bei	by	at, near
gegenüber	gaygen-oober	opposite
mit		with
nach	naKH	to
seit	zite	since
von	fon	from
zu	ts00	to, at

mit den Kindern   **seit dem letzten Jahr**
mit dayn kindern   zite daym letsten yar
with the children   since last year

The following prepositions can either take the accusative or the dative:

an		on, to
auf	owf	on
hinter		behind
in		in
neben	nayben	beside
über	oober	over, across
unter	oonter	under
vor	fohr	before, in front of
zwischen	tsvishen	between

The accusative is used whenever motion is shown, whereas the dative indicates position:

ich stelle die Vase auf den Tisch
ish shtell-uh dee vahz-uh owf dayn tish
I put the vase on the table

die Vase steht auf dem Tisch
dee vahz-uh shtayt owf daym tish
the vase is on the table

wir fahren über den Fluß
veer fahren oober dayn flooss
we are crossing the river

die Brücke über dem Fluß
dee broock-uh oober daym flooss
the bridge across the river

Adjectives and Adverbs

In German, there is no special ending to distinguish an adverb from an adjective (as '-ly' in English). The adverb is the same as the basic form of the adjective.

das Wetter ist schön
dass vetter ist shurn
the weather is beautiful

sie singt schön
zee zingt shurn
she sings beautifully

When an adjective is used on its own, ie not in front of a noun, it appears in its basic form, without an ending:

die Straße ist naß	**es ist zu spät**
dee shtr**ah**ss-uh ist nass	ess ist tsoo shpayt
the road is wet	it is too late

If, however, an adjective appears in front of a noun, it needs an ending in order to agree with the noun:

die nasse Straße	**ein später Zug**
dee n**a**ss-uh shtrahss-uh	ine shp**ay**ter tsook
the wet road	a late train

The adjective's ending further depends on whether it is used after a definite article (**der, die, das**) or after an indefinite article (**ein, eine**). As can be seen from the following tables, the endings vary according to gender and case of the noun.

Endings After Definite Articles

	m	f	n	pl
nom	–e	–e	–e	–en
acc	–en	–e	–e	–en
gen	–en	–en	–en	–en
dat	–en	–en	–en	–en

Endings After Indefinite Articles

	m	f	n
nom	–er	–e	–es
acc	–en	–e	–es
gen	–en	–en	–en
dat	–en	–en	–en

das große Hotel	**ein großes Hotel**
dass gr**oh**ss-uh hotel	ine gr**oh**ssess hotel
the big hotel	a big hotel

die großen Hotels
dee **groh**ssen hotelss
the big hotels

wir wohnen in dem großen Hotel
veer **voh**nen in daym **groh**ssen hotel
we are staying in the big hotel

die Zimmer eines großen Hotels
dee **ts**immer **ine**-ess **groh**ssen hotelss
the rooms of a big hotel

Comparatives and Superlatives

The comparative form of an adjective or adverb is used to express that something is bigger, better, more interesting etc than something else. In German, as for a number of English adjectives, this is shown by adding **-er**.

klein	**kleiner**
kline	kliner
small	smaller
schön	**schöner**
shurn	sh**ur**ner
beautiful	more beautiful

The superlative form of an adjective or adverb is used to express that something is the biggest, the best, the most interesting etc of all. In German, this is shown by adding **-ste**.

billig	**der/die/das billigste**
billish	dair/dee/dass **bi**llishst-uh
cheap	the cheapest
weich	**der/die/das weichste**
vysh	dair/dee/dass **vy**shst-uh
soft	the softest

Note that if adjectives contain an **a**, **o** or **u**, these will frequently change to **ä**, **ö** or **ü** in comparative and superlative forms:

lang	**länger**	**der/die/das längste**
lang	lenger	dair/dee/dass lengst-uh
long	longer	the longest

groß	**größer**	**der/die/das größte**
grohss	grurser	dair/dee/dass grursst-uh
big, tall	bigger, taller	the biggest, the tallest

dumm	**dümmer**	**der/die/das dümmste**
doomm	doommer	dair/dee/dass doommst-uh
stupid	more stupid	the most stupid

Some comparative and superlative forms are irregular completely:

gut	**besser**	**der/die/das beste**
goot	besser	dair/dee/dass best-uh
good	better	the best

hoch	**höher**	**der/die/das höchste**
hohKH	hurher	dair/dee/dass hurkst-uh
high	higher	the highest

viel	**mehr**	**der/die/das meiste**
feel	mair	dair/dee/dass myst-uh
much	more	the most

The word for 'than' is **als**:

er ist größer als ich
air ist grurser alss ish
he is taller than me

Possessive Adjectives

Possessive adjectives are words like 'my', 'your', 'our' etc. In German, they have to agree with the gender and number of the noun they refer to:

		m	f	n	pl
my		**mein**	**meine**	**mein**	**meine**
		mine	mi**ne**-uh	mine	mi**ne**-uh
your	(sing, familiar)	**dein**	**deine**	**dein**	**deine**
		dine	di**ne**-uh	dine	di**ne**-uh
	(sing, polite)	**Ihr**	**Ihre**	**Ihr**	**Ihre**
		eer	**eer**-uh	eer	**eer**-uh
his		**sein**	**seine**	**sein**	**seine**
		zine	zi**ne**-uh	zine	zi**ne**-uh
her		**ihr**	**ihre**	**ihr**	**ihre**
		eer	**eer**-uh	eer	**eer**-uh
our		**unser**	**unsere**	**unser**	**unsere**
		oonzer	**oo**nzer-uh	**oo**nzer	**oo**nzer-uh
your	(pl, familiar)	**euer**	**eure**	**euer**	**eure**
		oyer	**oy**r-uh	**oy**er	**oy**r-uh
	(pl, polite)	**Ihr**	**Ihre**	**Ihr**	**Ihre**
		eer	**eer**-uh	eer	**eer**-uh
their		**ihr**	**ihre**	**ihr**	**ihre**
		eer	**eer**-uh	eer	**eer**-uh

hast du deine Fahrkarte?
hast doo di**ne**-uh **fah**rkart-uh
have you got your ticket?

das ist mein Hotel
dass ist mine ho**tel**
this is my hotel

sind unsere Koffer schon hier?
zint **oo**nzer-uh **ko**ffer shohn heer
have our suitcases arrived yet?

Personal Pronouns

Subject Pronouns

I		**ich**	ish
you	(sing, familiar)	**du**(1)	doo
	(sing, polite)	**Sie**(2)	zee
he		**er**	air
she		**sie**	zee
it		**es**	ess
we		**wir**	veer
you	(pl, familiar)	**ihr**(3)	eer
	(pl, polite)	**Sie**(2)	zee
they		**sie**	zee

(1) **du** is used when speaking to one person and is the familiar form generally used when speaking to family, friends and children

(2) **Sie** is the polite form of address in the singular as well as the plural; it takes the third person plural of verbs

(3) **ihr** is the familiar form used when speaking to more than one person

Note that, when talking to strangers, unless they are children, you should always use **Sie**, never **du** or **ihr**.

It is important to remember that the German for 'it' is not automatically **es** but always depends on the noun which 'it' refers to. If the noun is masculine, use **er**; if it is feminine, use **sie**; only if the noun is neuter is **es** the pronoun to use.

> **ist der Zug schon da? – da kommt er**
> ist dair tsook shohn da – da kommt air
> has the train arrived yet? – here it comes

> **wo ist die Zeitung? – da liegt sie**
> vo ist dee tsytoong – da leekt zee
> where's the paper? – there it is

was macht das Kind? – es spielt

vass maKHt dass kint – ess shpeelt

what's the child doing? – he / she is playing

Direct Object Pronouns

These occur if you are using the pronoun as an object.

me		**mich** mish	it		**es**	ess
you	(sing, familiar)	**dich** dish	us		**uns**	oonss
	(sing, polite)	**Sie** zee	you	(pl, familiar)	**euch**	oysh
him		**ihn** een		(pl, polite)	**Sie**	zee
her		**sie** zee	them		**sie**	zee

ich habe sie gesehen

ish hahb-uh zee gezayen

I have seen her/them

kann ich dich morgen anrufen?

kann ish dish morgen anroofen

can I phone you tomorrow?

ich möchte euch einladen

ish mursht-uh oysh **ine**-lahden

I would like to invite you

Indirect Object Pronouns

If you are using an object pronoun to mean 'to me', 'to you' etc (although 'to' might not always be necessary in English), you use the following:

(to) me		**mir**	meer
(to) you	(sing, familiar)	**dir**	deer
	(sing, polite)	**Ihnen**	**ee**nen
(to) him		**ihm**	eem
(to) her		**ihr**	eer
(to) it		**ihm**	eem
(to) us		**uns**	oonss
(to) you	(pl, familiar)	**euch**	oysh
	(pl, polite)	**Ihnen**	**ee**nen
(to) them		**ihnen**	**ee**nen

sie hat es mir gegeben	**ich habe es ihm gesagt**
zee hat ess meer gegayben	ish hahb-uh ess eem gezahkt
she has given it to me	I told him

er hat ihnen einen Brief geschrieben
air hat eenen ine-en breef geshreeben
he has written them a letter

Reflexive Pronouns

These are used with reflexive verbs like **sich waschen** 'to wash (oneself)', **sich umdrehen** 'to turn around':

myself		**mich**	mish
yourself	(familiar)	**dich**	dish
	(polite)	**sich**	zish
himself		**sich**	zish
herself		**sich**	zish
itself		**sich**	zish
ourselves		**uns**	oonss
yourselves	(familiar)	**euch**	oysh
	(polite)	**sich**	zish
themselves		**sich**	zish

wir haben uns gut unterhalten	**Sie irren sich**
veer hahben oonss goot oonterhalten	zee eerren zish
we enjoyed ourselves	you are mistaken

ich habe mich geärgert
ish hahb-uh mish ge-airgert
I was annoyed

Possessive Pronouns

Possessive adjectives are words like 'mine', 'yours', 'ours' etc. In German, they have to agree with the gender and number of the noun they refer to:

	m	f	n	pl
mine	**meiner**	**meine**	**meins**	**meine**
	miner	mine-uh	mine-ss	mine-uh
yours (sing, familiar)	**deiner**	**deine**	**deins**	**deine**
	diner	dine-uh	dine-ss	dine-uh
(sing, polite)	**Ihrer**	**Ihre**	**Ihres**	**Ihre**
	eerer	eer-uh	eeress	eer-uh
his	**seiner**	**seine**	**seins**	**seine**
	ziner	zine-uh	zine-ss	zine-uh
hers	**ihrer**	**ihre**	**ihres**	**ihre**
	eerer	eer-uh	eeress	eer-uh
ours	**unserer**	**unsere**	**unseres**	**unsere**
	oonzerer	oonzer-uh	oonzer-ess	oonzer-uh
yours (pl, familiar)	**eurer**	**eure**	**eures**	**eure**
	oyrer	oyr-uh	oyress	oyr-uh
(pl, polite)	**Ihrer**	**Ihre**	**Ihres**	**Ihre**
	eerer	eer-uh	eeress	eer-uh
theirs	**ihrer**	**ihre**	**ihres**	**ihre**
	eerer	eer-uh	eeress	eer-uh

das sind meine	**ist das mein Glas oder Ihres?**
dass zint mine-uh	ist dass mine glahss oder eeress
these are mine	is that glass mine or yours?

möchten Sie Wein? – wir haben unseren schon bestellt
murshten zee vine – veer hahben oonzeren shohn beshtellt
would you like some wine? – we've already ordered ours

Verbs

The basic form of German verbs (the infinitive) usually ends in **-en**, occasionally in **-ln** or **-rn**.

gehen	to go, to walk
schlafen	to sleep
angeln	to fish

Present Tense

The present tense corresponds to 'I leave' and 'I am leaving' in English. To form the present tense in German, remove the verb ending (-en or -n) and add the endings to the stem of the verb, as shown in the tables below (the 'stem' of a verb is the past without the final '-en', '-eln' or '-ern'):

		machen (to do) maKH-en		**reden** (to talk) rayd-en	
I		ich	mach-e	ich	red-e
you	(sing, familiar)	du	mach-st	du	red-est
	(sing, polite)	Sie	mach-en	Sie	red-en
he/she/it		er/sie/es	mach-t	er/sie/es	red-et
we		wir	mach-en	wir	red-en
you	(pl, familiar)	ihr	mach-t	ihr	red-et
	(pl, polite)	Sie	mach-en	Sie	red-en
they		sie	mach-en	sie	red-en

See the section on Subject Pronouns page 21 for the use of the different words for 'you'.

Note that verbs ending in -t or -d, as **reden** above, insert an additional -e- to form some of their tenses.

Some common verbs are irregular:

haben [**hah**ben] to have			**sein** [zine] to be		
ich	habe	hahb-uh	ich	bin	
du	hast		du	bist	
Sie	haben	hahben	Sie	sind	zint
er/sie/es	hat		er/sie/es	ist	
wir	haben		wir	sind	
ihr	habt	hapt	ihr	seid	zite
Sie	haben		Sie	sind	
sie	haben		sie	sind	

dürfen [doorfen] to be allowed to

ich	darf	
du	darfst	
Sie	dürfen	doorfen
er/sie/es	darf	
wir	dürfen	
ihr	dürft	doorft
Sie	dürfen	
sie	dürfen	

fahren [fahren] to go, drive

ich	fahre	fahr-uh
du	fährst	fairst
Sie	fahren	fahren
er/sie/es	fährt	fairt
wir	fahren	
ihr	fahrt	
Sie	fahren	
sie	fahren	

können [kurnen] to be able to

ich	kann	
du	kannst	
Sie	können	kurnen
er/sie/es	kann	
wir	können	
ihr	könnt	kurnt
Sie	können	
sie	können	

mögen [murgen] to like

ich	mag	mahk
du	magst	mahkst
Sie	mögen	murgen
er/sie/es	mag	
wir	mögen	
ihr	mögt	murkt
Sie	mögen	
sie	mögen	

müssen [moossen] to have to

ich	muß	mooss
du	mußt	moosst
Sie	müssen	moossen
er/sie/es	muß	
wir	müssen	
ihr	müßt	moosst
Sie	müssen	
sie	müssen	

sehen [zayen] to see

ich	sehe	zay-uh
du	siehst	zeest
Sie	sehen	zayen
er/sie/es	sieht	zeet
wir	sehen	
ihr	seht	zayt
Sie	sehen	
sie	sehen	

werden [vairden] to become

ich	werde	vaird-uh
du	wirst	veerst
Sie	werden	vairden
er/sie/es	wird	veert
wir	werden	
ihr	werdet	vairdet
Sie	werden	
sie	werden	

wollen [vollen] to want

ich	will	vill
du	willst	villst
Sie	wollen	vollen
er/sie/es	will	
wir	wollen	
ihr	wollt	vollt
Sie	wollen	
sie	wollen	

Past Tense

To describe an action that has taken place in the past, both the imperfect and perfect tense can be used.

Imperfect

The imperfect describes events which have occurred once in the past or which were repeated, habitual or took place over a period of time. To form the imperfect, the following verb endings are used:

machen (to do)		reden (to talk)	
ich	mach-te	ich	red-ete
du	mach-test	du	red-etest
Sie	mach-ten	Sie	red-eten
er/sie/es	mach-te	er/sie/es	red-ete
wir	mach-ten	wir	red-eten
ihr	mach-tet	ihr	red-etet
Sie	mach-ten	Sie	red-eten
sie	mach-ten	sie	red-eten

als ich Student war, lebte ich in Köln
alss ish shtoodent var laypt-uh ish in kurln
when I was a student, I used to live in Cologne

wie war das Wetter in den Alpen?
vee var dass vetter in dayn alpen
what was the weather like in the Alps?

Both **haben** and **sein** are irregular in the imperfect tense:

haben [hahben] to have			sein [zine] to be		
ich	hatte	hatt-uh	ich	war	var
du	hattest		du	warst	varst
Sie	hatten		Sie	waren	vahren
er/sie/es	hatte		er/sie/es	war	
wir	hatten		wir	waren	
ihr	hattet		ihr	wart	vart
Sie	hatten		Sie	waren	
sie	hatten		sie	waren	

Perfect

The most common way of referring to the past is the perfect tense. The perfect is formed with the present tense of either **haben** or **sein** (see page 25) followed by the past participle of the verb. The past participle is formed by taking the stem of the verb and adding a prefix and ending as follows:

mach-en to do   **ge-mach-t** done
red-en to talk   **ge-red-et** talked

Most verbs take **haben** to form the perfect tense:

er hat es gemacht   **wir haben davon geredet**
air hat ess gemaкнt   veer hahben dafon geraydet
he has done it, he did it   we (have) talked about it

Some verbs take **sein**, mostly verbs of motion. Some of these are:

fahren to go, to drive   **ich bin gefahren**
fallen to fall   **ich bin gefallen**
fliegen to fly   **ich bin geflogen**
gehen to go   **ich bin gegangen**
kommen to come   **ich bin gekommen**
sein to be   **ich bin gewesen**
sterben to die   **ich bin gestorben**
werden to become   **ich bin geworden**

er ist nach London gefahren
air ist naкн london gefahren
he went to London

letztes Jahr sind wir in München gewesen
letstess yar zint veer in moonshen gevayzen
last year we were in Munich

Some common verbs have irregular past tenses. The following list shows the infinitive, the third person singular of the imperfect tense and the past participle.

Some Common Irregular Verbs

beginnen	to begin	begann	begonnen
bleiben	to stay	blieb	geblieben
bringen	to bring	brachte	gebracht
dürfen	to be allowed to	durfte	gedurft
essen	to eat	aß	gegessen
fahren	to go, to drive	fuhr	gefahren
finden	to find	fand	gefunden
fliegen	to fly	flog	geflogen
geben	to give	gab	gegeben
gehen	to go	ging	gegangen
haben	to have	hatte	gehabt
kennen	to know	kannte	gekannt
kommen	to come	kam	gekommen
können	to be able to	konnte	gekonnt
lassen	to let, to allow	ließ	gelassen
lesen	to read	las	gelesen
liegen	to lie	lag	gelegen
müssen	to have to	mußte	gemußt
nehmen	to take	nahm	genommen
schreiben	to write	schrieb	geschrieben
sehen	to see	sah	gesehen
sein	to be	war	gewesen
sitzen	to sit	saß	gesessen
sterben	to die	starb	gestorben
trinken	to drink	trank	getrunken
verlieren	to lose	verlor	verloren
werden	to become	wurde	geworden
wissen	to know	wußte	gewußt

Future

The future tense in German is formed by the verb **werden** and the infinitive of the verb concerned:

ich	werde	kommen	I will come etc
du	wirst	kommen	
Sie	werden	kommen	
er/sie/es	wird	kommen	
wir	werden	kommen	
ihr	werdet	kommen	
Sie	werden	kommen	
sie	werden	kommen	

er wird es nicht schaffen
air veert ess nisht shaffen
he's not going to manage it

was werden Sie morgen machen?
vass vairden zee morgen maкнen
what are you going to do tomorrow?

er wird morgen kommen
air veert morgen kommen
he'll come tomorrow

Note that German, like English, frequently uses the present tense for the future:

was machen Sie morgen?
vass maкнen zee morgen
what are you doing tomorrow?

er kommt morgen
air kommt morgen
he's coming tomorrow

Negatives

To make a sentence negative, German uses the word **nicht**:

ich verstehe	**ich verstehe nicht**
ish fairsh**tay**-uh	ish fairsh**tay**-uh nisht
I understand	I don't understand

If you want to say 'no' or 'not any' with nouns, use the word **kein** or **keine**:

ich habe kein Geld	**er hat keine Geduld**
ish h**ah**b-uh kine gelt	air hat **ki**ne-uh ged**oo**lt
I have no money	he hasn't got any patience

Imperatives

The imperative is used to express a command (such as 'come here!', 'let's go' etc). Generally, the imperative forms are similar to those of the infinitive. In fact, just adding **Sie** to the infinitive gives the polite form of the imperative:

warten to wait	**warten Sie!**
	varten zee
	wait!

The familiar form (singular) is identical with the infinitive without the final **-n**, or, in some cases, without the final **-en**:

warte!	but:	**komm!**
va**rt**-uh		komm
wait!		come (here)!

The corresponding plural form adds a **-t** to the singular:

wartet!	**kommt!**
va**rt**et	kommt
wait!	come (here)!

Questions

To form a question, the word order of subject and verb in the sentence change:

Sie sprechen Deutsch
zee shpre**shen** doytch
you speak German

sprechen Sie Deutsch?
shpre**shen** zee doytch
do you speak German?

Word order is also inverted in other cases, especially when a question word is used:

wann schließt das Museum?
van shleesst dass m00za**y**oom
when does the museum close?

ist mein Gepäck schon angekommen?
ist mine gepeck shohn **a**n-gekommen?
has my luggage arrived yet?

Dates

Dates are expressed with ordinal numbers (see below):

der erste Juli
dair **air**st-uh y**00**lee
the first of July

am ersten Juli
am **air**sten y**00**lee
on the first of July

der zwanzigste März
dair tsva**n**tsishst-uh mairts
the twentieth of March

am zwanzigsten März
am tsva**n**tsishsten mairts
on the twentieth of March

At the beginning of letters, the following form should be used:

Frankfurt, den 20. März
Frankfurt, March 20

Time

what time is it? wie spät ist es? [vee shpayt ist ess]
one o'clock ein Uhr [ine oor]
two o'clock zwei Uhr [tsvy oor]
it's one o'clock es ist ein Uhr [ess ist ine oor]
it's two o'clock es ist zwei Uhr [ess ist tsvy oor]
it's ten o'clock es ist zehn Uhr [ess ist tsayn oor]
five past one fünf nach eins [foonf nahKH ine-ss]
ten past two zehn nach zwei [tsayn nahKH tsvy]
quarter past one Viertel nach eins [feertel nahKH ine-ss]
quarter past two Viertel nach zwei [feertel nahKH tsvy]
*half past ten halb elf [halp elf]
twenty to ten zwanzig vor zehn [tsvantsish for tsayn]
quarter to two Viertel vor zwei [feertel for tsvy]
at half past four um halb fünf [oom halp foonf]
at eight o'clock um acht Uhr [oom aKHt oor]
14.00 14 Uhr [feertsayn oor]
17.30 siebzehn Uhr dreißig [zeeptsayn oor dryssish]
2 a.m. 2 Uhr morgens [tsvy oor morgens]
2 p.m. 2 Uhr nachmittags [tsvy oor nahKHmittahks]
10 a.m. 10 Uhr vormittags [tsayn oor formittahks]
10 p.m. 10 Uhr abends [tsayn oor ahbents]
noon Mittag [mittahk]
midnight Mitternacht [mitternaKHt]

an hour eine Stunde [ine-uh shtoond-uh]
a/one minute eine Minute [ine-uh minoot-uh]
two minutes zwei Minuten [tsvy minooten]
a second eine Sekunde [ine-uh zekoond-uh]
a quarter of an hour eine Viertelstunde [ine-uh feertelshtoond-uh]
half an hour eine halbe Stunde [ine-uh halb-uh shtoond-uh]
three quarters of an hour eine Dreiviertelstunde [ine-uh dryfeertel-shtoond-uh]

* Note the difference here. German for 'half past ten/three/five' etc is, literally, 'half eleven/four/six' etc.

Numbers

0	null [nooll]		110	hundertzehn [hoondert-tsayn]
1	eins [ine-ss]		200	zweihundert [tsvy-hoondert]
2	zwei [tsvy]		300	dreihundert [dry-hoondert]
3	drei [dry]		1,000	tausend [towzent]
4	vier [feer]		2,000	zweitausend [tsvy-towzent]
5	fünf [foonf]		10,000	zehntausend [tsayn-towzent]
6	sechs [zeks]		50,000	fünfzigtausend [foonftsish-towzent]
7	sieben [zeeben]		100,000	hunderttausend [hoondert-towzent]
8	acht [aKHt]		1,000,000	eine Million [ine-uh mill-yohn]
9	neun [noyn]			
10	zehn [tsayn]			
11	elf [elf]			
12	zwölf [tsvurlf]			
13	dreizehn [dry-tsayn]			
14	vierzehn [veer-tsayn]			
15	fünfzehn [foonf-tsayn]			
16	sechzehn [zesh-tsayn]			
17	siebzehn [zeep-tsayn]			
18	achtzehn [aKH-tsayn]			
19	neunzehn [noyn-tsayn]			
20	zwanzig [tsvantsish]			
21	einundzwanzig [ine-oont-tsvantsish]			
22	zweiundzwanzig [tsvy-oont-tsvantsish]			
23	dreiundzwanzig [dry-oont-tsvantsish]			
30	dreißig [dryssish]			
31	einunddreißig [ine-oont-dryssish]			
40	vierzig [feertsish]			
50	fünfzig [foonftsish]			
60	sechzig [zeshtsish]			
70	siebzig [zeeptsish]			
80	achtzig [aKHtsish]			
90	neunzig [noyntsish]			
100	hundert [hoondert]			

Ordinal numbers are formed by adding -te or -ste if the number ends in -ig. For example, fünfte [foonft-uh] (fifth), zwanzigste [tsvantsishst-uh] (twentieth).

1st	erste [airst-uh]
2nd	zweite [tsvite-uh]
3rd	dritte [dritt-uh]
4th	vierte [feert-uh]
5th	fünfte [foonft-uh]
6th	sechste [zekst-uh]
7th	siebte [zeept-uh]
8th	achte [aKHt-uh]
9th	neunte [noynt-uh]
10th	zehnte [tsaynt-uh]

In German, thousands are written with a full-stop. A comma is used for decimals.

German	English
10.000	10,000
2,83	2.83

Basic Phrases

yes
ja
yah

no
nein
nine

OK
okay

hello
hallo

good morning
guten Morgen
gooten morgen

good evening
guten Abend
gooten ahbent

good night
gute Nacht
goot-uh naкнt

goodbye
auf Wiedersehen
owf-veederzayn

please
bitte
bitt-uh

yes please
ja bitte
yah

thanks, thank you
danke
dank-uh

no thanks
nein danke
nine

thank you very much
vielen Dank
feelen

don't mention it
bitte
bitt-uh

how do you do?
guten Tag!
gooten tahk

how are you?
wie geht es dir/Ihnen?
gayt ess deer/eenen

fine, thanks
danke, gut
dank-uh goot

nice to meet you
freut mich
froyt mish

excuse me
(to get past)
entschuldigen Sie!
ent-shooldigen zee
(to get attention)
Entschuldigung!
ent-shooldigoong

sorry: (I'm) sorry
tut mir leid
t**oo**t meer lite

sorry?
(didn't understand) wie bitte?
vee b**i**tt-uh

I see/I understand
ich verstehe
ish fairst**ay**-uh

I don't understand
das verstehe ich nicht
n**i**sht

do you speak English?
sprechen Sie Englisch?
shpr**e**shen zee **e**ng-lish

I don't speak German
ich spreche kein Deutsch
ish shpr**e**sh-uh kine doytch

could you say it slowly?
könnten Sie das etwas
langsamer sagen?
k**u**rnten zee dass **e**tvass **l**angzahmer
z**ah**gen

could you repeat that?
können Sie das noch einmal
wiederholen?
k**u**rnen zee dass noкн **ine**-mahl

could you write it down?
könnten Sie es aufschreiben?
k**u**rnten zee ess **owf**-shryben

I'd like a ...
ich möchte gern ein ...
m**u**rsht-uh gairn

I'd like to ...
ich würde gern ...
v**oo**rd-uh

can I have a ...?
kann ich ein ... haben?
kan ish

how much is it?
was kostet das?
was k**o**stet das?

cheers!
(toast) Prost!
prohst

it is ...
es ist ...

where is it?
wo ist es?
vo

is it far from here?
ist es weit von hier?
fon heer

how long will it/does it take?
wie lange dauert es?
vee l**a**ng-uh d**o**wert ess

Conversion Tables

1 centimetre = 0.39 inches   1 inch = 2.54 cm

1 metre = 39.37 inches = 1.09 yards   1 foot = 30.48 cm

1 kilometre = 0.62 miles = 5/8 mile   1 yard = 0.91 m

1 mile = 1.61 km

km	1	2	3	4	5	10	20	30	40	50	100
miles	0.6	1.2	1.9	2.5	3.1	6.2	12.4	18.6	24.8	31.0	62.1

miles	1	2	3	4	5	10	20	30	40	50	100
km	1.6	3.2	4.8	6.4	8.0	16.1	32.2	48.3	64.4	80.5	161

1 gram = 0.035 ounces   1 kilo = 1000 g = 2.2 pounds

g	100	250	500
oz	3.5	8.75	17.5

1 oz = 28.35 g
1 lb = 0.45 kg

kg	0.5	1	2	3	4	5	6	7	8	9	10
lb	1.1	2.2	4.4	6.6	8.8	11.0	13.2	15.4	17.6	19.8	22.0

kg	20	30	40	50	60	70	80	90	100
lb	44	66	88	110	132	154	176	198	220

lb	0.5	1	2	3	4	5	6	7	8	9	10	20
kg	0.2	0.5	0.9	1.4	1.8	2.3	2.7	3.2	3.6	4.1	4.5	9.0

1 litre = 1.75 UK pints / 2.13 US pints

1 UK pint = 0.57 l   1 UK gallon = 4.55 l
1 US pint = 0.47 l   1 US gallon = 3.79 l

centigrade / Celsius $°C = (°F - 32) \times 5/9$

°C	-5	0	5	10	15	18	20	25	30	36.8	38
°F	23	32	41	50	59	64	68	77	86	98.4	100.4

Fahrenheit $°F = (°C \times 9/5) + 32$

°F	23	32	40	50	60	65	70	80	85	98.4	101
°C	-5	0	4	10	16	18	21	27	29	36.8	38.3

English

→

German

A
---

a, an* ein(e) **[ine(-uh)]**
  10 marks a bottle 10 Mark
  pro Flasche
about: about twenty etwa
  zwanzig **[etvah]**
  at about 5 o'clock gegen
  fünf Uhr **[gaygen]**
  a film about Germany ein
  Film über Deutschland
  [ober]
above über **[ober]**
abroad im Ausland **[owsslant]**
  to go abroad ins Ausland
  gehen
absolutely (I agree) genau
  [genow]
accelerator das Gaspedal
  [gahss-pedahl]
accept akzeptieren
  [aktsepteeren]
accident der Unfall **[oonfal]**
  there's been an accident es
  hat einen Unfall gegeben
  [gegayben]
accommodation die
  Unterkunft **[oonter-koonft]**
  see room
accurate genau **[genow]**
ache der Schmerz **[shmairts]**
  my back aches mein
  Rücken tut weh **[toot vay]**
across: across the road über
  die Straße **[ober]**
adapter der Adapter
address die Adresse **[adress-uh]**

what's your address? was ist
  Ihre Adresse? **[eer-uh]**

In German addresses, the
house number follows the
street name and the post
code precedes the town, eg:

Gerd Schuster
Mühlbachstr. 35
50462 Köln

address book das Adreßbuch
  [adressbooKH]
admission charge der Eintritt
  [ine-tritt]
adult der Erwachsene
  [airvaksen-uh]
advance: in advance im
  voraus **[forowss]**
aeroplane das Flugzeug
  [flooktsoyk]
after nach **[naKH]**
  after you nach Ihnen **[eenen]**
afternoon der Nachmittag
  [naKHmit-tahk]
  in the afternoon am
  Nachmittag
  this afternoon heute
  Nachmittag **[hoyt-uh]**
aftershave das After-shave
aftersun cream die Après-
  Lotion **[apray-lohts-yohn]**
afterwards danach **[danaKH]**
again wieder **[veeder]**
against gegen **[gaygen]**
age das Alter **[al-ter]**
ago: a week ago vor einer
  Woche **[for ine-er]**

an hour ago vor einer Stunde

agree: I agree ich bin einverstanden [ine-fair-shtanden]

AIDS Aids

air die Luft [looft]

by air mit dem Flugzeug [flooktsoyk]

air-conditioning die Klimaanlage [kleema-anlahg-uh]

airmail: by airmail per Luftpost [pair looftpost]

airmail envelope der Luftpost-Briefumschlag [looftposst breef-oomshlahk]

airport der Flughafen [flook-hahfen]

to the airport, please zum Flughafen bitte [tsoom]

airport bus der Flughafenbus [flook-hafenbooss]

aisle seat der Sitz am Gang

alarm clock der Wecker [vecker]

alcohol der Alkohol

alcoholic alkoholisch [alko-hohlish]

all: all the boys alle Jungen [al-uh]

all the girls alle Mädchen

all of it alles [al-ess]

all of them alle

that's all, thanks das ist alles, danke

allergic: I'm allergic to ... ich bin allergisch gegen ... [ish bin allairgish gaygen]

allowed: is it allowed? ist es erlaubt? [airlowpt]

all right okay

I'm all right ich bin okay

are you all right? bist du/sind Sie okay?

almond die Mandel

almost fast [fasst]

alone allein [al-ine]

alphabet das Alphabet [alfa-bayt]

a	ah	j	yot	s	ess
b	bay	k	kah	t	tay
c	tsay	l	el	u	oo
d	day	m	em	v	fow
e	ay	n	en	w	vay
f	eff	o	oh	x	eeks
g	gay	p	pay	y	œpsilon
h	hah	q	koo	z	tset
i	ee	r	air	ß	ess-tset

Alps die Alpen

already schon [shohn]

also auch [owкн]

although obwohl [opvohl]

altogether insgesamt

aluminium foil die Alufolie [ahloo-fohl-yuh]

always immer

am*: I am ich bin [ish]

a.m.: at seven a.m. um sieben Uhr morgens [oom – oor]

amazing (surprising) erstaunlich [airshtownlish] (very good) fantastisch

ambulance der Krankenwagen [kranken-vahgen]

call an ambulance! rufen Sie einen Krankenwagen [roofen zee ine-en]

 In the event of an emergency, dial 110. This puts you through to the police, who will summon an ambulance for you.

America Amerika [amaireeka]
American (adj) amerikanisch [amairikahnish]
  I'm American (man/woman) ich bin Amerikaner/ Amerikanerin
among unter [oonter]
amount die Menge [meng-uh] (money) der Betrag [betrahk]
amp: a 13 amp fuse eine dreizehn-Ampere- Sicherung [ampair zisheroong]
and und [oont]
angry wütend [vootent]
animal das Tier [teer]
ankle der Knöchel [knurshel]
anniversary (wedding) der Hochzeitstag [hoKH-tsites-tahk]
annoy: this man's annoying me dieser Mann belästigt mich [belestisht mish]
annoying ärgerlich [airgerlish]
another ein anderer [ine anderer]
  can we have another room? können wir ein anderes Zimmer haben?
  another beer, please noch ein Bier, bitte [noKH ine]

antibiotics die Antibiotika [anti-bee-ohteeka]
antifreeze das Frostschutzmittel [frost- shoots-mittel]
antihistamine das Antihistamin
antique: is it an antique? ist es antik? [anteek]
antique shop das Antiquitätengeschäft [antikvitayten-gesheft]
antiseptic das Antiseptikum
any: have you got any bread/tomatoes? haben Sie Brot/Tomaten? [hahben zee]
  sorry, I don't have any tut mir leid, ich habe keine [toot meer lite, ish hahbuh kine-uh]
anybody jemand [yaymant]
  does anybody speak English? spricht jemand Englisch?
  there wasn't anybody there es war keiner da [kyner]
anything etwas [etvass]

dialogues

  anything else? sonst noch etwas?
  nothing else, thanks sonst nichts, danke [nishts, dank- uh]

  would you like anything to drink? möchten Sie etwas trinken? [murshten]
  I don't want anything,

thanks ich möchte nichts, danke [nishts]

apart from abgesehen von [ap-gezay-en fon]
apartment die Wohnung [vohnoong]
apartment block der Wohnblock [vohnblock]
appendicitis die Blinddarm-entzündung [blint-darm-ent-tsoondoong]
aperitif der Aperitif [apairee-teef]
apology die Entschuldigung [ent-shooldigoong]
appetizer die Vorspeise [for-shpize-uh]
apple der Apfel
appointment der Termin [tairmeen]

dialogue

good afternoon, how can I help you? guten Tag, kann ich Ihnen behilflich sein? [gooten tahk, kan ish eenen behilflish zine]
I'd like to make an appointment ich möchte einen Termin vereinbaren [fair-ine-bahren]
what time would you like? welche Zeit wäre Ihnen recht? [velsh-uh tsite vair-uh eenen resht]
three o'clock drei Uhr [oor]

I'm afraid that's not possible, is four o'clock all right? tut mir leid, das ist nicht möglich, ist vier Uhr in Ordnung? [murglish]
yes, that will be fine ja, das ist mir recht [meer]
the name was ...? Ihr Name war ...? [eer nahm-uh vahr]

apricot die Aprikose [aprikohz-uh]
April der April [a-prill]
are*: we are wir sind [veer zint]
you are du bist/Sie sind [doo .../zee]
they are sie sind [zee]
area die Gegend [gaygent]
area code die Vorwahl [forvahl]
arm der Arm
arrange: will you arrange it for us? können Sie das für uns regeln? [raygeln]
arrival die Ankunft [ankoonft]
arrive ankommen
when do we arrive? wann kommen wir an? [van kommen veer an]
has my fax arrived yet? ist mein Fax schon angekommen?
we arrived today wir sind heute angekommen
art die Kunst [koonst]
art gallery die Kunstgalerie [koonstgal-leree]

artist der Künstler [k**oo**nstler]

as: as big as so groß wie [zoh grohss vee]

as soon as possible so bald wie möglich [m**ur**glish]

ashtray der Aschenbecher [**a**shen-besher]

ask fragen [fr**ah**gen]

I didn't ask for this das habe ich nicht bestellt [dass h**ah**b-uh ish nisht besht**e**llt]

could you ask him to ...? könnten Sie ihn bitten ...? [k**ur**nten zee een b**i**tten]

asleep: she's asleep sie schläft [shl**ay**ft]

aspirin das Kopfschmerzmittel [k**o**pf-shmairts-mittel]

asthma das Asthma [**a**st-mah]

astonishing erstaunlich [airsht**ow**nlish]

at: at the hotel im Hotel

at the station am Bahnhof

at six o'clock um 6 Uhr [oom]

at Günter's bei Günter [by]

athletics Leichtathletik [l**y**sht-at-laytik]

attractive attraktiv [atrakt**ee**f]

aubergine die Aubergine [ohbairj**ee**n-uh]

August der August [owg**oo**st]

Australia Australien [owstr**ah**lee-en]

Australian (adj) australisch [owstr**ah**lish]

I'm Australian (man/woman) ich bin Australier [owstr**ah**lee-er]/Australierin

Austria Österreich [**ur**ster-rysh]

Austrian (man/woman) der Österreicher [**ur**ster-rysher]/die Österreicherin (adj) österreichisch [**ur**ster-rysh-ish]

the Austrians die Österreicher

Austrian Alps die österreichischen Alpen

Austrian Tirol Tirol [tee-r**oh**l]

automatic (car) der Automatikwagen [owto-m**ah**tik-vahgen]

automatic teller (US) der Geldautomat [**ge**lt-owtomaht]

autumn der Herbst [hairpst]

in the autumn im Herbst

avenue die Allee [all**ay**]

average (not good) mittelmäßig [m**i**ttel-maysish] (ordinary) durchschnittlich [d**oo**rsh-shnitt-lish]

on average im Durchschnitt

awake: is he awake? ist er wach? [va**кн**]

away: go away! gehen Sie weg! [g**ay**-en zee vek]

is it far away? ist es weit? [vite]

awful furchtbar [f**oo**rsht-bar]

axle die Achse [**a**x-uh]

B

baby das Baby

baby food die Babynahrung [-nahroong]

baby's bottle das Fläschchen [flesh-shen]
baby-sitter der Babysitter
back (of body) der Rücken [rōocken]
(back part) die Rückseite [rōock-zite-uh]
at the back hinten
can I have my money back? kann ich mein Geld zurückbekommen? [tsōorōock-bekommen]
to come back zurückkommen
to go back zurückgehen [-gay-en]
backache die Rücken- schmerzen [rōocken-shmairtsen]
bacon der Speck [shpeck]
bad schlecht [shlesht]
a bad headache schlimme Kopfschmerzen [shlimm-uh]
badly schlecht [shlesht]
bag die Tasche [tash-uh]
(handbag) die Handtasche [hant-tash-uh]
(plastic) die Tüte [tōot-uh]
baggage das Gepäck [gepeck]
baggage check (US) die Gepäckaufbewahrung [gepeck-owfbevahroong]
baggage reclaim die Gepäckrückgabe [gepeck- rōock-gahb-uh]
bakery die Bäckerei [becker-ī]
balcony der Balkon [bal-kohn]
a room with a balcony ein Zimmer mit Balkon [ine tsimmer]

bald kahl
ball (large) der Ball [bal]
(small) die Kugel [kōogel]
ballet das Ballett [bal-ett]
ballpoint pen der Kugelschreiber [kōogel- shryber]
Baltic Sea die Ostsee [ost-zay]
banana die Banane [banahn-uh]
band (musical) die Band [bent]
bandage der Verband [fairband]
bank (money) die Bank

 Most banks are open from 9 a.m. to 4 p.m. or 4.30 p.m. Some close for an hour at lunchtime. On Thursdays, city centre branches will often be open until 6 p.m.; if you are changing money, make your transaction at one desk and then collect your money from another desk; the bank clerk is likely to say: **'Sie bekommen ihr Geld an der Kasse'** [zee bekommen eer gelt an dair kassuh]. The German unit of currency is the mark (**die Mark, die D-Mark, DM**) which consists of 100 **Pfennige (Pf)**. Denominations are 1, 2, 5, 10, 50 Pf, 1, 2, 5 DM (coins) and 10, 20, 50, 100, 200, 500, 1000 DM (notes).

bank account das Bankkonto [bank-konto]
bar die Bar

 In bars, it is not customary to pay for your drink at the same time as you order; a record of your orders will be kept (often on a beer mat) and you pay on leaving; you can expect table service in all bars and pubs. In cities some bars are normally open until early in the morning. Closing time is much less of a concept in Germany. The legal limit for driving is an alcohol level of 80 millilitres.

bar of chocolate die Tafel Schokolade [**tah**fel shoko-la**hd**-uh]
barber's der Frisör [friz**ur**]
basket der Korb [korp]
(in shop) der Einkaufskorb [**ine**-kowfs-korp]
bath das Bad [baht]
can I have a bath? kann ich ein Bad nehmen? [**nay**men]
bathroom das Bad [baht]
with a private bathroom mit eigenem Bad [**ī**-gen-em]
bath towel das Badehandtuch [**bah**duh-hant-tOOKH]
battery die Batterie [batter**ee**]
Bavaria Bayern [**by**-ern]
Bavarian Alps die Bayrischen Alpen [**by**-rishen]
be* sein [zine]
beach der Strand [shtrant]
beach mat die Strandmatte [**shtrant**-mat-uh]
beach umbrella der Sonnenschirm [**zo**nnen-sheerm]

In North Germany, you will find wicker beach chairs which have a top piece that goes over your head; they are called: **Strandkörbe** [strant-**kur**buh].

beans die Bohnen
runner beans die Stangenbohnen [**shtang**en-]
broad beans dicke Bohnen [**dick**-uh]
beard der Bart
beautiful schön [shurn]
because weil [vile]
because of ... wegen ... [**vay**gen]
bed das Bett
I'm going to bed ich gehe zu Bett [ish g**ay**-uh tsOO]
bed and breakfast Übernachtung mit Frühstück [OObern**a**KHtoong mit fr**OO**shtOOck]
bedroom das Schlafzimmer [shl**ah**f-tsimmer]
beef das Rindfleisch [**rint**-flysh]
beer das Bier [beer]
two beers, please zwei Bier, bitte [**bitt**-uh]

Some useful beer vocabulary:

Alsterwasser [**a**lster-vasser] shandy
Alt a darker beer, vaguely like bitter
Export lager

Faßbier [fassbeer] draught beer
ein großes Bier [ine grohssess beer] a large beer
eine Halbe [ine-uh halb-uh] half a litre
ein Helles [ine helless] a lager
ein kleines Bier [ine kline-ess beer] a small beer
eine Maß [mahss] a litre (in South Germany)
Pils strong lager
Starkbier [shtarkbeer] strong beer
Radler [rahtler] shandy
Weißbier [vice-beer] pale wheat-type beer
Weizenbier [vytsen-beer] pale wheat-type beer

beer mug der Bierkrug [beerkrook]
before vorher [forhair]
  before that davor [dafor]
  before me vor mir
begin: when does it begin? wann fängt es an? [van fengt ess an]
beginner (man/woman) der Anfänger [anfeng-er]/die Anfängerin
beginning: at the beginning am Anfang
behind hinten
  behind me hinter mir
beige beige [bayj]
Belgian (adj) belgisch [belgish]
Belgium Belgien [bel-gee-en]
believe glauben [glowben]
below unten [oonten]
  below ... unter ... [oonter]

belt der Gürtel [goortel]
bend (in road) die Kurve [koorv-uh]
Berlin Wall die (Berliner) Mauer [(bairleener) mow-er]
berth (on ship) die Kabine [kabeen-uh]
beside: beside the ... neben dem/der ... [nayben daym/dair]
best beste [best-uh]
better besser
  are you feeling better? geht es dir/Ihnen besser? [gayt ess deer/eenen]
between zwischen [tsvishen]
beyond jenseits (+gen) [yayn-zites]
bicycle das Fahrrad [fahr-raht]
big groß [grohss]
  too big zu groß [tsoo]
  it's not big enough es ist nicht groß genug [nisht – genook]
bike das Rad [raht]
  (motorbike) das Motorrad [motohr-raht]
bikini der Bikini
bill die Rechnung [reshnoong]
  (US: money) der Geldschein [gelt-shine]
  could I have the bill, please? kann ich bitte bezahlen? [kan ish bitt-uh betsahlen]
bin der Abfalleimer [apfal-ime-er]
bin liners die Mülltüten [mooll-tooten]
binding (ski) die Bindung [bindoong]

bird der Vogel [**foh**gel]

biro® der Kugelschreiber [k**oo**gel-shryber]

birthday der Geburtstag [geb**oo**rts-tahk]

happy birthday! herzlichen Glückwunsch zum Geburtstag! [**hairts**-lishen gl**oo**ckvoonsh tsoom]

biscuit das Plätzchen [pletsshen]

bit: a little bit ein bißchen [ine **biss**-shen]

a big bit ein großes Stück [gr**oh**sss sht**oo**ck]

a bit of ... ein Stück von ...

a bit expensive etwas teuer

bite (by insect) der Stich [shtish] (by dog) der Biß [biss]

bitter (taste etc) bitter

black schwarz [shvarts]

Black Forest der Schwarzwald [shvarts-valt]

blanket die Decke [**deck**-uh]

bless you! Gesundheit! [gez**oo**nt-hite]

blind blind [blint]

blinds die Jalousie [Jal**oo**zee]

blister die Blase [bl**ah**z-uh]

blocked (road, sink) verstopft [fairsht**o**pft]

block of flats der Wohnblock [**voh**nblock]

blond blond [blont]

blood das Blut [bloot]

high blood pressure hoher Blutdruck [bl**oo**t-droock]

blouse die Bluse [bl**oo**z-uh]

blow-dry (verb) fönen [**fur**nen]

I'd like a cut and blow-dry schneiden und fönen, bitte [shn**y**den oont]

blue blau [blow]

blusher das Rouge [r**oo**J]

boarding house die Pension [pangz-y**oh**n]

boarding pass die Bordkarte [**bor**tkart-uh]

boat das Boot [boht] (for passengers) das Schiff [shiff]

body der Körper [**kur**per]

boil (water, potatoes) kochen [k**o**KHen]

boiled egg ein gekochtes Ei [gek**o**KHtess ī]

bone der Knochen [k-n**o**KHen]

bonnet (of car) die Haube [**howb**-uh]

book das Buch [b**oo**KH]

to book buchen [b**oo**KHen], bestellen [besht**e**llen]

can I book a seat? kann ich einen Platz reservieren lassen? [rezair-v**ee**ren]

dialogue

I'd like to book a table for two ich möchte einen Tisch für zwei Personen bestellen [ish m**u**rsht-uh ine-en tish f**oo**r tsvy pairz**oh**nen]

what time would you like it booked for? für wann ist die Reservierung? [rezair-v**ee**roong]

half past seven halb acht

that's fine das geht in Ordnung [gayt in **o**rtnoong]
and your name? Ihr Name, bitte? [**nah**m-uh]

bookshop die Buchhandlung [b**oo**KH-hantloong]
bookstore (US) die Buchhandlung
boot (footwear) der Stiefel [sht**ee**fel]
(of car) der Kofferraum [**ko**ffer-rowm]
border (of country) die Grenze [**g**rents-uh]
bored: I'm bored ich habe langeweile [ish h**a**hb-uh l**a**ng-uh-vile-uh]
boring langweilig [l**a**ngvile-ish]
born: I was born in Manchester ich bin in Manchester geboren [geb**o**hren]
I was born in 1960 ich bin neunzehnhundertsechzig geboren
borrow leihen [l**y**-en]
may I borrow ...? kann ich ... leihen?
both beide [b**y**-duh]
bother: sorry to bother you with this es tut mir leid, Sie damit zu belästigen [ess t**oo**t meer lite zee dahmit ts**oo** bel**e**stigen]
bottle die Flasche [fl**a**sh-uh]
a bottle of dry white wine eine Flasche tr**o**ckenen Weißwein

bottle-opener der Flaschen-öffner [fl**a**shen-urfner]
bottom (of person) der Hintern
at the bottom of the hill am Fuß des Berges [f**oo**ss]
box die Schachtel [sha**K**Htel]
(larger) der Karton
box office die Kasse [k**a**ss-uh]
boy der Junge [y**oo**ng-uh]
boyfriend der Freund [froynt]
bra der BH [bay-h**a**h]
bracelet das Armband [**a**rmbant]
brake die Bremse [br**e**mz-uh]
brandy der Weinbrand [v**i**ne-brant]
bread das Brot [broht]
some more bread, please noch etwas Brot, bitte [**e**tvass]
white bread das Weißbrot [v**i**ce-broht]
brown bread das Graubrot [gr**o**w-broht]
wholemeal bread das Vollkornbrot [f**o**llkorn-broht]
break (verb) brechen [br**e**shen]
I've broken ... mir ist ... kaputtgegangen [meer – kap**oo**t-gegangen]
I think I've broken my wrist ich gla**u**be, ich habe mir das Handgelenk gebrochen [gebr**o**KHen]
breakdown die Panne [p**a**nn-uh]

If you break down on a motorway, go to one of the emergency telephones; arrows on the marker posts along the hard shoulder will direct you to the nearest one. The **Straßenwacht** [shtrahssenvakHt] will give free assistance. (You will have to pay for any parts.) The largest German motoring association is the **ADAC** [ah-day-ah-ts**ay**] which has links with other international motoring organizations. Note that it is compulsory to carry a warning triangle as well as a first-aid kit.

breakdown service die Pannenhilfe [p**a**nnen-hilf-uh]
break down (in car) eine Panne haben [**ine**-uh p**a**nn-uh h**a**hben]
I've broken down ich habe eine Panne
breakfast das Frühstück [fr**oo**shtック]
English/full breakfast ein englisches Frühstück [**e**ng-lish-ess]
break-in: I've had a break-in bei mir ist eingebrochen worden [by meer ist **ine**-gebrokHen v**o**rden]
breast die Brust [br**oo**st]
breathe atmen [**ah**tmen]
breeze die Brise [br**ee**z-uh]
brewery die Brauerei [brower-**i**]
bridge (over river) die Brücke [br**oo**ck-uh]

brief kurz [koorts]
briefcase die Aktentasche [**a**kten-tash-uh]
bright (light etc) hell
bright red hellrot [h**e**ll-r**oh**t]
brilliant (idea) glänzend [gl**e**ntsent]
(person) großartig [gr**oh**ss-artish]
bring bringen
I'll bring it back later ich bringe es später zurück [br**i**ng-uh ess shp**ay**ter tsoor**oo**ck]
Britain Großbritannien [grohss-brit**a**nnee-en]
British britisch [br**ee**tish]
brochure die Broschüre [brosh**oo**r-uh]
broken kaputt
bronchitis die Bronchitis [bron-sh**ee**tis]
brooch die Brosche [br**o**sh-uh]
broom der Besen [b**ay**zen]
brother der Bruder [br**oo**der]
brother-in-law der Schwager [shv**ah**ger]
brown braun [brown]
bruise der blaue Fleck [bl**ow**-uh]
brush die Bürste [b**oo**rst-uh]
(artist's) der Pinsel [p**i**nzel]
Brussels Brüssel [br**oo**ssel]
bucket der Eimer [**ime**-er]
buffet car der Speisewagen [shp**ize**-uh-vahgen]
buggy (for child) der Sportwagen [sh**o**rt-vahgen]
building das Gebäude [geb**oy**d-uh]

bulb (light bulb) die Birne [**beer**n-uh]

bumper die Stoßstange [sht**oh**ss-shtang-uh]

bunk das Bett

bureau de change die Wechselstube [**vek**sel-sht**oo**b-uh]

burglary der Einbruch [**ine**-brooкн]

burn die Verbrennung [fair-**bren**noong]
(verb) brennen

burnt: this is burnt das ist angebrannt [**an**-gebrannt]

burst: a burst pipe ein gepl**a**tztes Rohr

bus der Bus [**boo**ss]
what number bus is it to ...? welcher Bus fährt nach ...? [**vel**sher **boo**ss fairt naкн]
when is the next bus to ...? wann fährt der nächste Bus nach ...? [**nay**kst-uh]
what time is the last bus? wann fährt der letzte Bus? [**letst**-uh]
could you let me know when we get there? können Sie mir Bescheid sagen, wenn wir da sind? [**kur**nen zee meer besh**ite** z**ah**gen]

Get tickets from ticket machines at the bus stop or, in some areas, from the driver; in some parts of Germany tickets must be purchased in advance. Multiple tickets –

Mehrfahrten-karten [mair-fahrtenkarten] cut down the cost of travel considerably.

dialogue

does this bus go to ...?
fährt dieser Bus nach ...? [fairt]
no, you need a number ...
nein, Sie müssen mit der ... fahren
where does it leave from?
wo fährt er ab? [vo]

business das Geschäft [gesh**eft**]

bus station der Busbahnhof [**boo**ss-bahnhof]

bus stop die Bushaltestelle [**boo**ss-halt-uh-shtell-uh]

bust der Busen [**boo**zen]

busy (restaurant etc) voll [foll]
(telephone) besetzt [bez**etst**]
I'm busy tomorrow morgen bin ich beschäftigt [besh**ef**-tisht]

but aber [**ah**ber]

butcher's der Metzger [**metsger**]

butter die Butter [**boo**tter]

button der Knopf [k-nopf]

buy kaufen [**kow**fen]
where can I buy ...? wo kann ich ... bekommen? [voh]

by: by bus/car mit dem Bus/Auto [daym]
written by ... geschrieben von

by the window am Fenster
by the sea am Meer
by Thursday bis Donnerstag
bye auf Wiedersehen [owf-
veederzayn]

C

cabbage der Kohl
cable car die Drahtseilbahn
[drahtzile-bahn]
café das Café [kaffay]

Cafés serve coffee, tea
and cakes, alcoholic
drinks and snacks but not
full meals. Some **Konditoreien** (see
'cake shop') are also cafés, serving
coffee and cakes.

cagoule das Windhemd [vint-
hemt]
cake der Kuchen [kooKHen]
cake shop die Konditorei
[kondeetor-ī]
call (verb) rufen [roofen]
(to phone) anrufen [anroofen]
what's it called? wie heißt
das? [vee hyst dass]
he/she is called ... er/sie
heißt ...
please call a doctor bitte
rufen Sie einen Arzt
please give me a call at
7.30 a.m. tomorrow morning
könnten Sie mich morgen
früh um sieben Uhr dreißig
wecken? [kurnten zee mish

morgen froo – vecken]
please ask him to call me
sagen Sie ihm bitte, er
möchte mich anrufen
[mursht-uh]
call back: I'll call back later
ich komme später noch
einmal wieder [ish komm-uh
shpayter noKH ine-mahl veeder]
(phone back) ich rufe später
noch einmal an [roof-uh]
call round: I'll call round
tomorrow ich komme
morgen vorbei [komm-uh – for-
by]
camcorder der Camcorder
camera die Kamera
camera shop der Fotoladen
[foto-lahden]
camp (verb) zelten [tselten]
camping gas das Campinggas
[kemping-gahss]
campsite der Campingplatz
[kempingplats]

Sites are officially graded
on a scale beginning at
'good' and working up to
'excellent'. Even the lowest grade
have toilet and washing facilities
and a shop nearby on the site, while
the grandest are virtually open-air
hotels with swimming pools,
supermarkets and various other
comforts. Many sites, especially
those in popular holiday areas, are
nearly always full from June to
September, and you should arrive
early in the afternoon for a good

chance of getting in. Most campsites close down in the winter.

can (tin) die Dose [**doh**z-uh]
  a can of beer eine Dose Bier
can*: can you ...? kannst du/können Sie ...?
  [d**oo**/k**u**rnen zee]
  can I have ...? kann ich ... haben? [**hah**ben]
  I can't ... ich kann nicht...
  [nisht]
Canada Kanada
Canadian (adj) kanadisch
  [kan**ah**dish]
  I'm Canadian (man/woman) ich bin Kanadier [kan**ah**dee-er]/
  Kanadierin
canal der Kanal [kan**ahl**]
cancel (reservation) rückgängig machen [r**oo**ck-gengish ma**kH**en]
candle die Kerze [**kair**ts-uh]
candy (US) die Süßigkeiten [z**oo**ssish-kyten]
canoe das Kanu [kahn**oo**]
canoeing das Kanufahren [kahn**oo**-fahren]
can-opener der Dosenöffner [**doh**zen-urfner]
cap (hat) eine Mütze [m**oo**ts-uh]
  (of bottle) der Deckel
car das Auto [**owt**o]
  by car mit dem Auto
carafe die Karaffe [kar**aff**-uh]
  a carafe of house white, please eine Karaffe weißen Tafelwein, bitte

caravan der Wohnwagen [**voh**nvahgen]
caravan site der Wohnwagenplatz [**voh**nvahgen-plats]
carburettor der Vergaser [fair-**gah**zer]
card (birthday etc) die Karte [**kart**-uh]
  here's my (business) card hier ist meine Karte
cardigan die Strickjacke [**shtrick**-yack-uh]
cardphone das Kartentelefon
careful vorsichtig [**for**-zishtish]
  be careful! seien Sie vorsichtig! [**zy**-en zee]
caretaker der Hausmeister [**howss**-myster]
car ferry die Autofähre [**owt**o-fair-uh]
car hire die Autovermietung [**owt**o-fairmeetoong]
carnival der Karneval [**karn**-uh-val]
car park der Parkplatz [**park**plats]
carpet der Teppich [**teppish**]
carriage (of train) der Wagen [**vah**gen]
carrier bag die Tragetasche [**trahg**-uh-tash-uh]
carrot die Möhre [**mur**-uh]
carry tragen [**trah**gen]
carry-cot die Säuglingstragetasche [**zoyg**lings-trahg-uh-tash-uh]
carton (of orange juice etc) die Packung [**pack**oong]

carwash (place) die Autowaschanlage [**ow**to-vash-anlahg-uh]

case (suitcase) der Koffer

cash das Bargeld [**bahr**gelt] (verb) einlösen [**ine**-lurzen]

will you cash this for me? können Sie das für mich einlösen? [**kur**nen]

cash desk die Kasse [**kass**-uh]

cash dispenser der Geldautomat [**gelt**-owtomaht]

cassette die Kassette [kass**ett**-uh]

cassette recorder der Kassettenrecorder

castle das Schloß [shloss]

casualty department die Unfallstation [**oon**fal-shtats-yohn]

cat die Katze [**kats**-uh]

catch fangen

where do we catch the bus to ...? wo können wir den Bus nach ... bekommen?

cathedral der Dom [dohm]

Catholic (adj) katholisch [kat**oh**lish]

cauliflower der Blumenkohl [bl**oo**menkohl]

cave die Höhle [**hurl**-uh]

CD die CD [tsay-**day**]

ceiling die Decke [**deck**-uh]

celery der Sellerie [**zell**eree]

cellar (for wine) der Weinkeller [**vine**-keller]

cemetery der Friedhof [**freet**-hohf]

Centigrade* Celsius [**tsel**zee-oos]

centimetre* der Zentimeter [**tsenti**mayter]

central zentral [tsent**rahl**]

central heating die Zentralheizung [tsent**rahl**-hytsoong]

centre das Zentrum [**tsen**troom]

how do we get to the city centre? wie kommt man zum Stadtzentrum? [tsoom **shtat**-tsentroom]

cereal die Zerealien [tsairay-**ahl**ee-en]

certainly sicher [**zish**er]

certainly not ganz bestimmt nicht [gants besht**immt** nisht]

chair der Stuhl [sht**ool**]

chairlift der Sessellift [**zess**el-lift]

champagne der Champagner [shamp**an**-yer]

change (noun: money) das Wechselgeld [**veksel**-gelt]

to change (money) wechseln [**weks**eln]

to change a reservation umbuchen [**oom**b00KHen]

can I change this for ...? kann ich das gegen ... umtauschen? [**gay**gen ... **oom**-towshen]

I don't have any change ich habe kein Kleingeld [**hahb**-uh kine kl**ine**-gelt]

can you give me change for a 50 euro note? können Sie einen 50-Euro-Schein wechseln? [**kur**nen zee **ine**-en – **oy**ro-shine]

dialogue

do we have to change (trains/buses)? müssen wir umsteigen? [**moo**ssen veer **oo**m-shtygen]

yes, change at Düsseldorf ja, Sie müssen in Düsseldorf umsteigen

no, it's direct nein, das ist eine Dir**e**ktverbindung

changed: to get changed sich umziehen [zish **oo**m-tsee-en]
chapel die Kapelle [ka**pell**-uh]
charge der Preis [price]
charge (verb) verlangen [fair**lang**en]
charge card die Kreditkarte [kray**deet**-kart-uh]
see credit card
cheap billig [**bill**ish]

do you have anything cheaper? haben Sie etwas billigeres? [**hah**ben zee **e**tvass **bill**igeress]

check (verb) überprüfen [**oo**ber-pr**oo**fen]

could you check the ... please? könnten Sie die ... überprüfen, bitte? [**kurn**ten]
(US) der Scheck [sheck]
(in restaurant etc) die Rechnung [**resh**noong]
check-in der Check-in
check in (at hotel) sich **a**nmelden [zish]
(at airport) einchecken [**ine**-checken]

where do we have to check in? wo müssen wir einchecken?

cheek (of face) die Backe [**back**-uh]
cheerio! (bye-bye) tschüs! [ch**oo**ss]
cheers! (toast) Prost! [prohst]
(thanks) danke [**dank**uh]
cheese der Käse [**kayz**-uh]
chemist's die Apotheke [apo**tayk**-uh]

 German pharmacists sell prescribed and non-prescribed drugs. There are all-night pharmacists in bigger towns and cities; they work on a rota system and you can find the address of the one that is open on the door of any pharmacist as well as in local papers (look under **Nachtdienst** – night service).

cheque der Scheck [sheck]

do you take cheques? nehmen Sie Schecks? [**nay**men zee shecks]

cheque book das Scheckheft [**sheck**-heft]
cheque card die Scheckkarte [**sheck**-kart-uh]
cherry die Kirsche [**keersh**-uh]
chess Schach [shakH]
chest (body) die Brust [broost]
chewing gum der Kaugummi [**kow**-goommee]
chicken (as food) das Hähnchen [**hayn**shen]

chickenpox die Windpocken [**vi**ntpocken]

child das Kind [kint]
children die Kinder

child minder die Tagesmutter [**tah**gess-mootter]

children's pool das Kinderschwimmbecken [**ki**nder-shvimmbecken]

children's portion der Kinderteller [**ki**nder-teller]

chin das Kinn

china (noun) das Porzellan [portsell**ah**n]

Chinese (adj) chinesisch [shin**ay**zish]

chips die Pommes frites [pom frit]
(US) die Chips

chocolate die Schokolade [shokol**ah**d-uh]
milk chocolate die Milchschokolade [**mi**lsh-]
plain chocolate die Bitterschokolade
chocolates die Pralinen [pral**ee**nen]
hot chocolate der Kakao [kak**ow**]

choose wählen [**vay**len]

Christian name der Vorname [**fo**rnahm-uh]

Christmas Weihnachten [**vy**naкHten]
Christmas Eve der Heiligabend [hylish-**ah**bent]
merry Christmas! frohe Weihnachten [**fro**h-uh]

church die Kirche [**keersh**-uh]

cider der Apfelwein [**a**pfel-vine]

cigar die Zigarre [tsig**a**rr-uh]

cigarette die Zigarette [tsigar**ett**-uh]

cigarette lighter das Feuerzeug [**foy**er-tsoyk]

cinema das Kino [**kee**no]

circle der Kreis [krice]
(in theatre) der Balkon [balk**oh**n]

city die Stadt [shtatt]

city centre die Innenstadt [**i**nnenshtatt]

clean (adj) sauber [**zow**ber]
can you clean this for me? können Sie dies für mich reinigen? [**ku**rnen zee deess foor mish r**y**nigen]

cleaning solution (for contact lenses) die Reinigungslösung [**ry**nigoongs-lurzoong]

cleansing lotion (cosmetic) die Reinigungscreme [**ry**nigoongs-kraym]

clear klar

clever klug [klook]

cliff die Klippe [**kli**pp-uh]

climbing das Bergsteigen [**ba**irk-shtygen]

cling film die Frischhaltefolie [**fri**sh-halt-uh-fohlee-uh]

clinic die Klinik [**klee**nik]

cloakroom (for coats) die Garderobe [garder**oh**b-uh]

clock die Uhr [oor]

close schließen [shl**ee**ssen]

dialogue

what time do you close?
wann schließen Sie?
we close at 8 p.m. on
weekdays and 6 p.m. on
Saturdays wir schließen
wochentags um zwanzig
Uhr und samstags um
achtzehn Uhr [**vo**kHen-tahks
oom – **zams**-tahks]
do you close for lunch?
haben Sie mittags
geschlossen? [gesh**lo**ssen]
yes, between 1 and
2.30 p.m. ja, von dreizehn
Uhr bis vierzehn Uhr
dreißig

closed geschlossen [gesh**lo**ssen]
cloth (fabric) der Stoff [**sht**off]
(for cleaning etc) der Lappen
clothes die Kleider [**kly**der]
clothes line die Wäscheleine
[**ve**sh-uh-line-uh]
clothes peg die Wäsche-
klammer [**ve**sh-uh-klammer]
cloud die Wolke [**vo**lk-uh]
cloudy wolkig [**vo**lkish]
clutch (of car) die Kupplung
[**koo**ploong]
coach (bus) der Bus [**boo**ss]
(on train) der Wagen [**vah**gen]
coach station der
Busbahnhof [**boo**ssbahnhohf]
coach trip die Busreise [**boo**ss-
rize-uh]
coast die Küste [**kœo**st-uh]
on the coast an der Küste

coat (long coat) der Mantel
(jacket) die Jacke [**yack**-uh]
coathanger der Kleiderbügel
[**kly**derbœogel]
cockroach die Küchenschabe
[**kœo**shen-shahb-uh]
cocoa der Kakao [kak**ow**]
code (for phoning) die Vorwahl
[**for**vahl]
what's the (dialling) code for
Berlin? was ist die Vorwahl
für Berlin?
coffee der Kaffee [**kaff**ay]
two coffees, please zwei
Kaffee bitte

You can generally expect
to be served ground
coffee when ordering a
coffee. It is often served in a small
pot (**Kännchen** [**kenn**shen])
containing approximately two cups.
Note that the milk served with your
coffee is usually evaporated milk.
Italian coffees like **Cappuccino** and
Espresso are also quite popular.

coin die Münze [**mœo**nts-uh]
Coke® die Cola [**koh**la]
cold (adj) kalt
I'm cold mir ist kalt [meer]
I have a cold ich bin erkältet
[ish bin airk**el**tet]
collapse: he's collapsed er ist
zusammengebrochen [air ist
tsooz**a**mmengebrok**H**en]
collar der Kragen [**krah**gen]
collect sammeln
I've come to collect ... ich

komme, um ... abzuholen
[ish **komm**-uh oom ... **a**p-tsoo-hohlen]

collect call das R-Gespräch
[**air**-geshpraysh]

college das College

Cologne Köln [kurln]

colour die Farbe [**far**b-uh]
  do you have this in other
  colours? haben Sie dies
  noch in anderen Farben?
  [**hah**ben zee deess noкн in ander-en
  farben]

colour film der Farbfilm [**far**p-film]

comb (noun) der Kamm

come **ko**mmen

dialogue

  where do you come from?
  woher kommen Sie?
  [voh**air**]
  I come from Edinburgh ich
  komme aus Edinburgh
  [ish **ko**mm-uh owss]

come back zurückkommen
[tsoor**oo**ck-kommen]
  I'll come back tomorrow ich
  komme morgen zurück
  [**ko**mm-uh]

come in hereinkommen [hair-**ine**-kommen]

comfortable (hotel etc)
komfortabel [komfort**ah**bel]

compact disc die Compact-Disc

company (business) die Firma
[**feer**ma]

compartment (on train) das
Abteil [a**ptile**]

compass der Kompaß [**ko**mpass]

complain sich beschweren
[zish beshv**ai**ren]

complaint die Beschwerde
[beshv**ai**rd-uh]
  I have a complaint ich
  möchte mich beschweren
  [m**ur**sht-uh mish beshv**ai**ren]

completely völlig [**fur**lish]

computer der Computer
[ˈcomputerˈ]

concert das Konzert [konts**ai**rt]

concussion die Gehirn-
erschütterung [geh**eer**n-
airsh**oo**tteroong]

conditioner (for hair) der
Festiger

condom das Kondom
[kond**oh**m]

conference die Konferenz
[konf**ai**rents]

confirm bestätigen
[besht**ay**tigen]

congratulations! herzlichen
Glückwunsch! [**hair**tslishen
gl**oo**ckvoonsh]

connecting flight der
Anschlußflug [**a**nshlooss-flook]

connection (in travelling) die
Verbindung [fair**bi**ndoong]

conscious (medically) bei
Bewußtsein [by bev**oo**st-zine]

constipation die Verstopfung
[fair-sht**o**pfoong]

consulate das Konsulat

[konzool**aht**]

contact: where can I contact him? wo kann ich ihn erreichen? [vo – een air-**ry**shen]

contact lenses die Kontaktlinsen [kont**akt**-linzen]

contraceptive das Verhütungsmittel [fairh**oo**toongs-mittel]

convenient (time, location) günstig [g**oon**stish]

that's not convenient das ist nicht sehr günstig [nisht zair]

cook kochen [ko**KH**en]

not cooked (underdone) nicht gar [nisht gahr]

cooker der Herd [hairt]

cookie (US) das Plätzchen [**plets**-shen]

cooking utensils die Küchengeräte [k**oo**shen-gerayt-uh]

cool kühl [k**oo**l]

cork der Korken

corkscrew der Korkenzieher [**kor**ken-tsee-er]

corner: on the corner an der Ecke [**eck**-uh]

in the corner in der **E**cke

cornflakes die Corn-flakes

correct (right) richtig [**ri**shtish]

corridor der Gang

cosmetics die Kosmetika [kosma**yt**ika]

cost (verb) k**o**sten

how much does it cost? was kostet das? [vass **ko**stet dass]

cot (for baby) das Kinderbett

cotton die Baumwolle

[b**ow**mvoll-uh]

cotton wool die Watte [**vat**-uh]

couch (sofa) die Couch

couchette der Liegewagen [**lee**g-uh-vahgen]

cough (noun) der Husten [h**oo**sten]

cough medicine das Hustenmittel [h**oo**sten-mittel]

could: could you ...? könnten Sie...? [**kur**nten zee]

could I have ...? könnte ich ... haben? [**kur**nt-uh ish ... h**ah**ben]

I couldn't ... (wasn't able to) ich konnte nicht... [ish **ko**nnt-uh nisht]

country das Land [lant]

countryside die Landschaft [**lant**-shafft]

couple (man and woman) das Paar [pahr]

a couple of ... ein paar... [ine pahr]

courier der Reiseleiter [**rize**-uh-lyter]

course (of meal) der Gang

of course natürlich [nat**oo**rlish]

of course not natürlich nicht [nisht]

cousin (male) der Vetter [**fe**tter] (female) die Kusine [k**oo**z**ee**n-uh]

cow die Kuh [k**oo**]

crab die Krebs [krayps]

cracker (biscuit) der Kräcker [**kre**cker]

craft shop der Handwerksladen [**hant**vairkslahden]

crash (noun) der Zusammenstoß [tsoo-za**mm**en-shtohss]

I've had a crash ich hatte einen Unfall [ish h**a**tt-uh **ine**-en **oo**nfal]

crazy verrückt [fair-r** oo**ckt]

cream (on milk, in cake) die Sahne [**zah**n-uh]
(lotion) die Creme [kraym]
(colour) cremefarben [kr**aym**-farben]

creche (for babies) die Kinderkrippe [**k**inderkripp-uh]

credit card die Kreditkarte [kred**ee**t-kart-uh]

 Although credit cards and charge cards are accepted in a number of larger shops they are not as popular yet as in Great Britain and the US. Do not expect to be able to pay by credit card in supermarkets or at service stations.

dialogue

can I pay by credit card? kann ich mit Kreditkarte bezahlen? [bets**ah**len]

which card do you want to use? mit welcher Karte möchten Sie bezahlen? [v**e**lsher]

what's the number? was ist die Nummer? [n**oo**mmer]

and the expiry date? und das Ablaufdatum? [**a**plowf-dahtoom]

crisps die Chips [chips]

crockery das Geschirr [gesh**ee**r]

crossing (by sea) die Überfahrt [**oo**berfahrt]

crossroads die Kreuzung [kr**oy**tsoong]

crowd die Menge [m**e**ng-uh]

crowded (streets, bars) voll [foll]

crown (on tooth) die Krone [kr**oh**n-uh]

cruise (by ship) die Kreuzfahrt [kr**oy**ts-fahrt]

crutches die Krücken [kr**oo**ck-en]

cry weinen [v**y**nen]

cucumber die Gurke [g**oo**rk-uh]

cup die Tasse [t**a**ss-uh]

a cup of ... please eine Tasse ..., bitte [**ine**-uh]

cupboard der Schrank [shrank]

curly (hair) kraus [krowss]

current (electrical, in water) der Strom [shtrohm]
(in sea) die Strömung [shtr**u**rmoong]

curtains die Vorhänge [**f**orheng-uh]

cushion das Kissen

custom der Brauch [browкн]

Customs der Zoll [tsoll]

cut der Schnitt [shnitt]

cut (verb) schneiden [shn**y**den]

I've cut myself ich habe mich geschnitten [ish hahb-uh mish geshnitten]

cutlery das Besteck [beshteck]

cycling das Radfahren [rahtfahren]

cyclist (man/woman) der Radfahrer [rahtfahrer]/die Radfahrerin

Czech (adj) tschechisch [cheshish]

(language) Tschechisch

Czech Republic die Tschechische Republik [cheshish-uh rep00-bleek]

D

dad der Vater [fahter]

daily täglich [tayglish]

damage (verb) beschädigen [beshaydigen]

I'm sorry, I've damaged this tut mir leid, ich habe es beschädigt [t00t meer lite]

damaged beschädigt [beshaydisht]

damn! verdammt! [fairdamt]

damp feucht [foysht]

dance (noun) der Tanz [tants]

dance (verb) tanzen [tantsen]

would you like to dance? möchtest du/möchten Sie tanzen? [murshtest d00/murshten zee]

dangerous gefährlich [gefairlish]

Danish dänisch [daynish]

Danube die Donau [dohnow]

dark dunkel [doonkel]

it's getting dark es wird dunkel [veert]

date*: what's the date today? der Wievielte ist heute? [dair veefeelt-uh ist hoyt-uh]

let's make a date for next Monday wir sollten einen Termin für nächsten Montag vereinbaren [ine-en tairmeen f00r – fair-ine-bahren]

dates (fruit) die Datteln fpl

daughter die Tochter [toKHter]

daughter-in-law die Schwiegertochter [shveeger-toKHter]

dawn das Morgengrauen [morgen-growen]

at dawn bei Tagesanbruch [by tahgess-anbr00KH]

day der Tag [tahk]

the day after am Tag danach [danaKH]

the day after tomorrow übermorgen [00bermorgen]

the day before am Tag zuvor [ts00for]

the day before yesterday vorgestern [forgestern]

every day jeden Tag [yayden]

all day den ganzen Tag [dayn gantsen]

in two days' time in zwei Tagen [tahgen]

have a nice day schönen Tag noch [shurnen – noKH]

day trip der Tagesausflug [tahgess-owssfl00k]

dead tot [toht]

deaf taub [towp]

deal (business) das Geschäft [gesheft]

it's a deal abgemacht [ap-gemaKHt]

death der Tod [toht]

decaffeinated coffee koffeinfreier Kaffee [koffay-een-fry-er kaffay]

December der Dezember [daytsember]

decide entscheiden [ent-shyden]

we haven't decided yet wir haben uns noch nicht entschieden [veer hahben oonss noKH nisht ent-sheeden]

decision die Entscheidung [ent-shydoong]

deck (on ship) das Deck

deckchair der Liegestuhl [leeg-uh-shtool]

deduct abziehen [ap-tsee-en]

deep tief [teef]

definitely bestimmt [beshtimmt]

definitely not ganz bestimmt nicht [gants]

degree (qualification) der Abschluß [apshlooss]

delay die Verzögerung [fair-tsurgeroong]

deliberately absichtlich [apzishtlish]

delicatessen der Feinkostladen [fine-kost-lahden]

delicious köstlich [kurstlish]

deliver liefern [leefern]

delivery (of mail) die Zustellung [ts00-shtelloong]

Denmark Dänemark [dayn-uh-mark]

dental floss die Zahnseide [tsahnzide-uh]

dentist der Zahnarzt [tsahn-artst]

see **doctor**

dialogue

it's this one here es ist dieser hier [deezer heer]
this one? dieser?
no that one nein, dieser [nine]
here? hier? [heer]
yes ja [yah]

dentures das Gebiß [gebiss]

deodorant das Deodorant

department die Abteilung [ap-tyloong]

department store das Kaufhaus [kowfhowss]

departure die Abreise [ap-rize-uh]

(of plane) der Abflug [apflook]

departure lounge die Abflughalle [apflook-hal-uh]

depend: it depends es kommt darauf an [ess kommt darowf an]

it depends on ... es hängt von ... ab [hengt fon ... ap]

deposit (as security) die Kaution [kowts-yohn]

(as part payment) die

Anzahlung [**antsah**loong]
description die Beschreibung
[beshr**y**boong]
dessert der Nachtisch
[**na**KHtish]
destination das Reiseziel
[**rize**-uh-tseel]
develop entwickeln
[ent**vi**ckeln]

dialogue

could you develop these
films? können Sie diese
Filme entwickeln? [**kur**nen
zee **dee**z-uh film-uh]
when will they be ready?
wann sind sie fertig?
[**fair**tish]
tomorrow afternoon
morgen nachmittag
how much is the four-hour
service? was kostet der
Vier-Stunden-Service?
[sht**oo**nden]

diabetic (man/woman) der
Diabetiker [dee-ab**ay**tiker]/die
Diabetikerin
diabetic foods diabetische
Kost [dee-ab**ay**tish-uh]
dial (verb) wählen [**vay**len]
dialling code die Vorwahl
[**for**vahl]

see also **phone**

For direct international
calls from Germany, dial
the country code (given
below), the area code (minus the
first 0), and finally the subscriber
number:

UK: 0044   Australia: 0061
Ireland: 00353   New Zealand: 0064
US & Canada: 001

If you're calling from within the
former GDR, and not from a city, the
major snag is that codes change
according to the place from where
you're dialling. To find the dialling
code you're obliged to use the direct
phone service facilities to be found
in main post offices and railway
stations, or at least go there to find
out the code you require. Once you
have this code, it's easy enough to
call abroad from any booth.
see also **phone**

diamond der Diamant [dee-
am**ant**]
diaper (US) die Windel [**vi**ndel]
diarrhoea der Durchfall
[**door**shfal]
diary (business etc) der
Terminkalender [tairm**een**-
kalender]
(for personal experiences) das
Tagebuch [**tahg**-uh-bОoKH]
dictionary das Wörterbuch
[**vur**terbоoKH]
**didn't*
see **not**
die sterben [sht**air**ben]
diesel der Diesel
diet die Diät [dee-**ayt**]
I'm on a diet ich mache eine

Diät [ish maKH-uh **ine**-uh]
I have to follow a special diet
ich muß nach einer Diät
leben [mooss naKH **ine**-er –
la**y**ben]
difference der Unterschied
[**oon**tersheet]
what's the difference? was ist
der Unterschied?
different verschieden [fair-
sh**ee**den]
this one is different dieses ist
anders
a different table ein **a**nderer
Tisch
difficult schwer [shvair]
difficulty die Schwierigkeit
[shv**ee**rish-kite]
dinghy (rubber) das
Schlauchboot [shl**ow**KHboht]
(sailing) das Dingi [**d**ing-gee]
dining room das
Speisezimmer [shp**ize**-uh-
tsimmer]
dinner (evening meal) das
Abendessen [**ah**bentessen]
to have dinner zu **A**bend
essen [ts**oo**]
direct (adj) direkt [deer**ekt**]
is there a direct train? gibt es
eine direkte
Zugverbindung? [ts**oo**k-
fairbindoong]
direction die Richtung
[**r**ishtoong]
which direction is it? in
welcher Richtung ist es?
[**v**elsher]
is it in this direction? ist es in

dieser Richtung? [d**ee**zer]
directory enquiries die
Auskunft [**ow**sskoonft]

The number for
directory enquiries is
119.

dirt der Schmutz [shmoots]
dirty schmutzig [shm**oo**tsish]
disabled behindert
**is there access for the
disabled?** gibt es Zugang
für Behinderte? [geept ess
ts**oo**gang fŏŏr behindert-uh]
disappear verschwinden
[fairshv**i**nden]
it's disappeared es ist
verschwunden
[fairshv**oo**nden]
disappointed enttäuscht [ent-
t**oy**sht]
disappointing enttäuschend
[ent-t**oy**shent]
disaster die Katastrophe
[katastr**oh**f-uh]
disco die Diskothek
[diskot**ay**k]
discount der Rabatt [rabb**a**t]
is there a discount? gibt es
einen Rabatt? [geept ess **ine**-
en]
disease die Krankheit [krank-
hite]
disgusting widerlich
[v**ee**derlish]
dish (meal) das Gericht
[ger**i**sht]
(bowl) der Teller

dishcloth das Spültuch
[shp**oo**ltookH]

disinfectant das
Desinfektionsmittel
[dezinfekts-y**oh**ns-mittel]

disk (for computer) die Diskette
[disk**ett**-uh]

disposable diapers (US) die
Papierwindeln [pap**eer**-
vindeln]

disposable nappies die
Papierwindeln

distance die Entfernung [ent-
fairnoong]

in the distance weit weg [vite
vek]

distilled water destilliertes
Wasser [destill**eer**tess **va**sser]

district das Gebiet [geb**eet**]

disturb stören [sht**ur**-ren]

diversion (detour) die
Umleitung [**oo**m-lytoong]

diving board das Sprungbrett
[shpr**oo**ngbrett]

divorced geschieden
[gesh**ee**den]

dizzy: I feel dizzy mir ist
schwindlig [meer ist shv**int**lish]

do tun [toon]

what shall we do? was
sollen wir tun? [vass **zo**llen
veer]

how do you do it? wie
machen Sie das? [vee ma**kH**en
zee]

will you do it for me? können
Sie das für mich tun?
[**kur**nen]

dialogues

how do you do? guten Tag
[g**oo**ten tahk]
nice to meet you freut
mich [froyt mish]
what do you do? (work)
was machst du/machen
Sie beruflich? [vass ma**kH**st
doo/ ma**kH**en zee ber**oo**flish]
I'm a teacher, and you?
ich bin Lehrer, und Sie?
I'm a student ich bin
Student
what are you doing this
evening? was machst
du/machen Sie heute
abend? [ma**kH**st doo/ma**kH**en
zee h**oy**t-uh **ah**bent]
we're going out for a drink,
do you want to join us?
wir gehen einen trinken,
möchtest du/möchten
Sie mitkommen?
[m**ur**shtest doo/m**ur**shten zee]

do you want cream?
möchtest du/möchten Sie
Sahne?
I do, but she doesn't ich
ja, aber sie nicht [yah]

doctor der Arzt [artst]
we need a doctor wir
brauchen einen Arzt [veer
br**ow**kHen **ine**-en]
please call a doctor bitte
rufen Sie einen Arzt [**bitt**-uh
r**oo**fen zee]

British and other EU nationals are entitled to free medical care in Germany on production of a form E111, available from main post offices. Without this form, you'll have to pay in full for all medical treatment, which is expensive. Whether or not you get an E111, it's sensible to take out some form of travel insurance. For dental treatment, however, you should expect to be asked to pay part of the costs.

dialogue

where does it hurt? wo tut es weh? [vo toot ess vay]
right here genau hier [genow heer]
does that hurt now? tut es jetzt weh? [yetst]
yes ja
take this to the pharmacist gehen Sie hiermit zur Apotheke [gay-en zee heermit tsoor apotayk-uh]

document das Dokument [dok00ment]
dog der Hund [hoont]
doll die Puppe [poop-uh]
domestic flight der Inlandflug [inlant-fl00k]
don't* see not
don't do that! tu das/tun Sie das nicht! [too dass/toon zee dass nisht]

door die Tür [toor]
doorman der Portier [portyay]
double doppelt
double bed das Doppelbett
double room das Doppelzimmer [doppeltsimmer]
doughnut der Berliner [bairleener]
down: down here hier unten [heer oonten]
put it down over there setzen Sie es hier ab [zetsen zee ess heer ap]
it's down there on the right es ist hier unten rechts
it's further down the road es ist weiter die Straße entlang [vyter dee shtrahss-uh entlang]
downhill skiing der Abfahrtslauf [apfahrts-lowf]
downmarket (restaurant etc) weniger anspruchsvoll [vayniger anshprookHsfoll]
downstairs unten [oonten]
dozen das Dutzend [dootsent]
half a dozen sechs Stück [zeks shtook]
drain (in sink, street) der Abfluß [ap-flooss]
draught beer das Faßbier [fassbeer]
draughty: it's draughty es zieht [ess tseet]
drawer die Schublade [shooplahd-uh]
drawing die Zeichnung [tsyshnoong]
dreadful furchtbar [foorshtbar]

dream der Traum [trowm]
dress das Kleid [klite]
dressed: to get dressed sich anziehen [zish antsee-en]
dressing (for cut) der Verband [fairbant]
salad dressing die Salatsoße [zalahtzohss-uh]
dressing gown der Bademantel [bahd-uh-mantel]
drink (alcoholic) der Drink (non-alcoholic) das Getränk [getrenk]
drink (verb) trinken
a cold drink ein kaltes Getränk
can I get you a drink? kann ich Ihnen etwas zu trinken besorgen? [etvass tsoo – bezorgen]
what would you like to drink? was möchtest du/möchten Sie zu trinken? [murshtest doo/murshten zee]
no thanks, I don't drink nein danke, ich trinke nicht [trink-uh nisht]
I'll just have a drink of water ich möchte nur etwas Wasser
drinking water das Trinkwasser [trinkvasser]
is this drinking water? ist das Trinkwasser?
drive (verb) fahren
we drove here wir sind mit dem Auto gekommen [veer zint mit daym owto gekommen]
I'll drive you home ich fahre

Sie nach Hause [ish fahr-uh zee naKH howz-uh]
driver (man/woman) der Fahrer/die Fahrerin
driving licence der Führerschein [fOOrer-shine]
drop: just a drop please (of drink) nur einen Tropfen [noor ine-en]
drug (medical) das Medikament
drugs (narcotics) die Drogen fpl [drohgen]
drunk (adj) betrunken [betroonken]
drunken driving Trunkenheit am Steuer [troonken-hite am shtoyer]
dry (adj) trocken

 If you'd like a really dry wine, ask for it **'herb'** [hairp]

dry-cleaner die chemische Reinigung [shaymish-uh rynigoong]
duck die Ente [ent-uh]
due: he was due to arrive yesterday er sollte gestern ankommen [air zollt-uh]
when is the train due? wann kommt der Zug an?
dull (pain) dumpf [doompf] (weather) trüb [trOOp]
dummy (baby's) der Schnuller [shnooller]
during während [vairent]
dust der Staub [shtowp]

dusty staubig [**shtow**bish]
dustbin die Mülltonne [**mool**ltonn-uh]
Dutch (adj) holländisch [**hol**lendish]
(language) Holländisch
duty-free (goods) zollfreie Waren [**tsoll**fry-uh **vah**ren]
duty-free shop der Duty-free-Shop
duvet das Federbett [**fay**derbet]

E

each (every) jeder [**yay**der]
  how much are they each? was kosten sie pro Stück? [vass **kos**ten zee pro shtook]
ear das Ohr
earache Ohrenschmerzen [**ohr**en-shmairtsen]
early früh [froo]
  early in the morning früh am Morgen
  I called by earlier ich war schon einmal hier [shohn ine-mahl heer]
earring der Ohrring
east der Osten
  in the east im Osten
Easter Ostern [**ohs**tern]
easy leicht [lysht]
eat essen
  we've already eaten, thanks danke, wir haben schon gegessen [**hah**ben shohn]
eau de toilette das Eau de toilette

EC die EG [ay-**gay**]
economy class die Touristen-klasse [too**ris**ten-klass-uh]
egg das Ei [ī]
Eire Irland [**eer**lant]
either: either ... or ... entweder... oder... [**entvayder** ... **oh**der]
  either, I don't mind egal welcher [ay**gahl** velsher]
elastic der Gummi [**goo**mee]
elastic band das Gummiband [**goo**mmeebant]
elbow der Ellbogen
electric elektrisch [ay**lek**trish]
electric fire das elektrische Heizgerät [ay**lek**trish-uh **hites**-gerayt]
electrician der Elektriker [ay**lek**triker]
electricity der Strom [**shtrohm**]
  see **voltage**
elevator (US) der Aufzug [**owf**-tsook]
else: something else etwas anderes [**et**vass **an**deress]
  somewhere else woanders [vo-**an**ders]

dialogue

> **would you like anything else?** möchten Sie noch etwas? [**mur**shten]
> **no, nothing else, thanks** danke, das ist alles [**dank**-uh dass ist **al**-ess]

e-mail die E-Mail

embassy die Botschaft [**boht**-shafft]

emergency der Notfall [**noht**-fal]

this is an emergency! dies ist ein Notfall! [deess ist ine]

emergency exit der Notausgang [**noht**-owssgang]

empty leer [lair]

end das Ende [**end**-uh]

at the end of the street am Ende der Straße

end (verb) enden

when does it end? wann ist es zu Ende? [vann ist ess tsoo **end**-uh]

engaged (toilet, telephone) besetzt [be**zetst**]

(to be married) verlobt [fair**lohpt**]

engine der Motor [**moh**tohr]

England England [**eng**-lant]

English englisch [**eng**-lish]

I'm English (man/woman) ich bin Engländer [**eng**-lender]/Engländerin

do you speak English? sprichst du/sprechen Sie Englisch? [shprisht doo/**shpre**shen zee]

enjoy: to enjoy oneself sich amüsieren [zish amœ**zeeren**]

dialogue

how did you like the film? wie hat dir/Ihnen der Film gefallen? [vee hat deer/**eenen** dair]
I enjoyed it very much –

did you? er hat mir sehr gut gefallen – dir/Ihnen auch? [meer zair goot – deer/**eenen** owKH]

enjoyable unterhaltsam [oonter-**halt**-zahm]

(meal) angenehm [**an**-genaym]

enlargement (of photo) die Vergrößerung [fairgr**ur**sseroong]

enormous enorm [ay**norm**]

enough genug [gen**ook**]

there's not enough ... es ist nicht genug ... da [ess ist nisht]

it's not big enough es ist nicht groß genug

that's enough das genügt [dass gen**ookt**]

entrance der Eingang [**ine**-gang]

envelope der Umschlag [**oo**mshlahk]

epileptic (man/woman) der Epileptiker/die Epileptikerin

equipment (for climbing etc) die Ausrüstung [**ow**ss-rœstoong]

error der Fehler [**fay**ler]

especially besonders [be**zon**ders]

essential wesentlich [**vay**zentlish]

it is essential that ... es ist unbedingt notwendig, daß... [**oon**bedingt **noh**tvendish]

Estonia Estland [**est**lant]

EU die EU [ay-**oo**]

Em

euro der Euro [**oy**ro]

Eurocheque der Euroscheck [**oy**ro-sheck]

Eurocheque card die Euroscheckkarte [**oy**ro-sheck-kart-uh]

Europe Europa [oy**roh**pa]

European europäisch [oyroh**pay**ish]

even sogar [zo**gahr**], selbst [zelpst]

even if ... selbst wenn ... [ven]

evening der Abend [**ah**bent]

this evening heute abend [**hoy**t-uh]

in the evening am Abend

evening meal das Abendessen [**ah**bent-essen]

eventually schließlich [**shlee**sslish]

ever jemals [**yay**mahls]

dialogue

have you ever been to Heidelberg? waren Sie schon einmal in Heidelberg? [**vah**ren zee shohn **ine**-mahl]
yes, I was there two years ago ja, ich war vor zwei Jahren da [for – **yah**ren]

every jeder [**yay**der]

every day jeden Tag [**yay**den tahk]

everyone jeder [**yay**der]

everything alles [**al**-ess]

everywhere überall [** oo**ber-al]

exactly! genau! [ge**now**]

exam die Prüfung [pr**oo**foong]

example das Beispiel [**by**shpeel]

for example zum Beispiel [tsoom]

excellent hervorragend [hair**for**-rahgent]

excellent ausgezeichnet [owss-gets**y**shnet]

except außer [**ow**sser]

excess baggage das Übergewicht [**oo**bergevisht]

exchange rate der Wechselkurs [**veck**selkoorss]

exciting (day, holiday) aufregend [**owf**-raygent]

(film) spannend [**shp**annent]

excuse me (to get past) entschuldigen Sie! [ent-sh**oo**ldigen zee]

(to get attention) Entschuldigung! [ent-sh**oo**ldigoong]

(to say sorry) Verzeihung [fair-ts**y**-oong]

exhaust (pipe) der Auspuff [**ow**sspooff]

exhausted erschöpft [airsh**ur**pft]

exhibition die Ausstellung [**ow**ss-shtelloong]

exit der Ausgang [**ow**ssgang]

where's the nearest exit? wo ist der nächste Ausgang? [dair n**ay**kst-uh]

expect erwarten [air**var**ten]

expensive teuer [**toy**er]

experienced erfahren [air**fah**ren]

explain erklären [airkl**ai**ren]

can you explain that?
könnten Sie mir das
erklären? [**kur**nten zee meer]
express (mail) per Expreß
[pair eks**press**]
(train) der Schnellzug
[**shnell**ts**oo**k]
extension (telephone) der
Anschluß [**an**shlooss]
extension 21, please
Anschluß einundzwanzig
bitte [**bitt**-uh]
extension lead die
Verlängerungsschnur
[fair**leng**eroongs-shn**oo**r]
**extra: can we have an extra
one?** können wir noch eins
haben? [**kur**nen veer noKH ine-ss
hahben]
do you charge extra for that?
kostet das extra?
extraordinary
außergewöhnlich [**ow**sser-
gevurnlish]
extremely äußerst [**oy**sserst]
eye das Auge [**ow**g-uh]
**will you keep an eye on my
suitcase for me?** könnten
Sie auf meinen Koffer
aufpassen? [**kur**nten zee –
owfpassen]
eyebrow pencil der
Augenbrauenstift
[**ow**genbrowen-shtift]
eye drops die Augentropfen
[**ow**gen-tropfen]
eyeglasses (US) die Brille
[**brill**-uh]
eyeliner der Eyeliner

eye make-up remover der
Augen-Make-up-Entferner
[**ow**gen-'make-up'-entf**air**ner]
eye shadow der Lidschatten
[**leet**-shatten]

F

face das Gesicht [ge**zisht**]
factory die Fabrik [fa**breek**]
Fahrenheit* Fahrenheit
faint (verb) ohnmächtig
werden [**ohn**meshtish **vair**den]
she's fainted sie ist
ohnmächtig geworden [zee
ist – ge**vor**den]
I feel faint mir ist ganz
schwach [meer ist gants shv**aKH**]
fair (funfair) der Jahrmarkt
[**yahr**markt]
(trade) die Messe [**mess**-uh]
fair (adj) fair
fairly ziemlich [**tsee**mlish]
fake die Fälschung [**fel**shoong]
fall (verb) fallen [**fal**-en]
she's had a fall sie ist
hingefallen [zee ist **hin**-gefal-en]
(US: autumn) der Herbst
[**hair**pst]
false falsch [falsh]
family die Familie [fa**mee**lee-
uh]
famous berühmt [be**room**t]
fan (electrical) der Ventilator
[venti**lah**-tor]
(hand held) der Fächer [**fesh**er]
(sports) der Fan [fen]
fan belt der Keilriemen [**kile-**

reemen]
fantastic fantastisch
far weit [vite]

dialogue

is it far from here? ist es
weit von hier? [fon heer]
no, not very far nein, nicht
sehr weit [nisht zair]
well how far? wie weit
denn? [vee]
it's about 10 kilometres es
sind etwa zehn Kilometer
[etvah]

fare der Fahrpreis [**fahr**price]
farm der Bauernhof
[**bow**ernhohf]
fashionable modisch
[**moh**dish]
fast schnell
fat (person) dick
(on meat) das Fett
father der Vater [**fah**ter]
father-in-law der Schwiegervater [**shvee**ger-fahter]
faucet (US) der Wasserhahn
[**vas**serhahn]
fault der Fehler [**fay**ler]
sorry, it was my fault tut mir
leid, es war mein Fehler
[mine]
it's not my fault es ist nicht
meine Schuld [nisht m**ine**-uh
shoolt]
faulty defekt [day**fekt**]
favourite Lieblings- [**lee**plings]
fax das Fax [faks]

fax (verb) (person) per Fax
benachrichtigen [pair faks
ben**a**KH-rishtigen]
(document) faxen
February der Februar
[**fay**broo-ar]
feel fühlen [f**oo**len]
I feel hot mir ist heiß [meer ist
hice]
I feel unwell mir ist nicht gut
[nisht g**oo**t]
I feel like going for a walk mir
ist nach einem Spaziergang
[naKH]
how are you feeling? wie
fühlen Sie sich? [vee f**oo**len zee
zish]
I'm feeling better es geht mir
besser [ess gayt meer]
felt-tip (pen) der Filzstift [filts-
shtift]
fence der Zaun [tsown]
fender (US) die Stoßstange
[shtoh**ss**-shtang-uh]
ferry die Fähre [**fair**-uh]
festival das Festival [**festi**vahl]
fetch holen [**hoh**len]
I'll fetch him ich hole ihn
[**hoh**l-uh]
**will you come and fetch me
later?** können Sie mich
später abholen? [**kur**nen zee
mish shp**ay**ter **a**p-hohlen]
feverish: she's still feverish sie
hat noch immer Fieber [zee
hat noKH immer **fee**ber]
few: a few ein paar [ine pahr]
a few days ein paar Tage
fiancé: my fiancé mein

Verlobter [mine fairlohpter]
fiancée: my fiancée meine
Verlobte [mine-uh fairlohpt-uh]
field das Feld [felt]
fight der Kampf
fill füllen [fœllen]
fill in ausfüllen [owssfœllen]
  do I have to fill this in? muß
  ich das ausfüllen? [mooss
  ish dass owssfœllen]
fill up voll machen [foll
  maкHen]
  fill it up, please volltanken
  bitte [folltanken bitt-uh]
filling (in sandwich) der Belag
  [belahk]
  (in cake, tooth) die Füllung
  [fœlloong]
film der Film

dialogue

  **do you have this kind of
  film?** haben Sie diesen
  Film? [hahben zee deezen
  film?]
  yes, how many exposures?
  ja, wie viele Aufnahmen?
  [vee veel-uh owfnahmen]
  36 sechsunddreißig
  [seksoont-dryssish]

film processing die
  Filmentwicklung [film-
  entvickloong]
filter coffee der Filterkaffee
  [filter-kaffay]
filter papers das Filterpapier
  [filter-papeer]
filthy dreckig [dreckish]
find finden

I can't find it ich kann es
  nicht finden [ish kann ess
  nisht]
I've found it ich habe es
  gefunden [gefoonden]
find out herausfinden
  [herowss-finden]
  could you find out for me?
  könnten Sie das für mich
  herausfinden? [kurnten zee
  dass fœr mish]
fine (weather) schön [shurn]
  (punishment) die Geldstrafe
  [gelt-shtrahf-uh]

dialogues

  how are you? wie geht's?
  [vee gayts]
  I'm fine thanks danke, gut
  [goot]

  is that OK? ist das okay?
  that's fine thanks in
  Ordnung, danke [ortnoong]

finger der Finger [fing-er]
finish (verb) beenden [buh-
  enden]
  I haven't finished yet ich bin
  noch nicht fertig [ish bin noкH
  nisht fairtish]
  when does it finish? wann ist
  es zu Ende? [van ist ess tsoo
  end-uh]
fire das Feuer [foy-er]
  can we light a fire here?
  können wir hier ein Feuer
  machen? [kurnen veer heer –

maKHen]
it's on fire es brennt
fire alarm der Feueralarm
[foy-er-alarm]
fire brigade die Feuerwehr
[foy-er-vair]

In the event of a fire,
phone 112.

fire escape die Feuertreppe
[foy-er-trepp-uh], die
Feuerleiter [foy-er-lyter]
fire extinguisher der
Feuerlöscher [foy-er-lursher]
first erster [airster]
I was first ich war der/die
erste [dair/dee airst-uh]
at first zuerst [tsoo-airst]
the first time das erste Mal
first on the left die erste
Straße links
first aid die Erste Hilfe [airst-
uh hilf-uh]
first aid kit die Erste-Hilfe-
Ausrüstung [airst-uh hilf-uh
owssrœstoong]
first class erster Klasse [airster
klass-uh]
first floor der erste Stock
[airst-uh shtock]
(US) das Erdgeschoß [airt-
geshoss]
first name der Vorname
[fornahm-uh]
fish der Fisch [fish]
fishmonger's der
Fischhändler [fish-hentler]

fit (attack) der Anfall [an-fal]
it doesn't fit me es paßt mir
nicht [ess passt meer nisht]
fitting room der
Anproberaum [anprohb-uh-
rowm]
fix (arrange, sort out) regeln
[raygeln]
can you fix this? (repair)
können Sie das reparieren?
[kurnen zee dass repareeren]
fizzy sprudelnd [shproodelnt]
flag die Fahne [fahn-uh]
flannel der Waschlappen
[vashlappen]
flash (for camera) der Blitz
flat (apartment) die Wohnung
[vohnoong]
(adj) flach [flaKH]
I've got a flat tyre ich habe
einen Platten [ish hahb-uh ine-
en]
flavour der Geschmack
[geshmack]
flea der Floh
flight der Flug [flook]
flight number die
Flugnummer [flook-noommer]
flippers die Schwimmflossen
[shvimflossen]
flood die Flut [floot]
floor (of room) der Fußboden
[foossbohden]
(storey) das Stockwerk
[shtockvairk]
on the floor auf dem Boden
[owf daym bohden]
on the third floor im dritten
Stock

florist der Blumenhändler
[bl**oo**men-hentler]
flour das Mehl [mayl]
flower die Blume [bl**oo**m-uh]
flu die Grippe [gripp-uh]
fluent: he speaks fluent
German er spricht fließend
Deutsch [air shprisht fl**ee**ssent
doytch]
fly (insect) die Fliege [fl**ee**g-uh]
fly (verb) fliegen [fl**ee**gen]
fly in einfliegen [**ine**-fleegen]
fly out abfliegen [**ap**fleegen]
fog der Nebel [**nay**bel]
foggy: it's foggy es ist neblig
[**nay**blish]
folk dancing der Volkstanz
[**fo**llks-tants]
folk music die Volksmusik
[**fo**llks-m**oo**zeek]
follow folgen
follow me folgen Sie mir [zee
meer]
food das Essen
food poisoning die
Lebensmittelvergiftung
[**lay**bensmittel-fairg**i**ftoong]
food shop/store das
Lebensmittelgeschäft
[**lay**bensmittel-gesheft]
foot* der Fuß [f**oo**ss]
on foot zu Fuß [ts**oo**]
football der Fußball [**foo**ssbal]
football match das
Fußballspiel [**foo**ssbal-shpeel]
for für [f**œ**r]
do you have something
for ...? (headaches/diarrhoea etc)
haben Sie etwas gegen ...?

[h**ah**ben zee **e**tvass g**ay**gen]

dialogues

who's the bratwurst for?
für wen ist die Bratwurst?
[vayn]
that's for me das ist für
mich [mish]
and this one? und das
hier?
that's for her das ist für sie
[zee]

where do I get the bus for
Stuttgart? wo fährt der
Bus nach Stuttgart ab? [vo
fairt – naкн]
the bus for Stuttgart leaves
from Schillerstraße der
Bus nach Stuttgart fährt
von der Schillerstraße

how long have you been
here for? wie lange sind
Sie schon hier? [vee l**a**ng-uh
zint zee shohn heer]
I've been here for two
days, how about you? ich
bin seit zwei Tagen hier,
und Sie? [zite]
I've been here for a week
ich bin seit einer Woche
hier

forehead die Stirn [shteern]
foreign ausländisch
[**ow**sslendish]
foreigner (man/woman) der

Ausländer [**ow**sslender]/die Ausländerin

forest der Wald [vallt]

forget vergessen [fair**g**essen]

I forget, I've forgotten ich habe es vergessen [ish h**ah**b-uh ess]

fork (for eating) die Gabel [g**ah**bel]

(in road) die Abzweigung [ap-tsvygoong]

form (document) das Formular [form**oo**l**ah**r]

formal (dress) form**e**ll

fortnight zwei Wochen [tsvy v**o**KHen]

fortress die Festung [**f**estoong]

fortunately glücklicherweise [gl**oo**ck-lisher-vize-uh]

forward: **could you forward my mail?** könnten Sie meine Post nachsenden? [**kur**nten zee m**i**ne-uh posst na**KH**zenden]

forwarding address die Nachsendeadresse [na**KH**zend-uh-adress-uh]

foundation cream die Grundierungscreme [groond**ee**roongs-kraym]

fountain der Brunnen [br**oo**nnen]

foyer das Foyer [foy-y**ay**]

fracture der Bruch [brooKH]

France Frankreich [frank-rysh]

free frei [fry]

(no charge) kostenlos [**k**ostenlohss], gratis [gr**ah**tiss]

is it free (of charge)? ist es gratis?

freeway (US) die Autobahn [**ow**tobahn]

freezer die Gefriertruhe [gefr**ee**rtr**oo**-uh]

French (adj) französisch [frants**ur**zish]

(language) Französisch

French fries die Pommes frites [pom frit]

frequent häufig [h**oy**fish]

how frequent is the bus to Kiel? wie oft fährt der Bus nach Kiel? [vee oft fairt]

fresh frisch [frish]

fresh orange juice der natürliche Orangensaft [nat**oo**rlish-uh oro**n**Jenzaft]

Friday Freitag [**fry**tahk]

fridge der Kühlschrank [k**oo**lshrank]

fried gebraten [gebr**ah**ten]

fried egg das Spiegelei [shp**ee**gel-ī]

friend (man/woman) der Freund [froynt]/die Freundin [**fr**oyndin]

friendly freundlich [**fr**oyntlish]

from von [fon]

when does the next train from Bremen arrive? wann kommt der nächste Zug aus Br**e**men an? [der n**ay**kst-uh ts**oo**k owss]

from Monday to Friday von M**o**ntag bis Fr**e**itag

from next Thursday ab nächsten D**o**nnerstag

dialogue

where are you from?
woher kommst du/
kommen Sie? [voh**air**
kommst d00/**ko**mmen zee]
I'm from Slough ich bin
aus Slough [ish bin owss]

front die Vorderseite [**fo**rderzite-uh]
in front vorn [forn]
in front of the hotel vor dem
Hotel [for]
at the front vorn [forn]
frost der Frost
frozen gefroren
frozen food die Tiefkühlkost
[**tee**fk00lkost]
fruit das Obst [ohpst]
fruit juice der Fruchtsaft
[fr00KHtzaft]
fry braten [**bra**hten]
frying pan die Bratpfanne
[bra**ht**-pfan-uh]
full voll [foll]
it's full of ... es ist voller...
I'm full ich bin satt [ish bin zatt]
full board die Vollpension
[**fo**llpangz-yohn]
fun: it was fun es hat Spaß
gemacht [ess hat shpahss
gema**KH**t]
funfair das Volksfest [**fo**llks-fest]
funicular railway die Seilbahn
[**zi**le-bahn]
funny (strange) seltsam
[**ze**ltzahm]
(amusing) komisch [**ko**hmish]

furniture die Möbel [m**ur**bel]
further weiter [**vy**ter]
it's further down the road es
ist weiter die Straße entlang

dialogue

**how much further is it to
the castle?** wie weit ist es
noch bis zum Schloß?
[vee vite ist ess noKH bis tsoom]
about 3 kilometres etwa
drei Kilometer [**et**vah]

fuse (noun) die Sicherung
[**zi**sheroong]
the lights have fused die
Sicherung ist durchgebrannt
[**do**orsh-gebrannt]
fuse box der
Sicherungskasten
[**zi**sheroongs-kasten]
fuse wire der Schmelzdraht
[shm**e**lts-draht]
future die Zukunft [ts00koonft]
in future in Zukunft

G

gallon* die Gallone [gal**oh**n-uh]
game das Spiel [shpeel]
(meat) das Wild [vilt]
garage (for fuel) die Tankstelle
[**ta**nk-shtell-uh]
(for repairs) die Werkstatt
[**va**irkshtatt]
(for parking) die Garage

[gar**ah**J-uh]
garden der Garten
garlic der Knoblauch
[k-n**oh**blowKH]
gas das Gas [gahss]
(US: gasoline) das Benzin
[bents**een**]
gas cylinder (camping gas) die
Gasflasche [g**ah**ss-flash-uh]
gasoline (US) das Benzin
[bents**een**]
see petrol
gas permeable lenses
luftdurchlässige
Kontaktlinsen [**loo**ft-doorsh-
lessig-uh kont**ak**t-linzen]
gas station (US) die Tankstelle
[tank-sht**ell**-uh]
gate das Tor [tohr]
(at airport) der Flugsteig [fl**ook**-
shtike]
gay schwul [shv**oo**l]
gay bar die Schwulenkneipe
[shv**oo**len-k-nipe-uh]
gear (in car etc) der Gang
gearbox das Getriebe
[get**ree**b-uh]
gear lever der Schaltknüppel
[sh**al**t-k-n**oo**ppel]
general allgemein [al-gem**ine**]
Geneva Genf
gents' (toilet) die
Herrentoilette [h**ai**ren-twalett-
uh]
genuine echt [esht]
German (man/woman) der/die
Deutsche [d**oy**tch-uh]
(adj) deutsch [doytch]
(language) Deutsch

the Germans die Deutschen
German measles die Röteln
[r**ur**teln]
Germany Deutschland
[d**oy**tch-lant]
get (obtain) bekommen
(fetch) holen [h**oh**len]
(become) werden [v**air**den]
**will you get me another one,
please?** bringen Sie mir
bitte noch eins [noKH ine-ss]
**do you know where I can get
them?** wissen Sie, wo ich sie
bek**o**mmen kann?
how do I get to ...? wie
komme ich nach...? [vee
k**o**mm-uh ish naKH]
to get old alt werden [v**air**den]

dialogue

can I get you a drink?
möchtest du/möchten
Sie etwas trinken?
[m**u**rshtest d**oo**/m**u**rshten zee
etvass]
no, I'll get this one, what
would you like? nein, das
ich meine Runde, was
möchten Sie? [m**ine**-uh
r**oo**nd-uh]
a glass of red wine ein
Glas Rotwein

get back (return)
zurückkommen [ts**oo**r**oo**ck-
kommen]
get in (arrive) ankommen [**an**-
kommen]

get off aussteigen [**ow**ss-shtygen]

where do I get off? wo muß ich aussteigen? [vo mooss ish]

get on (to train etc) einsteigen [**ine**-shtygen]

get out (of car etc) aussteigen [**ow**ss-shtygen]

get up (in the morning) aufstehen [**ow**f-shtay-en]

gift das Geschenk [geshenk]

gift shop der Geschenkladen [geshenk-lahden]

gin der Gin

a gin and tonic, please einen Gin Tonic, bitte [**ine**-en]

girl das Mädchen [**may**dshen]

girlfriend die Freundin [fr**oy**ndin]

give geben [**gay**ben]

I gave it to him ich habe es ihm gegeben [ish h**ah**b-uh ess eem geg**ay**ben]

will you give this to ...? bitte geben Sie dies ...

give back zurückgeben [ts**oor**ook-gayben]

glad froh

glass das Glas [glahss]

a glass of wine ein Glas Wein

glasses (spectacles) die Brille [br**i**ll-uh]

gloves die Handschuhe [hant-shoo-uh]

glue der Klebstoff [kl**ay**p-shtoff]

go gehen [**gay**-en]

(by car, train etc) fahren

we'd like to go to the Black Forest wir möchten zum Schwarzwald fahren [veer m**ur**shten tsoom]

where are you going? wohin gehen/fahren Sie? [voh**i**n]

where does this bus go? wohin fährt dieser Bus? [fairt]

let's go gehen wir

she's gone (left) sie ist gegangen

where has he gone? wohin ist er gegangen?

I went there last week ich war letzte Woche da

hamburger to go Hamburger zum Mitnehmen [tsoom]

go away weggehen [vek-gay-en]

go away! gehen Sie weg!

go back (return) zurückgehen [ts**oor**ook-gay-en]

go down (the stairs etc) hinuntergehen [hin**oo**nter-gay-en]

go in hineingehen [hin-**ine**-gay-en]

go out (in the evening) ausgehen [**ow**ss-gay-en]

do you want to go out tonight? möchten Sie heute abend ausgehen? [m**ur**shten zee h**oy**t-uh ahbent]

go through gehen durch [**gay**-en doorsh]

go up (the stairs etc) hinaufgehen [hin**ow**f-gay-en]

goat die Ziege [ts**ee**g-uh]

God Gott

goggles (ski) die Skibrille
[sheebrill-uh]

gold das Gold [gollt]

golf Golf

golf course der Golfplatz
[golf-plats]

good gut [goot]

good! gut!

it's no good es hat keinen
Zweck [ess hat kine-en tsveck]

goodbye auf Wiedersehen
[owf-veederzayn]

good evening guten Abend
[gooten ahbent]

Good Friday der Karfreitag
[kar-frytahk]

good morning guten Morgen
[gooten morgen]

good night gute Nacht [goot-
uh nakHt]

goose die Gans [ganss]

got: we've got to ... wir
müssen ... [veer mossen]

I've got to ... ich muß ...
[mooss]

have you got any ...? haben
Sie ...? [hahben zee]

government die Regierung
[regeeroong]

gradually allmählich [al-
maylish]

grammar die Grammatik

gram(me) das Gramm

granddaughter die Enkelin
[enk-uh-lin]

grandfather der Großvater
[grohssfahter]

grandmother die Großmutter
[grohssmootter]

grandson der Enkel

grapefruit die Grapefruit

grapefruit juice der
Grapefruitsaft [-zaft]

grapes die Trauben [trowben]

grass das Gras [grahss]

grateful dankbar

gravy die Soße [zohss-uh]

great (excellent) großartig
[grohss-artish]

that's great! das ist toll! [tol]

a great success ein großer
Erfolg [grohss-er]

Great Britain Großbritannien
[grohss-britannee-en]

Greece Griechenland
[greeshenlant]

greedy gefräßig [gefrayssish]

Greek griechisch [greeshish]

green grün [grOOn]

green card (car insurance) die
grüne Karte [grOOn-uh kart-uh]

greengrocer's der Gemüse-
händler [gemOOz-uh-hentler]

grey grau [grow]

grill (on cooker) der Grill

grilled gegrillt

grocer's der
Lebensmittelhändler
[laybensmittel-hentler]

ground der Boden [bohden]

on the ground auf dem
Boden

ground floor das Erdgeschoß
[airt-geshoss]

group die Gruppe
[groop-uh]

guarantee die Garantie
[garantee]

is it guaranteed? ist darauf
Garantie? [dar**owf**]
guest der Gast
guesthouse die Pension
[pangz-**yohn**]

To escape the formality of
a hotel, look for one of
the plentiful **Pensionen**
which may be rooms above a bar or
a restaurant or simply space in a
private house; in urban areas these
cost about the same as a hotel but
in the countryside are usually less
expensive. An increasingly prevalent
budget option (especially in busy
holiday areas) is bed and breakfast
accommodation in a private house
(look for signs saying
Fremdenzimmer or **Zimmer frei**).
These are seldom other than a really
good deal. However, very few
German cities have private rooms on
offer other than to relieve
congestion when there's a trade fair
on. Also in the more rural areas, and
particularly plentiful along the main
touring routes, are country inns or
guesthouses (**Gasthäuser**). These
are often in an atmospheric old
building and the cost includes
breakfast. Farmhouse holidays are
increasingly popular and in many
ways are the best bargains of all.
Full lists of these are available from
local tourist offices and the only
major snag is that this option is
really only feasible if you have your
own transport.

guide (person) der Reiseleiter
[**ry**-zuh-lyter]
guidebook der Reiseführer
[**ry**-zuh-fOOrer]
guided tour die Rundfahrt
[**roo**ntfahrt]
(on foot) der Rundgang
[**roo**ntgang]
guitar die Gitarre [git**arr**-uh]
gum (in mouth) das Zahnfleisch
[ts**ahn**-flysh]
gun das Gewehr [gev**air**]
gym das Fitneßstudio [**fit**ness-
shtOOdee-oh]

H

hair das Haar [hahr]
hairbrush die Haarbürste
[**hah**rbOOrst-uh]
haircut der Haarschnitt
[**hah**rshnit]
hairdresser der Frisör [friz**ur**]

Hairdressers are
usually closed on
Mondays.

hairdryer der Fön® [furn]
hair gel das Haargel [**hah**r-gayl]
hairgrip die Haarklemme
[**hah**rklem-uh]
hair spray das Haarspray
[**hah**r-shpray]
half* halb [halp]
half an hour eine halbe
Stunde [**ine**-uh halb-uh sht**oo**nd-
uh]

half a litre ein halber Liter [halber leeter]

about half that etwa die Hälfte [etvah dee helft-uh]

half board die Halbpension [halp-pangz-yohn]

half-bottle die halbe Flasche [halb-uh flash-uh]

half fare der halbe Fahrpreis [halb-uh fahr-price]

half price: at half price zum halben Preis [tsoom halben price]

hall (in house) die Diele [deel-uh]

ham der Schinken [shinken]

German ham will normally be thinly sliced and slightly smoked. If you want ham as you'd normally get it at home, you should ask for 'gekochter Schinken'.

hamburger der Hamburger [hemburger]

hammer der Hammer

hand die Hand [hant]

handbag die Handtasche [hant-tash-uh]

handbrake die Handbremse [hantbremz-uh]

handkerchief das Taschentuch [tashen-tOOKH]

handle (on door) die Klinke [klink-uh]

(on suitcase etc) der Griff

hand luggage das Handgepäck [hant-gepeck]

hang-gliding das Drachen-fliegen [draKHen-fleegen]

hangover der Kater [kahter]

I've got a hangover ich habe einen Kater [ish hahb-uh ine-en]

happen geschehen [geshay-en]

what's happening? was ist los? [lohss]

what has happened? was ist passiert? [passeert]

happy glücklich [glOOcklish]

I'm not happy about this ich bin damit nicht zufrieden [ish bin dahmit nisht tsOOfreeden]

harbour der Hafen [hahfen]

hard hart

(difficult) schwer [shvair]

hard-boiled egg ein hartgekochtes Ei [hartgekoKHtess ī]

hard lenses harte Kontaktlinsen [hart-uh kontakt-linzen]

hardly kaum [kowm]

hardly ever fast nie [fasst nee]

hardware shop die Eisenwarenhandlung [īzenvahren-hantloong]

hat der Hut [hoot]

hate (verb) hassen

have* haben [hahben]

can I have a ...? kann ich ein ... haben? [kan ish]

can we have some ...? können wir etwas ... haben? [kurnen veer etvass]

do you have ...? hast du/haben Sie...? [dOO/... zee]

what'll you have? (drink) was möchtest du/möchten Sie? [vass **mur**shtest d00/**mur**shten zee]

I have to leave now ich muß jetzt gehen [mooss yetst **gay**-en]

do I have to ...? muß ich ...?

hayfever der Heuschnupfen [**hoy**-shnoopfen]

hazelnuts die Haselnüsse [**hah**zel-n00ss-uh]

he* er [air]

head der Kopf

headache die Kopfschmerzen [**kopf**-shmairtsen]

headlights die Scheinwerfer [sh**ine**-vairfer]

headphones die Kopfhörer [**kopf**-hur-rer]

health food shop der Bioladen [**bee**-oh-lahden]

healthy gesund [gez**oo**nt]

hear hören [**hur**-ren]

dialogue

can you hear me? können Sie mich hören? [**kur**nen zee mish]

I can't hear you ich kann Sie nicht hören [ish kan zee nisht]

hearing aid das Hörgerät [**hur**-gerayt]

heart das Herz [hairts]

heart attack der Herzinfarkt

[**hairts**-infarkt]

heat die Hitze [**hits**-uh]

heater (in room) der Ofen [**oh**fen]

(in car) die Heizung [**hyt**soong]

heating die Heizung [**hyt**soong]

heavy schwer [shvair]

heel (of foot) die Ferse [**fairz**-uh]

(of shoe) der Absatz [**ap**zats]

could you heel these? können Sie mir hier die Absätze erneuern? [**kur**nen zee meer heer dee **ap**sets-uh airn**oy**ern]

heelbar die Absatzbar [**ap**zatsbar]

height (of mountain) die Höhe [**hur**-uh]

(of person) die Größe [gr**urss**-uh]

helicopter der Hubschrauber [**h00p**-shrowber]

hello hallo

Shaking hands when meeting people (whether they are friends, business partners or strangers) is routine in Germany. It may sometimes be regarded as impolite or standoffish not to shake hands.

helmet (for motorcycle) der Helm

help die Hilfe [**hilf**-uh]

(verb) helfen

help! Hilfe!

can you help me? können

Sie mir helfen? [**kur**nen zee meer]

thank you very much for your help vielen Dank für Ihre Hilfe [**feel**en dank fœr **eer**-uh]

helpful hilfreich [**hilf**-rysh]

hepatitis die Hepatitis [hepat**eet**iss]

her*: I haven't seen her ich habe sie nicht gesehen [zee]

give it to her geben Sie es ihr [**eer**]

with her mit ihr

for her für sie

that's her das ist sie

that's her towel das ist ihr Handtuch

herbal tea der Kräutertee [kr**oy**ter-tay]

herbs die Kräuter [kr**oy**ter]

here hier [heer]

here is/are ... hier ist/sind [zint]

here you are (offering) bitte [**bitt**-uh]

hers*: that's hers das gehört ihr [dass geh**urt** eer]

hey! he! [hay]

hi! hallo!

hide verstecken [fairsht**ecken**]

high hoch [hohKH]

highchair der Hochstuhl [**hoh**KH-sht00l]

highway (US) die Autobahn [**ow**tobahn]

hill der Berg [bairk]

him*: I haven't seen him ich habe ihn nicht gesehen [een]

give it to him geben Sie es

ihm [eem]

with him mit ihm

for him für ihn

that's him das ist er [air]

hip die Hüfte [h**œft**-uh]

hire: for hire zu vermieten [ts00 fairm**eet**en]

(verb) mieten [**meet**en]

where can I hire a bike? wo kann ich ein Fahrrad mieten? [vo kan ish ine f**ah**r-raht]

see also **rent**

his*: it's his car es ist sein Auto [zine]

that's his das ist seins [**zine**-ss]

hit (verb) schlagen [**shlah**gen]

hitch-hike trampen [tr**empen**]

hobby das Hobby

hold (verb) halten

hole das Loch [loKH]

holiday der Urlaub [**00r**lowp]

on holiday im Urlaub

Holland Holland [**hol**-lant]

home das Zuhause [ts00h**owz**-uh]

at home (in my house etc) zu Hause

(in my country) bei uns [by **oonss**]

we go home tomorrow wir fahren morgen nach Hause [veer f**ah**ren **m**orgen naKH]

honest ehrlich [**air**lish]

honey der Honig [**hoh**nish]

honeymoon die Flitterwochen [fl**itt**ervoKHen]

hood (US: of car) die Haube [**howb**-uh]

hope hoffen

I hope so hoffentlich [**h**offentlish]

I hope not hoffentlich nicht [nisht]

hopefully hoffentlich [**h**offentlish]

horn (of car) die Hupe [h**oo**p-uh]

horrible schrecklich

horse das Pferd [pfairt]

horse riding Reiten [**r**yten]

hospital das Krankenhaus [**k**ranken-howss]

hospitality die Gastfreund-schaft [**g**ast-froynt-shafft]

thank you for your hospitality vielen Dank für Ihre Gastfreundschaft [**f**eelen dank f**oo**r **ee**r-uh]

hot heiß [hice]
  (spicy) scharf [sharf]

I'm hot mir ist heiß [meer]

it's hot today es ist heiß heute [**h**oyt-uh]

hotel das Hotel
  see **room**

An immensely complicated grading system applies to German hotels, with no fewer than 80 classifications according to price and services provided. Despite this, they're all more or less the same: clean, comfortable and functional with conveniences like TV, phone and en suite bathroom usually taken for granted in the medium range establishments upwards. You should always call into the nearest tourist office to check any special deals which they may have with local establishments; this can result in you spending less than the figures quoted on the official hotel lists which every tourist office provides. Many tourist offices charge a few euros for finding you a room, but others perform the service gratis. You should take care not to turn up in a large town or city when there's a trade fair or **Messe** taking place.

hotel room: in my hotel room in meinem Hotelzimmer [m**ine**-em hot**e**l-tsimmer]

hot spring die Thermalquelle [tairm**ah**l-kvell-uh]

hour die Stunde [sht**oo**nd-uh]

house das Haus [howss]

house wine der Tafelwein [**tah**fel-vine]

hovercraft das Luftkissenboot [**loo**ft-kissenboht]

how wie [vee]

how many? wie viele? [**f**eel-uh]

how do you do? guten Tag! [g**oo**ten tahk]

dialogues

how are you? wie geht es dir/Ihnen? [gayt ess deer/**ee**nen]

fine, thanks, and you? danke, gut, und dir/Ihnen? [dank-uh g**oo**t]

how much is it? was kostet das?
75 euros fünfundsiebzig Euro
I'll take it ich nehme es [ish **naym**-uh ess]

humid feucht [foysht]
humour der Humor [hoom**ohr**]
Hungarian ungarisch [**oo**ngahrish]
Hungary Ungarn [**oo**ngarn]
hungry hungrig [**hoo**ngrish]
I'm hungry ich habe Hunger [ish ha**h**buh h**oo**ng-er]
are you hungry? hast du/haben Sie Hunger? [d**oo**/ha**h**ben zee]
hurry (verb) sich beeilen [zish buh-**i**len]
I'm in a hurry ich habe es eilig [ish ha**h**b-uh ess **i**lish]
there's no hurry es eilt nicht [**i**lt nisht]
hurry up! beeilen Sie sich!
hurt (verb) weh tun [vay t**oo**n]
it really hurts es tut echt weh [t**oo**t esht vay]
husband der Mann
hydrofoil das Tragflächenboot [tra**h**kfleshenboht]
hypermarket der Verbrauchermarkt [fair-bro**w**kHer-markt]

I
■

I ich [ish]
ice das Eis [ice]
with ice mit Eis
no ice, thanks kein Eis, danke [kine ice, **d**ank-uh]
ice cream das Eis [ice]
ice-cream cone die Tüte Eiskrem [t**oo**t-uh **ice**-kraym]
ice lolly das Eis am Stiel [ice am shteel]
ice rink die Schlittschuhbahn [shl**i**tt-sh**oo**-bahn]
ice skates die Schlittschuhe [shl**i**tt-sh**oo**-uh]
idea die Idee [ee**day**]
idiot der Idiot [eedee-**oh**t]
if wenn [ven]
ignition die Zündung [ts**oo**ndoong]
ill krank
I feel ill ich fühle mich krank [ish f**oo**l-uh mish]
illness die Krankheit [kr**a**nkhite]
imitation (leather etc) nachgemacht [na**kH**-gema**kH**t]
immediately sofort [zof**or**t]
important wichtig [v**i**shtish]
it's very important es ist sehr wichtig [ist zair]
it's not important es ist nicht wichtig [nisht]
impossible unmöglich [oon-m**ur**glish]
impressive beeindruckend [be-**ine**-droockent]

improve verbessern [fair-bessern]

I want to improve my German ich möchte mein Deutsch aufbessern [ish mursht-uh mine doytch **owf**-bessern]

in: it's in the centre es ist im Zentrum

in my car in meinem Auto

in Munich in München

in two days from now in zwei Tagen [**tah**gen]

in May im Mai

in English auf Englisch [owf eng-lish]

in German auf Deutsch [doytch]

is he in? ist er da?

in five minutes in fünf Minuten [min**oo**ten]

inch* der Zoll [tsoll]

include enthalten [ent-halten]

does that include meals? ist das einschließlich der Mahlzeiten? [**ine**-shleeslish dair **mahl**-tsyten]

is that included? ist das im Preis enthalten? [**price**]

inconvenient ungünstig [**oong**CONstish]

incredible (very good, amazing) unglaublich [oon-g**low**plish]

Indian indisch [indish]

indicator (on car) der Blinker

indigestion die Magenverstimmung [**mah**gen-fair-shtimmoong]

indoor pool das Hallenbad [hallenbaht]

indoors drinnen

inexpensive billig [billish]

infection die Infektion [infekts-**yoh**n]

infectious ansteckend [anshteckent]

inflammation die Entzündung [ent-ts**CON**doong]

informal (clothes, occasion, meeting) zwanglos [tsvang-lohss]

information die Information [informats-**yoh**n]

do you have any information about ...? haben Sie Informationen über ...? [**hah**ben zee informats-**yoh**nen **CON**ber]

information desk der Informationsschalter [informats-**yoh**ns-shalter]

injection die Spritze [shprits-uh]

injured verletzt [**fair**letst]

she's been injured sie ist verletzt [zee]

in-laws die Schwiegereltern [shv**ee**ger-eltern]

inner tube der Schlauch [shl**owKH**]

innocent unschuldig [**oon**-shooldish]

insect das Insekt [inzekt]

insect bite der Insektenstich [inz**ek**ten-shtish]

do you have anything for insect bites? haben Sie etwas für Insektenstiche? [**hah**ben zee **et**vass f**CON**r]

insect repellent das Insektenbekämpfungsmittel [inzekten-bekempfoongs-mittel]

inside innen

inside the hotel im Hotel

let's sit inside setzen wir uns nach drinnen [zetsen veer oonss naKH]

insist: I insist ich bestehe darauf [ish beshtay-uh darowf]

insomnia die Schlaflosigkeit [shlahf-lohzish-kite]

instant coffee der Pulverkaffee [poolver-kaffay]

instead statt dessen [shtatt]

instead of ... anstelle von ... [anshtell-uh fon]

give me that one instead geben Sie mir statt dessen das [gayben zee meer shtatt dessen dass]

insulin das Insulin [inzooleen]

insurance die Versicherung [fairzisheroong]

intelligent intelligent [intelligent]

interested: I'm interested in ... ich interessiere mich für ... [ish interesseer-uh mish foor]

interesting interessant

that's very interesting das ist sehr interessant [zair]

international international [internats-yonahl]

Internet das Internet

interpret dolmetschen [dolmetchen]

interpreter (man/woman) der Dolmetscher [dolmetcher]/die Dolmetscherin

intersection (US) die Kreuzung [kroytsoong]

interval (at theatre) die Pause [powz-uh]

into in

I'm not into ... ich stehe nicht auf ... [ish shtay-uh nisht owf]

introduce vorstellen [forshtellen]

may I introduce ...? darf ich Ihnen ... vorstellen? [ish eenen]

invitation die Einladung [ine-lahdoong]

invite einladen [ine-lahden]

Ireland Irland [eerlant]

Irish irisch [eerish]

I'm Irish (man/woman) ich bin Ire/Irin [ish bin eer-uh/eerin]

iron (for ironing) das Bügeleisen [boogel-izen]

can you iron these for me? könnten Sie diese Sachen für mich bügeln? [kurnten zee deez-uh zaKHen foor mish boogeln]

is* ist

island die Insel [inzel]

it* es; er; sie [ess, air, zee]

it is ... es ist ...

is it ...? ist es...?

where is it? wo ist es? [vo]

it's him er ist es

it was ... es war... [var]

Italian (adj) italienisch [ital-yaynish]

(language) Italienisch

Italy Italien [itahlee-en]

itch: it itches es juckt [ess yoockt]

J

jack (for car) der Wagenheber [**vah**gen-hayber]
jacket die Jacke [**y**ackuh]
jam die Marmelade [marm-uh-**lah**d-uh]
jammed: it's jammed es klemmt
January der Januar [yan**oo**ar]
jar das Glas [glahss]
jaw der Kiefer [**keef**er]
jazz der Jazz
jealous eifersüchtig [**i**ferz∞shtish]
jeans die Jeans
jellyfish die Qualle [kvall-uh]
jersey der Pullover [pooll**oh**ver]
jetty der Steg [shtayk]
Jewish jüdisch [y∞dish]
jeweller's das Juweliergeschäft [yoov-uh-**leer**-gesheft]
jewellery der Schmuck [shmoock]
job die Arbeit [**arb**ite]
jogging das Joggen
  I'm going jogging ich gehe joggen [ish g**ay**-uh]
joke der Witz [vits]
journey die Reise [**rize**-uh]
  have a good journey! gute Reise! [g**oo**t-uh]
jug die Kanne [**kann**-uh]
  a jug of water ein Krug mit Wasser [kr**oo**k mit **vass**er]
juice der Saft [zaft]
July der Juli [y**oo**lee]
jump (verb) springen [shpringen]
jumper der Pullover [pooll**oh**ver]
jump leads das Starthilfekabel [shtart-hilf-uh-kahbel]
junction die Kreuzung [kr**oy**tsoong]
June der Juni [y**oo**nee]
just (only) nur [noor]
  just two nur zwei
  just for me nur für mich [foor mish]
  just here genau hier [gen**ow** heer]
  not just now nicht jetzt [nisht yetst]
  we've just arrived wir sind gerade angekommen [veer zint ger**ah**d-uh an-gekommen]

K

keep behalten
  keep the change der Rest ist für Sie [dair rest ist foor zee]
  can I keep it? kann ich es behalten?
  please keep it bitte behalten Sie es
ketchup der Ketchup
kettle der Wasserkessel [**vass**er-kessel]
key der Schlüssel [shl∞ssel]
  the key for room 201, please den Schlüssel für Zimmer zweihunderteins, bitte [dayn – foor ts**imm**er]
key ring der Schlüsselring

[shlﬀssel-ring]
kidneys die Nieren [**neeren**]
kill töten [**turten**]
kilo* das Kilo [**keelo**]
kilometre* der Kilometer
[**keelo-mayter**]
  **how many kilometres is it
  to ...?** wieviel Kilometer
  sind es nach ...? [**veefeel**]
kind (generous) nett
  that's very kind das ist sehr
  nett [**zair**]

dialogue

  which kind do you want?
  welche möchtest
  du/möchten Sie? [**velsh**-uh
  murshtest dﬀ/**murshten zee**]
  I want this/that kind ich
  möchte diese hier/die da
  [ish **mursht**-uh **deez**-uh
  heer/dee da]

king der König [**kurnish**]
kiosk der Kiosk
kiss der Kuß [**kooss**]
  (verb) küssen [**koossen**]
kitchen die Küche [**koosh**-uh]
kitchenette die Kochnische
[koKHneesh-uh]
Kleenex® die Papiertücher
[papeer-toosher]
knee das Knie [k-nee]
knickers das Höschen [hurss-
shen]
knife das Messer
knitwear die Strickwaren
[shtrick-vahren]

knock (verb) klopfen
knock down anfahren
  he's been knocked down er
  ist angefahren worden [air ist
  an-gefahren **v**orden]
knock over (object) umstoßen
  [**oom**-shtohssen]
  (pedestrian) anfahren
know (somebody, a place)
  kennen
  (something) wissen [**vissen**]
  I don't know ich weiß nicht
  [ish vice nisht]
  I didn't know that das wußte
  ich nicht [**voost**-uh]
  **do you know where I can
  find ...?** wissen Sie, wo ich
  ... finden kann?

L

label das Etikett
ladies' (toilets) die
  Damentoilette [**dah**men-
  twalett-uh]
ladies' wear die
  Damenkleidung [**dah**men-
  klydoong]
lady die Dame [**dahm**-uh]
lager das helle Bier [**hell**-uh
  beer]
  see **beer**
lake der See [zay]
Lake Constance der
  Bodensee [**boh**denzay]
Lake Lucerne der
  Vierwaldstätter See [**feer**valt-
  shtetter zay]

lamb das Lamm
lamp die Lampe [lamp-uh]
lane (on motorway) die Spur
[shpoor]
(small road) die Gasse [gass-uh]
language die Sprache
[shprahKH-uh]
language course der
Sprachkurs [shprahKH-koors]
large groß [grohss]
last letzter [letster]
last week letzte Woche [letst-
uh voKH-uh]
last Friday letzten Freitag
[letsten]
last night gestern abend
[gestern ahbent]
what time is the last train to
Hamburg? wann fährt der
letzte Zug nach Hamburg?
[vann fairt]
late spät [shpayt]
sorry I'm late tut mir leid,
daß ich zu spät komme [toot
meer lite dass ish tsoo shpayt
komm-uh]
the train was late der Zug
hatte Verspätung [dair tsook
hatt-uh fairshpaytoong]
we must go, we'll be late wir
müssen gehen, sonst
kommen wir zu spät [veer
moossen gay-en zonst kommen veer
tsoo]
it's getting late es wird spät
[ess veert]
later später [shpayter]
I'll come back later ich
komme später wieder [ish

komm-uh – veeder]
see you later bis später
later on nachher [naKH-hair]
latest spätester [shpaytester]
by Wednesday at the latest
spätestens bis Mittwoch
[shpaytestens biss]
Latvia Lettland [lettlant]
laugh (verb) lachen [laKHen]
launderette der Waschsalon
[vash-zallong]
laundromat (US) der
Waschsalon
laundry (clothes) die Wäsche
[vesh-uh]
(place) die Wäscherei [vesherī]
lavatory die Toilette [twalett-
uh]
law das Gesetz [gezets]
lawn der Rasen [rahzen]
lawyer der Rechtsanwalt
[reshts-anvallt]
laxative das Abführmittel
[apfoor-mittel]
lazy faul [fowl]
lead (electrical) das Kabel
[kahbel]
lead (verb) führen [fooren]
where does this road lead to?
wohin führt diese Straße?
[vohin foort deez-uh shtrahss-uh]
leaf das Blatt
leaflet der Prospekt
leak die undichte Stelle
[oondisht-uh shtell-uh]
(verb) lecken
the roof leaks das Dach ist
undicht
learn lernen [lairnen]

least: not in the least nicht im mindesten [nisht]

at least mindestens

leather das Leder [**lay**der]

leave verlassen [fair**lass**en]

I am leaving tomorrow ich reise morgen ab [ish **rize**-uh **mor**gen ap]

he left yesterday er ist gestern abgereist [**ap**-geryst]

may I leave this here? kann ich das hierlassen? [**heer**lassen]

I left my coat in the bar ich habe meinen Mantel in der Bar gelassen [**hahb**-uh mine**-**en]

when does the bus for Saarbrücken leave? wann fährt der Bus nach Saarbrücken? [vann fairt dair booss naKH]

leek der Lauch [lowKH]

left links

on the left links

to the left nach links [naKH]

turn left biegen Sie links ab [**bee**gen zee – ap]

there's none left es ist alle [**al**uh]

left-handed linkshändig [**links**-hendish]

left luggage (office) die Gepäckaufbewahrung [ge**peck**-owfbevahroong]

leg das Bein [bine]

lemon die Zitrone [tsit**rohn**-uh]

lemonade die Limonade [limon**ah**d-uh]

lemon tea der Zitronentee [tsit**rohn**entay]

lend leihen [**ly**-en]

will you lend me your ... ? könnten Sie mir Ihr ... leihen? [**kur**nten zee meer eer]

lens (of camera) das Objektiv [ob-yek**teef**]

lesbian die Lesbierin [lesbee-**erin**]

less weniger [**vay**niger]

less than weniger als

less expensive nicht so teuer [nisht zoh]

lesson die Stunde [sht**oond**-uh]

let (allow) lassen

will you let me know? können Sie mir Bescheid sagen? [**kur**nen zee meer beshite **zah**gen]

I'll let you know ich werde Ihnen Bescheid sagen [ish vaird-uh **ee**nen]

let's go for something to eat gehen wir etwas essen [**gay**-en veer **et**vass]

let off absetzen [**ap**zetsen]

will you let me off at ...? können Sie mich in ... absetzen? [**kur**nen zee mish]

letter der Brief [breef]

do you have any letters for me? ist ein Brief für mich angekommen? [ine breef foor mish **an**-gekommen]

letterbox der Briefkasten [**breef**kasten]

Letterboxes in Germany are yellow. Collection times are indicated at the front. A red dot denotes Sunday collection.

lettuce der Kopfsalat [kopfzalaht]
lever der Hebel [haybel]
library die Bücherei [boosherī]
licence die Genehmigung [genaymigoong]
(driving) der Führerschein [foorer-shine]
lid der Deckel
lie (tell untruth) lügen [loogen]
lie down sich hinlegen [zish hinlaygen]
life das Leben [layben]
lifebelt der Rettungsgürtel [rettoongs-goortel]
lifeguard (on beach) der Rettungsschwimmer [rettoongs-shvimmer]
life jacket die Schwimmweste [shvimm-vest-uh]
lift (in building) der Aufzug [owf-ts00k]
could you give me a lift? könnten Sie mich mitnehmen? [kurnten zee mish mitnaymen]
would you like a lift? kann ich Sie mitnehmen?
lift pass (for ski lift) der Liftpaß [liftpas]
a daily/weekly lift pass ein Liftpaß für einen Tag/eine

Woche [foor ine-en tahk/ine-uh voKH-uh]
light das Licht [lisht]
(not heavy) leicht [lysht]
do you have a light? (for cigarette) haben Sie Feuer? [hahben zee foyer]
light green hellgrün [hellgroon]
light bulb die Glühbirne [gloobeern-uh]
I need a new light bulb ich brauche eine neue Birne [noy-uh]
lighter (cigarette) das Feuerzeug [foyer-tsoyk]
lightning der Blitz [blits]
like mögen [murgen]
I like it es gefällt mir [ess gefelt meer]
I don't like it es gefällt mir nicht [nisht]
I like going for walks ich gehe gern spazieren [ish gay-uh gairn]
I like you ich mag dich [ish mahk dish]
do you like ...? magst du/mögen Sie...? [mahkst doo/murgen zee]
I'd like a beer ich möchte gern ein Bier [mursht-uh gairn]
I'd like to go swimming ich würde gern schwimmen gehen [voord-uh]
would you like a drink? möchtest du/möchten Sie etwas trinken?
would you like to go for a

walk? möchtest du/möchten Sie einen Spaziergang machen?

what's it like? wie ist es? [vee]

I want one like this ich möchte so eins [zoh ine-ss]

lime die Limone [limohn-uh]

lime cordial der Limonensaft [limohnenzaft]

line (on paper) die Linie [leenee-uh]

(telephone) die Leitung [lytoong]

could you give me an outside line? könnten Sie mir ein Amt geben? [kurnten zee meer ine amt gayben]

lips die Lippen

lip salve der Lippen-Fettstift [fett-shtift]

lipstick der Lippenstift [lippen-shtift]

liqueur der Likör [likur]

listen zuhören [tsoo-hur-ren]

Lithuania Litauen [litowen]

litre* der Liter [leeter]

a litre of white wine ein Liter Weißwein

little klein [kline]

just a little, thanks danke, nur ein bißchen [dank-uh noor ine biss-shen]

a little milk etwas Milch [etvass]

a little bit more ein bißchen mehr [mair]

live leben [layben]

we live together wir wohnen zusammen [veer vohnen tsoozammen]

dialogue

where do you live? wo wohnen Sie? [vo vohnen zee]
I live in London ich wohne in London

lively lebhaft [layp-haft]

liver die Leber [layber]

loaf das Brot [broht]

lobby (in hotel) das Foyer [foy-yay]

lobster der Hummer [hoommer]

local örtlich [urtlish]

can you recommend a local restaurant? können Sie ein Restaurant am Ort empfehlen? [kurnen zee ine restorong am ort empfaylen]

lock das Schloß [shloss]

(verb) abschließen [ap-shleessen]

it's locked es ist abgeschlossen [ap-geshlossen]

lock in einschließen [ine-shleessen]

lock out ausschließen [owss-shleessen]

I've locked myself out ich habe mich ausgesperrt [ish hahb-uh mish owss-geshpairt]

locker (for luggage etc) das Schließfach [shleessfaKH]

lollipop der Lutscher [lootcher]

London London [lon-don]

long lang

how long will it/does it take?
wie lange dauert es? [vee lang-uh dowert ess]

a long time eine lange Zeit [ine-uh lang-uh tsite]

one day/two days longer ein Tag/zwei Tage länger [leng-er]

long distance call das Ferngespräch [fairn-geshpraysh]

look: I'm just looking, thanks danke, ich sehe mich nur um [dank-uh, ish zay-uh mish noor oom]

you don't look well du siehst nicht gut aus [doo zeest nisht goot owss]

look out! passen Sie auf! [passen zee owf]

can I have a look? kann ich mal sehen? [kann ish mahl zay-en]

look after sich kümmern um [zish k‫oommern oom]

look at ansehen [anzay-en]

look for suchen [zookHen]

I'm looking for ... ich suche... [ish zookH-uh]

look forward to sich freuen auf [zish froyen owf]

I'm looking forward to it ich freue mich darauf [ish froy-uh mish darowf]

loose (handle etc) lose [lohz-uh]

lorry der Lastwagen [lasst-vahgen]

lose verlieren [fairleeren]

I've lost my way ich habe mich verlaufen [ish hahb-uh mish fairlowfen]

I'm lost, I want to get to ... ich weiß nicht, wo ich bin, ich möchte nach ... [vice nisht vo ish bin ish mursht-uh nakH]

I've lost my handbag ich habe meine Handtasche verloren [fairlohren]

lost property (office) das Fundbüro [foont-b‫ooroh]

lot: a lot, lots viel [feel]

not a lot nicht sehr viel [nisht zair]

a lot of people viele Leute [feel-uh]

a lot bigger viel größer

I like it a lot ich mag es sehr [ish mahk ess zair]

lotion die Lotion [lohts-yohn]

loud laut [lowt]

lounge (in house) das Wohnzimmer [vohn-tsimmer]
(in hotel) die Lounge
(in airport) der Warteraum [vart-uh-rowm]

love die Liebe [leeb-uh]
(verb) lieben [leeben]

I love Germany ich liebe Deutschland

lovely herrlich [hairlish]

low (prices, bridge) niedrig [needrish]

luck das Glück [gl‫oock]

good luck! viel Glück [feel]

luggage das Gepäck [gepeck]

luggage trolley der Kofferkuli [koffer-kooli]

lump (on body) die Beule

[b**oy**l-uh]

lunch das Mittagessen
[m**i**ttahkessen]

lungs die Lungen [**loo**ng-en]

Luxembourg Luxemburg
[**loo**ksemboorg]

luxurious luxuriös [looksooree-**ur**ss]

luxury der Luxus [**loo**ksooss]

M

machine die Maschine
[mash**ee**n-uh]

mad (insane) verrückt [fair-r**oo**ckt]

(angry) böse [b**ur**z-uh]

made: what is it made of?
woraus ist es? [v**oh**rowss]
(food) was ist da drin? [vass]

magazine die Zeitschrift
[ts**i**te-shrift]

maid (in hotel) das
Zimmermädchen [ts**i**mmer-maydshen]

maiden name der
Mädchenname [m**ay**dshen-nahm-uh]

mail die Post
is there any mail for me? ist
Post für mich da? [f**oo**r mish]

mailbox der Briefkasten
[br**ee**fkasten]
see letterbox

main Haupt- [h**ow**pt]

main course das
Hauptgericht [h**ow**pt-gerisht]

main post office die

Hauptpost [h**ow**pt-posst]

main road die Hauptstraße
[h**ow**pt-shtrahss-uh]

mains switch der
Hauptschalter [h**ow**pt-shalter]

make (brand name) die Marke
[m**ark**-uh]
(verb) machen [m**a**kHen]
I make it 200 euros nach
meiner Rechnung sind das
zweihundert Euro [nakH
m**i**ne-er r**e**shnoong zint dass]

make-up das Make-up

man der Mann

manager der Geschäftsführer
[gesh**e**fts-f**oo**rer]
can I see the manager? kann
ich den Geschäftsführer
sprechen? [dayn – shpr**e**shen]

manageress die
Geschäftsführerin [gesh**e**fts-f**oo**rerin]

manual (car) ein Auto mit
Handschaltung [**ow**to mit h**a**nt-shaltoong]

many viele [f**ee**l-uh]
not many nicht viele [n**i**sht]

map (of city) der Stadtplan
[sht**a**t-plahn]
(road map) die Straßenkarte
[shtr**ah**ssen-kart-uh]
(geographical) die Landkarte
[l**a**ntkart-uh]

March der März [mairts]

margarine die Margarine
[margar**ee**n-uh]

market der Markt

marmalade die
Orangenmarmelade [or**on**Jen-

marmel**ahd**-uh]

married: I'm married ich bin
verheiratet [ish bin
fairh**y**rahtet]

are you married? sind Sie
verheiratet? [zint zee]

mascara die Wimperntusche
[**v**impern-toosh-uh]

match (football etc) das Spiel
[shpeel]

matches die Streichhölzer
[sht**r**ysh-hurltser]

material (fabric) der Stoff
[shtoff]

matter: it doesn't matter das
macht nichts [ma**k**Ht nishts]

what's the matter? was ist
los? [vass ist lohss]

mattress die Matratze
[mat**r**ats-uh]

May der Mai [my]

may: may I have another one?
kann ich noch eins haben?
[ish no**k**H ine-ss ha**h**ben]

may I come in? darf ich
hereinkommen? [hair**ine**-
kommen]

may I see it? kann ich es
sehen? [z**ay**-en]

maybe vielleicht [feel**y**sht]

mayonnaise die Mayonnaise
[my-oh-n**ay**z-uh]

me* mich [mish]

that's for me das ist für
mich

send it to me schicken Sie es
mir [meer]

me too ich auch [ish ow**k**H]

meal die Mahlzeit [m**ah**ltsite]

dialogue

> **did you enjoy your meal?**
> hat es Ihnen geschmeckt?
> [**ee**nen gesh**m**eckt]
>
> **it was excellent, thank you**
> es war ausgezeichnet,
> danke [var owss-gets**y**shnet,
> dank-uh]

mean (verb) bedeuten
[bed**oy**ten]

what do you mean? was
meinen Sie damit? [vass
m**ine**-en zee]

dialogue

> **what does this word
> mean?** was bedeutet
> dieses Wort? [vass bed**oy**tet
> d**ee**zess vort]
>
> **it means ... in English** auf
> Englisch bedeutet es ...
> [owf **eng**-lish]

measles die Masern [m**ah**zern]

meat das Fleisch [flysh]

mechanic der Mechaniker
[mesh**ah**niker]

medicine die Medizin
[medits**ee**n]

medium (size) mittlerer

medium-dry (wine)
halbtrocken [h**al**p-trocken]

medium-rare (steak) medium
[m**ay**dee-oom]

medium-sized mittelgroß
[m**i**ttelgrohss]

meet treffen

nice to meet you freut mich [froyt mish]

where shall I meet you? wo treffen wir uns? [vo – veer oonss]

meeting die Besprechung [beshpreshoong]

meeting place der Treffpunkt [treff-poonkt]

melon die Melone [melohn-uh]

men die Männer [menner]

mend reparieren [repareeren]

could you mend this for me? können Sie das reparieren? [kurnen zee]

menswear die Herrenkleidung [hairen-klydoong]

mention erwähnen [airvaynen]

don't mention it gern geschehen [gairn geshay-en]

menu die Speisekarte [shpize-uh-kart-uh]

may I see the menu, please? kann ich bitte die Speisekarte haben? [bitt-uh]

see **Menu Reader** on page 213

message die Nachricht [naKHrisht]

are there any messages for me? ist eine Nachricht für mich hinterlassen worden? [ine-uh – foor mish]

I want to leave a message for ... ich möchte eine Nachricht für ... hinterlassen [ish mursht-uh]

metal das Metall

metre* der Meter [mayter]

microwave (oven) der Mikrowellenherd [meekrovellen-hairt]

midday der Mittag

at midday mittags [mittahgs]

middle: **in the middle** in der Mitte [dair mitt-uh]

in the middle of the night mitten in der Nacht

the middle one der mittlere [mittler-uh]

midnight die Mitternacht [mitter-naKHt]

at midnight um Mitternacht [oom]

might: **I might** vielleicht [feelysht]

I might not vielleicht nicht [nisht]

I might want to stay another day vielleicht bleibe ich noch einen Tag länger [blibe-uh ish noKH ine-en tahk leng-er]

migraine die Migräne [migrayn-uh]

mild (taste, weather) mild [milt]

mile* die Meile [mile-uh]

milk die Milch [milsh]

milkshake der Milchshake

millimetre* der Millimeter [millimayter]

minced meat das Hackfleisch [hackflysh]

mind: **never mind** macht nichts [maKHt nishts]

I've changed my mind ich habe es mir anders überlegt [ish hahb-uh ess meer anders ooberl**ay**kt]

dialogue

do you mind if I open the window? macht es Ihnen etwas aus, wenn ich das Fenster öffne? [maкнт ess **ee**nen etvass owss venn ish] **no, I don't mind** nein, das ist mir gleich [meer gl**y**sh]

mine*: it's mine es gehört mir [geh**u**rt meer]
mineral water das Mineral-wasser [miner**ah**lvasser]
mint (sweet) das Pfefferminz [pfefferm**i**nts]
minute die Minute [min**oo**t-uh]
in a minute gleich [gl**y**sh]
just a minute Moment mal [m**oh**ment mahl]
mirror der Spiegel [shp**ee**gel]
Miss Frau [frow]
Miss! (waitress etc) Fräulein [fr**oy**line]
miss (bus, train) verpassen [fairp**a**ssen]
(regret absence of) vermissen [fairm**i**ssen]
I missed the bus ich habe den Bus verpaßt [ish h**a**h-uh dayn booss fairp**a**sst]
missing: to be missing fehlen [f**ay**len]
there's a suitcase missing ein Koffer fehlt
mist der Nebel [n**ay**bel]
mistake der Fehler [f**ay**ler]

I think there's a mistake ich glaube, da ist ein Fehler [ish gl**ow**b-uh]
sorry, I've made a mistake tut mir leid, ich habe einen Fehler gemacht [t**oo**t meer lite ish h**ah**b **ine**-en]
misunderstanding das Mißverständnis [miss-f**ai**rshtentniss]
mix-up: sorry, there's been a mix-up tut mir leid, etwas ist schiefgelaufen [t**oo**t meer lite, etvass ist sh**ee**f-gelowfen]
mobile phone das Handy [h**e**ndi]
modern modern [mod**ai**rn]
modern art gallery die Galerie für moderne Kunst [gal-er**ee** f**oo**r mod**ai**rn-uh koonst]
moisturizer die Feuchtigkeitscreme [f**oy**shtishkites-kraym]
moment: I'll be back in a moment ich bin gleich wieder da [glysh v**ee**der]
Monday Montag [m**oh**ntahk]
money das Geld [gelt]
month der Monat [m**oh**naht]
monument das Denkmal [d**e**nkmahl]
moon der Mond [mohnt]
moped das Moped [m**oh**pet]
more* mehr [mair]
can I have some more water, please? kann ich bitte noch etwas Wasser haben? [ish b**i**tt-uh noкн etvass]
more expensive/interesting

teurer/interessanter [**toy**rer]
more than 50 über fünfzig
[**oo**ber]
more than that mehr als das
a lot more viel mehr [feel]

dialogue

would you like some
more? möchten Sie noch
etwas? [**mur**shten zee noкн
etvass]
no, no more for me, thanks
nein danke, das ist genug
[nine dank-uh dass ist gen**oo**k]
how about you? und Sie?
[oont zee]
I don't want any more,
thanks ich möchte nichts
mehr, danke [**ni**shts]

morning der Morgen
 this morning heute morgen
 [**hoy**t-uh]
 in the morning am Morgen
most: I like this one most of all
 dies gefällt mir am besten
 [deess gefellt meer]
 most of the time die meiste
 Zeit [dee **my**st-uh tsite]
 most tourists die meisten
 Touristen [**my**sten]
 mostly meistens [**my**stens]
mother die Mutter [**moo**tter]
motorbike das Motorrad
 [mot**ohr**-raht]
motorboat das Motorboot
 [mot**ohr**-boht]
motorway die Autobahn
[**ow**tobahn]
mountain der Berg [bairk]
 in the mountains in den
 Bergen [dayn **bai**rgen]
mountaineering das
 Bergsteigen [**bairk**-shtygen]
mouse die Maus [mowss]
moustache der Schnurrbart
 [**shnoo**rr-bart]
mouth der Mund [moont]
mouth ulcer die Mundfäule
 [**moo**nt-foyl-uh]
move bewegen [bev**ay**gen]
 (move house) umziehen [**oo**m-
 tsee-en]
 he's moved to another room
 er ist in ein anderes Zimmer
 gezogen [air ist in ine **a**nderess
 ts**i**mmer gets**oh**gen]
 could you move your car?
 könnten Sie Ihr Auto
 wegfahren? [**ku**rnten zee eer
 owto veckfahren]
 could you move up a little?
 könnten Sie etwas
 aufrücken? [etvass **ow**f-r**oo**cken]
 where has it moved to? (shop,
 gallery) wo ist es jetzt? [vo]
movie der Film
movie theater (US) das Kino
 [**kee**no]
Mr Herr [hair]
Mrs Frau [frow]
Ms Frau [frow]
much viel [feel]
 much better/worse viel
 besser/schlechter [**shle**shter]
 much hotter viel heißer
 not much nicht viel [nisht]

not very much nicht sehr viel
[zair]

I don't want very much ich
möchte nicht so viel

mud der Dreck

mug (for drinking) die Tasse
[**ta**ss-uh]

I've been mugged ich bin
überfallen worden [ish bin
ooberfallen **vo**rden]

mum die Mutter [**moo**tter]

mumps der Mumps [moomps]

Munich München [**moo**nshen]

museum das Museum
[moo**zay**oom]

mushrooms die Pilze [**pi**lts-uh]

music die Musik [moo**zeek**]

musician der Musiker
[**moo**ziker]

Muslim moslemisch
[mos**lay**mish]

mussels die Muscheln
[**moo**sheln]

must*: I must ich muß... [ish
mooss]

I mustn't drink alcohol ich
darf keinen Alkohol trinken
[**kine**-en]

mustard der Senf [zenf]

my*: my room mein Zimmer
[mine]

my family meine Familie
[**mine**-uh]

my parents meine Eltern

myself: I'll do it myself ich
mache es selbst [ish maKH-uh
ess **ze**lpst]

by myself allein [al**line**]

N

nail (finger, metal) der Nagel
[**nah**gel]

nail varnish der Nagellack
[**nah**gel-lack]

name der Name [**nah**muh]

The familiar du and first
names are used in
informal relationships, for
example, between friends and
relatives, or when talking to
children. In formal situations, or
when talking to older people you
don't know, Sie is used, combined
with the address Herr or Frau (Mr or
Mrs/Ms) + surname. In less formal
situations, Germans immediately
adopt first name terms.

my name's John ich heiße
John [ish h**ice**-uh]

what's your name? wie
heißen Sie? [vee h**ice**-en zee]

what is the name of this
street? wie heißt diese
Straße? [vee hysst]

napkin die Serviette [zairvee-
ett-uh]

nappy die Windel [**vi**ndel]

narrow eng

nasty (person) gemein [ge**mine**]
(weather, accident) furchtbar
[**foo**rshtbar]

national national [nats-yoh**nahl**]

nationality die
Staatsangehörigkeit [sht**ah**ts-

an-gehurishkite]
natural natürlich [nat**oo**rlish]
nausea die Übelkeit [**oo**belkite]
navy (blue) marineblau
[mar**ee**n-uh-blow]
near nah
  is it near the city centre? ist
  es nahe dem Stadtzentrum?
  [n**ah**-uh daym]
  **do you go near the
  Brandenburg Gate?** fahren
  Sie in die Nähe des
  Brandenburger Tores? [f**ah**ren
  zee in dee n**ay**-uh]
  where is the nearest ...? wo
  ist der nächste ...? [vo ist dair
  n**ay**kst-uh]
nearby in der Nähe [dair n**ay**-
uh]
nearly fast [fasst]
necessary notwendig
[n**oh**tvendish]
neck der Hals [halss]
necklace die Halskette
[h**a**lskett-uh]
necktie (US) die Krawatte
[krav**a**tt-uh]
need: I need ... ich brauche ...
[ish br**ow**KH-uh]
  do I need to pay? muß ich
  bezahlen? [mooss]
needle die Nadel [n**ah**del]
negative (film) das Negativ
[n**ay**gateef]
neither: neither (one) of them
keiner (von ihnen) [k**ine**-er
fon **ee**nen]
  neither ... nor ... weder ...
  noch ... [v**ay**der ... noKH]

nephew der Neffe [neff-uh]
net (in sport) das Netz
Netherlands die Niederlande
[n**ee**derland-uh]
network map der
  Nahverkehrsplan
  [n**ah**fairkairs-plahn]
never nie [nee]

dialogue

have you ever been to
Mainz? waren Sie schon
einmal in Mainz? [v**ah**ren
zee shohn **ine**-mahl]
no, never, I've never been
there nein, ich war noch
nie da [noKH]

new neu [noy]
news (radio, TV etc) die
  Nachrichten [n**a**KHrishten]
newsagent's der
  Zeitungshändler [ts**y**toongs-
  hentler]
newspaper die Zeitung
  [ts**y**toong]
newspaper kiosk der
  Zeitungskiosk [ts**y**toongs-kee-
  osk]
New Year Neujahr [n**oy**-yahr]
Happy New Year! frohes
  neues Jahr [fr**oh**-ess n**oy**ess yar]

Many Germans celebrate
New Year's Eve at a
Silvester-party; midnight
firework displays are traditional
events.

New Year's Eve Silvester
[zilvester]
New Zealand Neuseeland
[noyzaylant]
New Zealander: I'm a New
Zealand (man/woman) ich
bin Neuseeländer
[noyzaylender]/
Neeseeländerin
next nächster [naykster]
the next turning/street on the
left die nächste
Abzweigung/Straße links
[naykst-uh]
at the next stop an der
nächsten Haltestelle
[naysten]
next week nächste Woche
next to neben [nayben]
nice (food) gut [goot]
(looks, view etc) hübsch [hoopsh]
(person) nett
niece die Nichte [nisht-uh]
night die Nacht [naKHt]
at night nachts
good night gute Nacht [goot-
uh]

dialogue

do you have a single room
for one night? haben Sie
ein Einzelzimmer für
eine Nacht? [hahben zee ine
ine-tsel-tsimmer foor ine-uh]
yes ja [yah]
how much is it per night?
was kostet es pro Nacht?
it's 150 euros for one night

eine Übernachtung kostet
hundertfünfzig Euro
[oober-naKHtoong]
thank you, I'll take it
danke, ich nehme es
[naym-uh]

nightclub der Nachtklub
[naKHtkloob]
nightdress das Nachthemd
[naKHt-hemt]
night porter der Nachtportier
[naKHt-port-yay]
no nein [nine]
I've no change ich habe kein
Kleingeld [kine]
there's no ... left es ist kein ...
übrig [oobrish]
no way! auf keinen Fall [owf
kine-en fal]
oh no! (upset) nein!
nobody keiner [kine-er]
there's nobody there es ist
keiner da
noise der Lärm [lairm]
noisy: it's too noisy es ist zu
laut [tsoo lowt]
non-alcoholic alkoholfrei
[alkohohlfry]
none keiner [kine-er]
nonsmoking compartment das
Nichtraucherabteil
[nishtrowKHer-aptile]
noon der Mittag [mittahk]
no-one keiner [kine-er]
nor: nor do I ich auch nicht
[owKH nisht]
normal normal [normahl]
north der Norden

in the north im Norden
north of Leipzig nördlich
von Leipzig [**nurt**lish fon]
northeast der Nordosten
[nort-**o**sten]
northern nördlich [**nurt**lish]
North Sea die Nordsee
[**nor**tzay]
northwest der Nordwesten
[nort**ves**ten]
Northern Ireland Nordirland
[nort-**ee**rlant]
Norway Norwegen [**nor**vaygen]
Norwegian (adj) norwegisch
[**nor**vaygish]
nose die Nase [**nah**z-uh]
nosebleed Nasenbluten
[**nah**zen-bl**oo**ten]
not* nicht [nisht]
no, I'm not hungry nein, ich
habe keinen Hunger [**kine**-
en]
I don't want any, thank you
ich möchte keine, danke
[m**ur**sht-uh **kine**-uh d**ank**-uh]
it's not necessary es ist nicht
nötig
I didn't know that das wußte
ich nicht [**voo**st-uh]
not that one – this one nicht
den – diesen [dayn – **dee**zen]
note (banknote) der
Geldschein [**gelt**-shine]
notebook das Notizbuch
[noht**ee**ts-b**oo**KH]
notepaper (for letters) das
Briefpapier [**bree**f-papeer]
nothing nichts [nishts]
nothing for me, thanks nichts

für mich, danke
nothing else sonst nichts
[zonst]
novel der Roman [rom**ahn**]
November der November
now jetzt [yetst]
number die Nummer
[**noo**mmer]
I've got the wrong number
ich habe mich verwählt
[**hah**b-uh mish fairv**ay**lt]
what is your phone number?
was ist Ihre Telefon-
nummer? [**eer**-uh telef**ohn**-
noommer]
number plate das
Nummernschild [**noo**mmern-
shilt]
Nuremburg Nürnberg [n**oo**rn-
bairk]
nurse (female) die
Krankenschwester [**kran**ken-
shvester]
(male) der Krankenpfleger
[**kran**ken-pflayger]
nursery slope der
Anfängerhügel [**an**fenger-
h**oo**gel]
nut (for bolt) die
Schraubenmutter
[shr**ow**benmootter]
nuts die Nüsse [n**oo**ss-uh]

O

occupied (toilet) besetzt
[bez**e**tst]
o'clock*: it's nine o'clock es ist

neun Uhr [oor]
October der Oktober
odd (strange) merkwürdig
[mairk-voordish]
of* von (+dat) [fon]
  the name of the hotel der
  Name des Hotels
off (lights) aus [owss]
  it's just off Goethestraße es
  ist ganz in der Nähe der
  Goethestraße [gants in dair
  nay-uh]
  we're off tomorrow wir
  reisen morgen ab [veer ryzen]
offensive anstößig [an-
shturssish]
office das Büro [booroh]
often oft
  not often nicht oft [nisht]
  how often are the buses?
  wie oft fahren die Busse?
  [vee]
oil (for car, for salad) das Öl [url]
ointment die Salbe [zalb-uh]
OK okay
  are you OK? sind Sie okay?
  is that OK with you? ist das in
  Ordnung? [ortnoong]
  is it OK if I ...? kann ich ... ?
  that's OK thanks (it doesn't
  matter) danke, das ist in
  Ordnung
  I'm OK (nothing for me, I've got
  enough) nein, danke [nine]
  (I feel OK) mir geht's gut [meer
  gayts goot]
  is this train OK for ...? fährt
  dieser Zug nach ...?
  I said I'm sorry, OK ich habe

doch gesagt, es tut mir leid
[hahb-uh dokн gezahkt]
old alt

dialogue

how old are you? wie alt
bist du/sind Sie? [vee alt
bist doo/zint zee]
I'm twenty-five ich bin
fünfundzwanzig
and you? und du/Sie?
[oont]

old-fashioned altmodisch
[altmohdish]
old town (old part of town) die
  Altstadt [alt-shtatt]
  in the old town in der
  Altstadt
olive oil das Olivenöl [oleeven-
url]
olives die Oliven [oleeven]
omelette das Omelette
[omlett]
on* auf [owf]
  on the street/beach auf der
  Straße/am Strand
  is it on this road? ist es auf
  dieser Straße?
  on the plane im Flugzeug
  on Saturday am Samstag
  on television im Fernsehen
  I haven't got it on me ich
  habe es nicht bei mir [hahb-
  uh ess nisht by meer]
  this one's on me (drink) diese
  Runde ist auf meine
  Rechnung [deez-uh roond-uh

ist owf **mine**-uh **r**eshnoong]

the light wasn't on das Licht war nicht an

what's on tonight? was gibt es h**eu**te **a**bend? [vass geept ess]

once (one time) einmal [**ine**-mahl]

at once (immediately) sofort [z**o**fort]

one* ein(e) [**ine**(-uh)]
(as figure) eins [ine-ss]

the white one der w**ei**ße [dair]

one-way ticket die einfache Fahrkarte [**ine**-faкн-uh f**a**hr-kart-uh]

onion die Zwiebel [tsv**ee**bel]

only nur [n**oo**r]

only one nur einer

it's only 6 o'clock es ist erst sechs Uhr [airst]

I've only just got here ich bin gerade erst **a**ngekommen [ger**a**hd-uh airst]

on/off switch der Ein/Aus-Schalter [ine-**ow**ss-shalter]

open (adj) **o**ffen

open (verb) öffnen [**u**rfnen]

when do you open? wann machen Sie auf? [van ma**кн**en zee owf]

I can't get it open ich bekomme es nicht auf [bek**o**mm-uh]

in the open air im Freien [fry-en]

opening times die Öffnungszeiten [**u**rfnoongs-

tsyten]

open ticket die unbeschränkte Fahrkarte [**oo**nbeshrenkt-uh f**a**hrkart-uh]

opera die Oper [**oh**per]

operation (medical) die Operation [operats-y**oh**n]

operator (telephone) die Vermittlung [fairmittloong]

opposite: the opposite direction die entgegengesetzte Richtung [entg**a**ygen-gezetst-uh r**i**shtoong]

the bar opposite die Kneipe gegenüber [gaygen-**oo**ber]

opposite my hotel gegenüber m**ei**nem Hotel

optician der Augenarzt [**ow**genartst]

or oder [**oh**der]

orange (fruit) die Apfelsine [apfelz**ee**n-uh], die Orange [or**o**nJ-uh]
(colour) orange

orange juice der Orangensaft [oronJen-zaft]

orchestra das Orchester [ork**e**ster]

order: can we order now? können wir jetzt bestellen? [k**u**rnen veer yetst besht**e**llen]

I've already ordered, thanks d**a**nke, ich habe schon bestellt [h**a**hb-uh shohn]

I didn't order this das habe ich nicht bestellt

out of order außer Betrieb [**ow**sser betr**ee**p]

ordinary normal [norm**a**hl]

107

other andere [**a**nder-uh]
the other one der andere
the other day (recently)
neulich [**n**oylish]
I'm waiting for the others ich
warte auf die anderen [dee
anderen]
do you have any others?
haben Sie noch andere?
[**h**ahben zee noкн]
otherwise sonst [zonst]
our* unser [**oo**nzer]
ours* unserer [**oo**nzerer]
out: he's out (not at home) er ist
nicht da [air ist nisht]
three kilometres out of town
drei Kilometer außerhalb
der Stadt [**ow**sserhalp dair
shtatt]
outdoors draußen [**drow**ssen]
outside ... außerhalb ... (+gen)
[**ow**sser-halp]
can we sit outside? können
wir draußen sitzen?
[**drow**ssen]
oven der Backofen [**b**ack-
ohfen]
over: over here hier [heer]
over there dort drüben
[**dr∞**ben]
over 500 über fünfhundert
[**∞**ber]
it's over (finished) es ist vorbei
[for-b**y**]
overcharge: you've
overcharged me Sie haben
mir zuviel berechnet [zee
hahben meer ts∞feel bereshnet]
overcoat der Mantel

overnight (travel) über Nacht
[**∞**ber naкнt]
overtake überholen
[**∞**berhohlen]
owe: how much do I owe you?
was bin ich Ihnen schuldig?
[vass bin ish **ee**nen sh∞ldish]
own: my own ... mein eigener
... [mine **ī**gener]
are you on your own? sind
Sie allein hier? [zint zee all**ine**
heer]
I'm on my own ich bin allein
hier
owner (man/woman) der
Besitzer [bez**i**tser]/die
Besitzerin

P

pack (verb) packen
pack: a pack of ... (food, drink
etc) eine Packung ... [**ine**-uh
pack**oong**]
package das Paket [pak**ay**t]
package holiday die
Pauschalreise [powsh**ah**lrize-uh]
packed lunch das Lunchpaket
[-pak**ay**t]
packet: a packet of cigarettes
eine Schachtel Zigaretten
[sh**a**кнtel tsigar**e**tten]
padlock das Vorhängeschloß
[**f**orheng-uh-shloss]
page (of book) die Seite [z**ite**-
uh]
could you page Mr ...?
können Sie Herrn ...

ausrufen lassen? [**kur**nen zee hairn ... **ows**sroofen]

pain der Schmerz [shmairts]

I have a pain here ich habe hier Schmerzen [ish hahb-uh heer]

painful schmerzhaft [shm**ai**rts-haft]

painkillers das Schmerzmittel [shm**ai**rts-mittel]

paint die Farbe [**f**arb-uh]

painting (picture) das Gemälde [gemeld-uh]

pair: a pair of ... ein Paar ... [ine pahr]

Pakistani (adj) pakistanisch [pakist**ah**nish]

palace der Palast

pale blaß [blass]

pale blue zartblau [tsartblow]

pan die Pfanne [pf**ann**-uh]

panties das Höschen [**hurs**-shen]

pants (underwear: men's) die Unterhose [**oo**nter-hohz-uh] (women's) das Höschen [**hurs**-shen] (US) die Hose [**h**ohz-uh]

pantyhose die Strumpfhose [shtr**oo**mpf-hohz-uh]

paper das Papier [pap**eer**] (newspaper) die Zeitung [**tsy**toong]

a piece of paper ein Stück Papier [ine sht**oo**ck]

paper handkerchiefs die Papiertaschentücher [pap**eer**-tashent**oo**sher]

parcel das Paket [pak**ay**t]

pardon?, (US) **pardon me?** (didn't understand) wie bitte? [vee bitt-uh]

parents: my parents meine Eltern [**mine**-uh eltern]

parents-in-law die Schwiegereltern [shv**ee**ger-eltern]

park der Park (verb) parken

can I park here? kann man hier parken? [heer]

parking lot (US) der Parkplatz [**p**arkplats]

part ein Teil [tile]

partner (boyfriend, girlfriend) der Partner/die Partnerin

party (group) die Gruppe [gr**oo**pp-uh] (celebration) die Fete [f**ay**t-uh]

pass (in mountains) der Paß [pas]

passenger der Passagier [passa**J**eer]

passport der Paß [pas]

past*: in the past in der Vergangenheit [dair fairg**a**ngen-hite]

just past the information office kurz hinter dem Auskunftsbüro [k**oo**rts]

path der Weg [vayk]

pattern das Muster [m**oo**ster]

pavement der Bürgersteig [b**oo**rgershtike]

on the pavement auf dem Bürgersteig

pay (verb) zahlen [ts**ah**len]

can I pay, please? kann ich

zahlen, bitte? [**bitt**-uh]
it's already paid for es ist
schon bezahlt [shohn bets**ah**lt]

dialogue

> who's paying? wer
> bezahlt? [vair bets**ah**lt]
> I'll pay ich bezahle
> no, you paid last time, I'll
> pay nein, du hast letztes
> Mal bezahlt, ich bezahle
> [letstess mahl]

pay phone der
Münzfernsprecher [m**oo**nts-
fairnshpresher]
peaceful friedlich [**free**tlish]
peach der Pfirsich [**pfeer**zish]
peanuts die Erdnüsse
[airtn**oo**ss-uh]
pear die Birne [**beern**-uh]
peas die Erbsen [**air**psen]
peculiar eigenartig [**ī**gen-artish]
pedestrian crossing der
Fußgängerüberweg
[**foo**ssgeng-er-**oo**bervayk]

Most German pedestrians
will stop at a red light on
a pedestrian crossing
whether there are cars about or not,
even at night! Police are often quick
to hand out on-the-spot fines for
jaywalkers.

pedestrian precinct die
Fußgängerzone [**foo**ssgeng-er-
tsohn-uh]

peg (for washing) die
Wäscheklammer [**vesh**-uh-
klammer]
(for tent) der Hering [**hair**ing]
pen der Stift [shtift]
pencil der Bleistift [**bly**-shtift]
penfriend (boy/girl) der
Brieffreund [**breef**-froynt]/die
Brieffreundin
penicillin das Penizillin
[penitsill**een**]
penknife das Taschenmesser
[**tash**en-messer]
pensioner (man/woman) der
Rentner/die Rentnerin
people die Leute [**loyt**-uh]
the other people in the hotel
die **a**nderen Leute im Hotel
too many people zu viele
Leute [ts**oo** feel-uh]
pepper (spice) der Pfeffer
(vegetable) die Paprikaschote
[**pa**prika-shoht-uh]
peppermint (sweet) das
Pfefferminz [**pfeffermints**]
per: per night pro Nacht
[na**kH**t]
how much per day? was
kostet es pro Tag? [tahk]
per cent Prozent [prots**ent**]
perfect perfekt [pair**fekt**]
perfume das Parfüm [par**foom**]
perhaps vielleicht [feel**ysht**]
perhaps not vielleicht nicht
period (of time) die Zeit [tsite]
(menstruation) die Periode
[pairee-**oh**d-uh]
perm die Dauerwelle
[**dow**ervell-uh]

permit die Genehmigung
[gen**ay**-migoong]
person die Person [pairz**ohn**]
personal stereo der
  Walkman®
petrol das Benzin [bents**een**]

Types of petrol are
Normal [norm**ahl**] (2/3
star, always unleaded),
Super verbleit [z**oo**per fair-**bl**ite] (4
star, leaded) and **Super unverbleit**
[**oo**nfair-blite] (4 star, unleaded).
Cash payment is the norm.

petrol can der
  Reservekanister [rez**ai**rv-uh-
  kanister]
petrol station die Tankstelle
  [**tank**-shtell-uh]
pharmacy die Apotheke
  [apot**ayk**-uh]
  see **chemist**
phone das Telefon [telef**ohn**]
  (verb) anrufen [**an**-r**oo**fen]

Phone boxes are yellow
and are either operated by
coins (**Münzfernsprecher**
[m**oo**nts-fairn-shpresher]) or cards
(**Kartentelefon** [karten-telefohn]).
Phonecards (**Telefonkarten**) can be
purchased from post offices and
some shops. A phonecard is worth
buying, especially if you're intending
to call home. However, an easier
option is to use the direct phone
service facilities of the main post
office (**Hauptpost**): a phone booth

will be allocated to you from the
counter marked **Fremdgespräche**,
which is also where you pay once
you've finished.
see **speak** and **dialling code**

phone book das Telefonbuch
  [telef**ohn**-b**oo**KH]
phonecard die Telefonkarte
  [-**kart**-uh]
phone number die
  Telefonnummer [-**noo**mmer]
photo das Foto
  excuse me, could you take a
  photo of us? entschuldigen
  Sie, könnten Sie ein Foto
  von uns machen? [k**u**rnten zee
  ine]
phrase book der
  Sprachführer [shprahKH-f**oo**rer]
piano das Klavier [klav**eer**]
pickpocket der Taschendieb
  [**t**ashen-deep]
pick up: **will you be there to**
  pick me up? werden Sie da
  sein, um mich abzuholen?
  [oom mish **a**pts**oo**-hohlen]
picnic das Picknick
picture das Bild [bilt]
pie (meat) die Pastete [past**ayt**-
  uh]
  (fruit) der Kuchen [k**oo**KHen]
piece das Stück [sht**oo**ck]
  a piece of ... ein Stück ...
  [ine]
pill die Pille [p**i**ll-uh]
  I'm on the pill ich nehme die
  Pille [ish **n**aym-uh dee]
pillow das Kopfkissen

pillow case der Kopfkissenbezug [kopfkissen-betsook]

pin die Nadel [nahdel]

pineapple die Ananas [ananas]

pineapple juice der Ananassaft [ananas-zaft]

pink rosa [rohza]

pipe (for smoking) die Pfeife [pfife-uh]
(for water) das Rohr

pipe cleaner der Pfeifenreiniger [pfyfen-ryniger]

pity: it's a pity das ist schade [shahd-uh]

pizza die Pizza [peetsa]

place der Platz [plats]
is this place taken? ist dieser Platz besetzt? [deezer – bezetst]
at your place bei dir/Ihnen [by deer/eenen]
at his place bei ihm [eem]

plain (not patterned) uni [oonee]

plane das Flugzeug [flooktsoyk]
by plane mit dem Flugzeug [daym]

plant die Pflanze [pflants-uh]

plaster (for cut) das Heftpflaster

plaster cast der Gipsverband [gips-fairbant]

plastic das Plastik
(credit cards) die Kreditkarten [kredeet-karten]

plastic bag die Plastiktüte [plastik-toot-uh]

plate der Teller

platform der Bahnsteig [bahnshtike]

which platform is it, please? welches Gleis, bitte? [velshess glice bitt-uh]

play (verb) spielen [shpeelen]
(noun: in theatre) das Stück [shtook]

playground der Spielplatz [shpeel-plats]

pleasant angenehm [an-genaym]

please bitte [bitt-uh]
yes please ja bitte [yah]
could you please ...? könnten Sie bitte ...? [kurnten zee]
please don't bitte nicht [nisht]

pleased to meet you! freut mich! [froyt mish]

pleasure die Freude [froyd-uh]
my pleasure ganz meinerseits [gants mine-er-zites]

plenty: plenty of ... viel ... [feel]
we've plenty of time wir haben viel Zeit
that's plenty, thanks das reicht, danke [rysht]

pliers die Zange [tsang-uh]

plug (electrical) der Stecker [shtecker]
(for car) die Zündkerze [tsoontkairts-uh]
(in sink) der Stöpsel [shturpsel]

plumber der Klempner

p.m.* (in the afternoon) nachmittags [naкHmittahks]
(in the evening) abends [ahbents]

poached egg das pochierte Ei [posheert-uh ī]
pocket die Tasche [tash-uh]
point: two point five zwei Komma fünf
 there's no point es hat keinen Sinn [kine-en zin]
points (in car) die Kontakte [kontakt-uh]
poisonous giftig [giftish]
Poland Polen
Polish polnisch
police die Polizei [politsī]
 call the police! rufen Sie die Polizei! [roofen zee dee]

The German police are not renowned for their friendliness, but they usually treat foreigners with courtesy. It's important to remember that you are expected to carry your ID (your passport, or at least a student card or driving licence) at all times. Traffic offences or any other misdemeanours will result in a rigorous checking of documentation, and on-the-spot fines are best paid without argument. Throughout Germany the number to ring for the police is 110.

policeman der Polizist [politsist]
police station die Polizeiwache [politsī-vaкн-uh]
policewoman die Polizistin [politsistin]
polish die Creme [kraym]

polite höflich [hurflish]
polluted verschmutzt [fairshmootst]
pony der Pony [ponnee]
pool (for swimming) das Schwimmbecken [shvimm-becken]
poor (not rich) arm
 (quality) schlecht [shlesht]
pop music die Popmusik [pop-moozeek]
pop singer (male/female) der Popsänger [popzenger]/die Popsängerin
population die Bevölkerung [befurlkeroong]
pork das Schweinefleisch [shvine-uh-flysh]
port (for boats) der Hafen [hahfen]
 (drink) der Portwein [portvine]
porter (in hotel) der Portier [port-yay]
portrait das Porträt [portray]
posh (restaurant, people) vornehm [fornaym]
possible möglich [murglish]
 is it possible to ...? ist es möglich, zu ...?
 as ... as possible so ... wie möglich [zo ... vee]
post (mail) die Post [posst]
 (verb) absenden
 could you post this for me? könnten Sie das für mich aufgeben? [kurnten zee dass foor mish owf-gayben]
postbox der Briefkasten [breefkasten]

postcard die Postkarte [**po**sstkart-uh]
poster das Plakat [plak**ah**t]
post office die Post

The German postal service is generally fast and reliable. There is no distinction between first and second class post; most deliveries within Germany reach their destination on the next day. Post offices are normally open from 9 a.m. till 6 p.m. Monday to Friday but closed on Saturday afternoons. Some may close for one or two hours at lunchtime.

poste restante postlagernd [**po**sst-lahgernt]
pots and pans das Kochgeschirr [**ko**KHgesheer]
potato die Kartoffel
potato chips (US) die Chips [chips]
potato salad der Kartoffelsalat [kart**o**ffel-zal**ah**t]
pottery (objects) die Töpferwaren [**tur**pfer-vahren]
pound* (money, weight) das Pfund [pfoont]
power cut der Stromausfall [shtr**oh**m-owssfal]
power point die Steckdose [sht**eck**-dohz-uh]
practise: I want to practise my German ich will mein Deutsch üben [ish vill mine doytch **oo**ben]

prawns die Krabben
prefer: I prefer ... ich mag lieber ... [ish mahk l**ee**ber]
pregnant schwanger [shv**ang**-er]
prescription (for chemist) das Rezept [rayts**ept**]
present (gift) das Geschenk [gesh**enk**]
president der Präsident [prezee**dent**]
pretty hübsch [h**oo**psh]
it's pretty expensive es ist ganz schön teuer [gants shurn t**oy**er]
price der Preis [price]
priest der Geistliche [**gy**stlish-uh]
prime minister der Premierminister [premy**ay**-minister]
printed matter die Drucksache [dr**oo**ck-zaKH-uh]
priority (in driving) die Vorfahrt [**fo**rfahrt]

Where there are no priority signs, traffic coming from the right has priority. Priority signs are either a yellow lozenge (priority road) or a red-rimmed triangle with an arrow (indicating priority for the next crossroads).

prison das Gefängnis [gef**eng**-niss]
private privat [priv**ah**t]
private bathroom das eigene

Bad [**ee**gen-uh baht]

private room das Einzelzimmer [**ine**-tseltsimmer]

probably wahrscheinlich [vahrsh**ine**-lish]

problem das Problem [probl**ay**m]

no problem! kein Problem [kine]

program(me) das Programm [progr**a**m]

promise: I promise ich verspreche es [fairshr**e**sh-uh]

pronounce: how is this pronounced? wie spricht man das aus? [vee shprisht man dass owss]

properly (repaired, locked etc) richtig [**ri**shtish]

protection factor der Lichtschutzfaktor [**li**sht-shoots-faktor]

Protestant evangelisch [ayvang**ay**lish]

public convenience die öffentliche Toilette [**ur**fentlish-uh twalett-uh]

public holiday der gesetzliche Feiertag [ge**zetz**lish-uh **fire**-tahk]

pudding (dessert) der Nachtisch [**na**kHtish]

pull ziehen [**tsee**-en]

pullover der Pullover [pool**oh**ver]

puncture die Reifenpanne [**ry**fen-pann-uh]

purple violett [vee-oh-l**e**tt]

purse (for money) das Portemonnaie [port-mon**ay**]

(US) die Handtasche [hant-tash-uh]

push schieben [**shee**ben]

pushchair der Sportwagen [**shp**ort-vahgen]

put tun [toon]

where can I put ...? wo kann ich ... hinstellen? [**hin**-shtellen]

could you put us up for the night? könnten Sie uns heute nacht unterbringen? [**oo**nss **hoy**t-uh na**kH**t **oo**nterbringen]

pyjamas der Schlafanzug [shl**ah**f-antsook]

Q

quality die Qualität [kvalit**ayt**]

quarantine die Quarantäne [kvarant**ay**n-uh]

quarter das Viertel [**fee**rtel]

quayside: on the quayside am Kai [ky]

question die Frage [fr**ah**g-uh]

queue die Schlange [shl**ang**-uh]

quick schnell [shnell]

that was quick das war schnell [vahr]

what's the quickest way there? wie komme ich am schnellsten dorthin? [vee komm-uh ish am shnellsten dort-hin]

fancy a quick drink? wollen wir schnell einen trinken gehen? [**vo**llen veer – **ine**-en

trinken g**ay**-en]

quickly schnell [sh**nell**]

quiet (place, hotel) ruhig [**roo**ish]

quiet! Ruhe! [**roo**-uh]

quite (fairly) ziemlich [ts**ee**mlish]

(very) ganz [gants]

that's quite right ganz recht [resht]

quite a lot eine ganze Menge [**ine**-uh g**ants**-uh m**eng**-uh]

R

rabbit das Kaninchen [kan**ee**nshen]

race (for runners, cars) das Rennen

racket (squash, tennis etc) der Schläger [shl**ay**ger]

radiator (in room) der Heizkörper [**hites**-kurper] (of car) der Kühler [k**oo**ler]

radio das Radio [**rah**dee-oh] on the radio im Radio

rail: by rail per Bahn [pair]

railway die Eisenbahn [**Tz**enbahn]

rain der Regen [**ray**gen] in the rain im Regen it's raining es regnet [**ray**gnet]

raincoat der Regenmantel [**ray**genmantel]

rape die Vergewaltigung [fairgev**al**-tigoong]

rare (steak) englisch [**eng**-lish]

rash (on skin) der Ausschlag [**ow**ss-shlahk]

raspberry die Himbeere [**him**bair-uh]

rat die Ratte [**ratt**-uh]

rate (for changing money) der Wechselkurs [**veksel**-koorss]

rather: it's rather good es ist ganz gut [gants g**oo**t] I'd rather ... ich würde lieber ... [ish v**oo**rd-uh l**ee**ber]

razor (electric) der Rasierapparat [raz**eer**-apparaht]

razor blades die Rasierklingen [raz**eer**-klingen]

read lesen [**lay**zen]

ready fertig [**fair**tish] are you ready? bist du/sind Sie fertig? I'm not ready yet ich bin noch nicht fertig [noKH nisht]

dialogue

when will it be ready? wann ist es fertig? [vann] it should be ready in a couple of days es müßte in ein paar Tagen fertig sein [m**oo**sst-uh]

real echt [esht]

really wirklich [**veer**klish] that's really great das ist echt toll [esht tol]

rearview mirror der Rückspiegel [r**oo**ck-shpeegel]

reasonable (prices etc) vernünftig [fairn**oo**nftish]

receipt die Quittung

[kvittoong]

recently kürzlich [koortslish]

reception (in hotel, for guests) der Empfang

at reception am Empfang

reception desk die Rezeption [retsepts-yohn]

receptionist die Empfangsperson [empfangs-pairzohn]

recognize erkennen [airkennen]

recommend: could you recommend ...? könnten Sie ... empfehlen? [kurnten zee ... empfaylen]

record (music) die Schallplatte [shallplat-uh]

red rot [roht]

red wine der Rotwein [rohtvine]

refund (verb) erstatten [airshtatten]

can I have a refund? kann ich das Geld zurückbekommen? [kan ish dass gelt tsoorück-bekommen]

region das Gebiet [gebeet]

registered: by registered mail per Einschreiben [pair ine-shryben]

registration number die Autonummer [owto-noommer]

relative der/die Verwandte [fairvant-uh]

religion die Religion [religyohn]

remember: I don't remember ich kann mich nicht

erinnern [ish kan mish nisht air-innern]

I remember ich erinnere mich [air-inner-uh]

do you remember? erinnern Sie sich? [zee zish]

rent die Miete [meet-uh]
(verb) mieten [meeten]

for rent zu vermieten [tsoo fairmeeten]

dialogue

I'd like to rent a car ich möchte ein Auto mieten [ish mursht-uh ine owto]

for how long? für wie lange? [foor vee lang-uh]

two days zwei Tage [tahg-uh]

this is our range das ist unser Angebot [oonzer angeboht]

I'll take the ... ich nehme den ... [naym-uh dayn]

is that with unlimited mileage? ist das ohne Kilometerbeschränkung? [ohn-uh keelo-mayter-beshrenkoong]

it is ja [yah]

can I see your licence please? kann ich bitte Ihren Führerschein sehen? [eeren foorer-shine]

and your passport und Ihren Paß [pas]

is insurance included? ist Versicherung inbegriffen?

yes, but you have to pay the first 200 euros yourself ja, aber die ersten zweihundert Euro müssen Sie selbst bezahlen [zelpst betsahlen]
can you leave a deposit of ...? könnten Sie eine Anzahlung von ... leisten? [ine-uh an-tsahloong – lysten]

rented car das Mietauto [meet-owto]
repair (verb) reparieren [repareeren]
can you repair it? können Sie es reparieren? [kurnen zee]
repeat wiederholen [veederhohlen]
could you repeat that? können Sie das noch einmal wiederholen? [kurnen zee dass noKH ine-mahl]
reservation die Reservierung [rezairveeroong]
I'd like to make a reservation ich möchte eine Reservierung vornehmen [mursht-uh ine-uh – for-naymen]

dialogue

I have a reservation ich habe eine Reservierung [ish hahb-uh]
yes sir, what name please? auf welchen Namen, bitte? [owf velshen nahmen]

reserve reservieren [rezairveeren]

dialogue

can I reserve a table for tonight? kann ich für heute abend einen Tisch reservieren? [kan ish foor hoyt-uh ahbent ine-en tish]
yes madam, for how many people? ja, für wieviele Personen? [foor vee veel-uh pairzohnen]
for two für zwei [tsvy]
and for what time? und für welche Zeit? [velsh-uh tsite]
for eight o'clock für acht Uhr [oor]
and could I have your name please? und kann ich bitte Ihren Namen haben? [eeren nahmen]
see alphabet

rest: I need a rest ich brauche Erholung [ish browKH-uh airhohloong]
the rest of the group der Rest der Gruppe
restaurant das Restaurant [restorong]

 Italian, Greek, Turkish and Chinese restaurants are very popular with Germans, while for traditional German food you're best advised to

try a **Gasthaus** [gast-howss] (inn)
or even a **Brauhaus** [brow-howss].
Look out for the set-price menu
(**Tageskarte** [tahgess-kart-uh])
which usually offers 3-course meals
at very reasonable prices.

rest room (US) die Toilette
[twalett-uh]
retired: I'm retired ich bin im
Ruhestand [ish bin im r00-uh-
shtant]
return (ticket) die Rückfahrkarte [rOOck-fahrkart-uh]

dialogue

a return to Heilbronn eine
Rückfahrkarte nach
Heilbronn
coming back when? wann
soll die Rückfahrt sein?
[rOOck-fahrt]

reverse charge call das R-
Gespräch [air-geshpraysh]
reverse gear der
Rückwärtsgang
[rOOckvairtsgang]
revolting ekelhaft [aykelhaft]
Rhine der Rhein [rine]
rib die Rippe [ripp-uh]
rice der Reis [rice]
rich (person) reich [rysh]
(food) schwer [shvair]
ridiculous lächerlich
[lesherlish]
right (correct) richtig [rishtish]
(not left) rechts [reshts]

you were right Sie hatten
recht [resht]
that's right das stimmt
[shtimmt]
this can't be right das kann
nicht stimmen [nisht
shtimmen]
right! okay!
is this the right road for ...?
ist dies die Straße nach ...?
[deess]
on the right rechts
turn right biegen Sie rechts
ab [beegen zee – ap]
right-hand drive die
Rechtssteuerung [reshts-
shtoyeroong]
ring (on finger) der Ring
I'll ring you ich rufe Sie an
[ish r00f-uh zee]
ring back zurückrufen
[ts00rOOck-r00fen]
ripe (fruit) reif [rife]
rip-off: it's a rip-off das ist
Wucher [vooKHer]
rip-off prices Wucherpreise
[vooKHer-prize-uh]
risky riskant
river der Fluß [flooss]
road die Straße [shtrahss-uh]
is this the road for ...? ist dies
die Straße nach ...? [deess dee
– naKH]
down the road die Straße
entlang
road accident der Verkehrsunfall [fairkairss-oonfal]
road map die Straßenkarte
[shtrahssen-kart-uh]

roadsign das Verkehrszeichen
[fairkairs-tsyshen]

rob: I've been robbed ich bin
bestohlen worden [ish bin
beshtohlen vorden]

rock der Felsen [felzen]
(music) der Rock

on the rocks (with ice) mit Eis
[ice]

roll (bread) das Brötchen
[brurtchen]

roof das Dach [daKH]

roof rack der
Dachgepäckträger [daKH-
gepeck-trayger]

room das Zimmer [tsimmer]

in my room in meinem
Zimmer [mine-em]

dialogue

do you have any rooms?
haben Sie Zimmer frei?
[fry]

for how many people? für
wie viele Personen? [foor
vee veel-uh pairzohnen]

for one/for two für eine
Person/für zwei Personen

yes, we have rooms free
ja, wir haben Zimmer frei

for how many nights will it
be? für wie lange? [foor vee
lang-uh]

just for one night nur für
eine Nacht [ine-uh naKHt]

how much is it? was kostet
es?

... with bathroom and ...

without bathroom ... mit
Bad und ... ohne Bad
[ohn-uh baht]

can I see a room with
bathroom? kann ich ein
Zimmer mit Bad sehen?
[zay-en]

ok, I'll take it gut, ich
nehme es [naym-uh]

room service der Zimmer-
service [tsimmer'service']

rope das Seil [zile]

rosé (wine) der Roséwein
[rohzay-vine]

roughly (approximately)
ungefähr [oongefair]

round: it's my round das ist
meine Runde [mine-uh roond-
uh]

roundabout (for traffic) der
Kreisverkehr [krice-fairkair]

round trip ticket die
Rückfahrkarte [rOck-fahrkart-
uh]

see return

route die Strecke [shtreck-uh]

what's the best route?
welches ist der beste Weg?
[velshess ist dair best-uh vayk]

rubber (material) das Gummi
[goommee]
(eraser) der Radiergummi
[radeer-goommee]

rubber band das Gummiband
[goommee-bant]

rubbish (waste) der Abfall [ap-
fal]
(poor quality goods) der Mist

rubbish! (nonsense) Quatsch!
[kvatch]
rucksack der Rucksack
[**roo**ckzack]
rude unhöflich [**oon**-hurflish]
ruins die Ruinen [roo-**ee**nen]
rum der Rum [roomm]
  rum and coke ein Rum mit
  Cola [**koh**la]
run (person) rennen, laufen
[**low**fen]
  how often do the buses run?
  wie oft fahren die Busse?
  [vee oft **fah**ren dee **boo**ss-uh]
  I've run out of money ich
  habe kein Geld mehr [ish
  hahb-uh kine gelt mair]
rush hour die Rush-hour

S

sad traurig [**trow**rish]
saddle der Sattel [**zatt**el]
safe (not in danger) sicher
[**zi**sher]
  (not dangerous) ungefährlich
[**oon**-gefairlish]
safety pin die
  Sicherheitsnadel [**zi**sher-hites-
  nahdel]
sail das Segel [**zay**gel]
sailboard das Windsurfbrett
[**vint**-surfbrett]
sailboarding das Windsurfen
[**vint**-surfen]
salad der Salat [zal**aht**]
salad dressing die Salatsoße
[zal**aht**-zohss-uh]

sale: for sale zu verkaufen
[ts00 fair**kow**fen]
salmon der Lachs [lacks]
salt das Salz [zalts]
same: the same derselbe
[dair**zelb**-uh]
  the same man/woman
  derselbe Mann/dieselbe
  Frau [dee**zelb**-uh]
  the same as this dasselbe
  wie das [dass**elb**-uh vee]
  the same again, please
  dasselbe nochmal, bitte
  [no**KH**mahl **bitt**-uh]
  it's all the same to me das ist
  mir ganz egal [meer gants
  ay**gahl**]
sand der Sand [zant]
sandals die Sandalen
[zan**dah**len]
sandwich das belegte Brot
[be**layk**t-uh broht]
sanitary napkin (US) die
  Damenbinde [**dah**menbind-uh]
sanitary towel die
  Damenbinde [**dah**menbind-uh]
sardines die Sardinen
[zar**dee**nen]
Saturday Samstag [**zam**stahk]
sauce die Soße [**zoh**ss-uh]
saucepan der Kochtopf
[**ko**KHtopf]
saucer die Untertasse [**oon**ter-
tass-uh]
sauna die Sauna [**zow**nah]
sausage die Wurst [voorst]
**say: how do you say ... in
German?** was heißt ... auf
Deutsch? [vass hyst ... owf

doytch]

what did he say? was hat er gesagt? [gezahkt]

I said ... ich sagte ... [zahkt-uh]

he said ... er sagte ...

could you say that again? könnten Sie das wiederholen? [kurnten zee dass veeder-hohlen]

scarf (for neck) der Schal [shahl]

(for head) das Kopftuch [kopftooKH]

scenery die Landschaft [lantshafft]

schedule (US) der Fahrplan [fahrplahn]

scheduled flight der Linienflug [leen-yenflook]

school die Schule [shool-uh]

scissors: a pair of scissors eine Schere [shair-uh]

scotch der Scotch

Scotch tape der Tesafilm® [tayzahfilm]

Scotland Schottland [shottlant]

Scottish schottisch [shottish]

I'm Scottish (man/woman) ich bin Schotte [shott-uh]/ Schottin

scrambled eggs die Rühreier [roor-ier]

scratch der Kratzer [kratser]

screw die Schraube [shrowb-uh]

screwdriver der Schraubenzieher [shrowben-tsee-er]

scrubbing brush (for hands) die Handbürste [hant-boorst-uh]

(for floors) die Scheuerbürste [shoyer-boorst-uh]

sea das Meer [mair]

by the sea am Meer

seafood die Meeresfrüchte [mairess-frøosht-uh]

seafood restaurant das Fischrestaurant [fish-restorong]

seafront die Strandpromenade [shtrantpromenahd-uh]

seagull die Möwe [murv-uh]

search (verb) suchen [zooKHen]

seashell die Muschel [mooshel]

seasick: I feel seasick ich bin seekrank [ish bin zaykrank]

I get seasick ich werde leicht seekrank [vaird-uh lysht]

seaside: by the seaside am Meer [mair]

seat der Sitzplatz [zitsplats]

is this anyone's seat? sitzt hier jemand? [zitst heer yaymant]

seat belt der Sicherheitsgurt [zisherhites-goort]

seaweed der Tang

secluded abgelegen [apgelaygen]

second (adj) zweiter [tsvyter]

(of time) die Sekunde [zekoond-uh]

just a second! Moment mal! [mahl]

second class zweiter Klasse [tsvyter klass-uh]

second-hand gebraucht [gebrowKHt]

see sehen [**zay**-en]

can I see? kann ich mal sehen?

have you seen ...? haben Sie ... gesehen? [**hah**ben zee ... ge**zay**-en]

I saw him this morning ich habe ihn heute morgen gesehen

see you! bis später! [shp**ayter**]

I see (I understand) ich verstehe [fair**stay**-uh]

self-catering apartment die Ferienwohnung [**fay**ree-en-**vohn**oong]

self-service die Selbstbedienung [**zelpst**-bedeenoong]

sell verkaufen [fair**kow**fen]

do you sell ...? haben Sie ...? [**hah**ben zee]

Sellotape® der Tesafilm® [**tay**zahfilm]

send senden [**zen**den]

I want to send this to England ich möchte dies nach England senden [ish **mursht**-uh deess]

senior citizen (man/woman) der Rentner/die Rentnerin

separate getrennt

separated: I'm separated ich lebe getrennt [ish **layb**-uh]

separately (pay, travel) getrennt

September der September [zep**tember**]

septic vereitert [fair-**ī**tert]

serious ernst [airnst]

service charge (in restaurant) die Bedienung [bed**een**oong]

service station die Tankstelle (mit Werkstatt) [**tank**shtell-uh mit **vair**kshtatt]

serviette die Serviette [zairvee-**ett**-uh]

set menu die Tageskarte [**tah**gess-kart-uh]

several mehrere [**mair**er-uh]

sew nähen [**nay**-en]

could you sew this back on? können Sie das wieder annähen? [**kur**nen zee dass **vee**der an-**nay**-en]

sex der Sex

sexy sexy

shade: in the shade im Schatten [**shat**ten]

shake: let's shake hands geben wir uns die Hand [**gay**ben veer oonss dee hant]

shallow (water) seicht [zysht]

shame: what a shame! wie schade! [vee sh**ah**d-uh]

shampoo das Shampoo

can I have a shampoo and set? können Sie mir die Haare waschen und legen? [**kur**nen zee meer dee **hah**r-uh **vash**en oont **lay**gen]

share (room, table etc) sich teilen [zish **ty**len]

sharp (knife, taste) scharf [sharf]

(pain) stechend [**shte**shent]

shattered (very tired) todmüde [**toht**mœd-uh]

shaver der Rasierapparat [razeer-**app**araht]

shaving foam die Rasierseife

[raz**eer**-zife-uh]

shaving point die Steckdose
für Rasierapparate
[sht**eck**dohz-uh foor raz**eer**-
apparaht-uh]

she* sie [zee]
 is she here? ist sie hier?
 [heer]

sheet (for bed) das Laken
 [**lah**ken]

shelf das Brett

shellfish die Schaltiere [**shahl**-
teer-uh]

sherry der Sherry

ship das Schiff [shiff]
 by ship mit dem Schiff

shirt das Hemd [hemt]

shit! Scheiße! [sh**ice**-uh]

shock der Schock [shock]
 I got an electric shock from ...
 ich habe einen elektrischen
 Schlag von ... bekommen
 [ish hahb-uh **ine**-en ayl**ek**trishen
 shlahk fon]

shock-absorber der
Stoßdämpfer [sht**ohss**-
dempfer]

shocking (behaviour, prices)
skandalös [skandal**urss**]
 (custom etc) schockierend
 [shock**eer**ent]

shoe der Schuh [shoo]
 a pair of shoes ein Paar
 Schuhe [pahr sh**oo**-uh]

shoelaces die Schnürsenkel
 [shn**ũũr**-zenkel]

shoe polish die Schuhcreme
 [sh**oo**-kraym]

shoe repairer der

Schuhmacher [sh**oo**-
makHer]

shop das Geschäft [gesh**eft**]

 Shops generally open
between 8.30 and 10 a.m.
and close at 6.30 p.m.
Mondays to Fridays. On Saturdays,
shops close at 2 p.m. except for the
first Saturday in each month when,
at least in the town centres, shops
do not close until 6 p.m. On
Thursdays many shops remain open
until about 8 p.m. (**langer
Donnerstag**). Sunday opening is
under debate, but do not expect to
be able to do any shopping on a
Sunday.

shopping: I'm going shopping
ich gehe einkaufen [ish g**ay**-
uh **ine**-kowfen]

shopping centre das
Einkaufszentrum [**ine**-kowfss-
tsentroom]

shop window das
Schaufenster [sh**ow**fenster]

shore (of sea) der Strand
 [shtrant]
 (of lake) das Ufer [**oo**fer]

short (time, journey) kurz
 [koorts]
 (person) klein [kline]

shortcut die Abkürzung [ap-
k**oo**rtsoong]

shorts die Shorts

should: what should I do? was
soll ich machen? [vass zoll ish
m**a**kHen]

he shouldn't be long er
kommt sicher bald [air kommt
zisher balt]

you should have told me das
hätten Sie mir sagen sollen
[hetten zee meer zahgen zollen]

shoulder die Schulter
[shoolter]

shout (verb) schreien [shry-en]

show (in theatre) die
Vorstellung [for-shtelloong]

could you show me?
könnten Sie mir das zeigen?
[kurnten zee meer dass tsygen]

shower (in bathroom) die
Dusche [doosh-uh]

with shower mit Dusche

shower gel das Duschgel
[doosh-gayl]

shut (verb) schließen
[shleessen]

when do you shut? wann
machen Sie zu? [vann maкнen
zee tsoo]

when do they shut? wann
machen sie zu?

they're shut sie sind
geschlossen [geshlossen]

I've shut myself out ich habe
mich ausgesperrt [ish hahb-uh
mish owss-geshpairt]

shut up! halt den Mund!
[dayn moont]

shutter (on camera) der
Verschluß [fairshlooss]

shutters (on window) die
Fensterläden [fenster-layden]

shy (person) schüchtern
[shooshtern]

(animal) scheu [shoy]

sick (ill) krank

I'm going to be sick (vomit)
ich muß mich übergeben
[ish mooss mish oobergayben]

side die Seite [zite-uh]

the other side of town das
andere Ende der Stadt
[ander-uh end-uh dair shtatt]

side lights das Standlicht
[shtantlisht]

side salad die Salatbeilage
[zalaht-bylahg-uh]

side street die Seitenstraße
[zyten-shtrass-uh]

sidewalk (US) der Bürgersteig
[boorgershtike]

sight: the sights of ... die
Sehenswürdigkeiten von ...
[zay-ens-voordish-kyten fon]

sightseeing: we're going
sightseeing wir machen
eine Rundfahrt [veer maкнen
ine-uh roont-fahrt]
(on foot) wir machen einen
Rundgang [ine-en roont-gang]

sightseeing tour die
Rundfahrt [roont-fahrt]

sign das Schild [shilt]
(roadsign) das Verkehrs-
zeichen [fairkairs-tsyshen]

signal: he didn't give a signal
(driver) er hat nicht geblinkt
(cyclist) er hat keine
Richtung angezeigt [kine-uh
rishtoong an-getsykt]

signature die Unterschrift
[oonter-shrift]

signpost der Wegweiser

[**vay**k-vyzer]

silence die Ruhe [**roo**-uh]

silk die Seide [**zy**duh]

silly (person) albern [**al**-bairn]
(thing to do etc) dumm [doomm]

silver das Silber [**zil**ber]

silver foil die Alufolie [**ah**loo-fohl-yuh]

similar ähnlich [**ayn**lish]

simple (easy) einfach [**ine**-fakH]

since: since yesterday seit gestern [zite]
since I got here seit ich hier bin [heer]

sing singen [**zing**en]

singer (man/woman) der Sänger [**zeng**er]/die Sängerin

single (not married) unverheiratet [**oon**-fair-hyrahtet]
a single to ... eine einfache Fahrt nach ... [**ine**-uh **ine**-fakH-uh fahrt nakH]

single bed das Einzelbett [**ine**-tsel-bett]

single room das Einzelzimmer [**ine**-tsel-tsimmer]

sink (in kitchen) die Spüle [shp**oo**l-uh]

sister die Schwester [shv**es**ter]

sister-in-law die Schwägerin [shv**ay**gerin]

sit: can I sit here? kann ich mich hier hinsetzen? [ish mish heer **hin**zetsen]
is anyone sitting here? sitzt hier jemand? [zitst heer **yay**mant]

sit down sich hinsetzen [zish **hin**zetsen]
do sit down nehmen Sie Platz [**nay**men zee plats]

size die Größe [**grur**ss-uh]

ski der Ski [shee]
(verb) skifahren [**shee**fahren]
a pair of skis ein Paar Skier [pahr **shee**-er]

ski boots die Skistiefel [**shee**-shteefel]

skiing das Skifahren [**shee**fahren]
we're going skiing wir gehen Skilaufen [veer **gay**-en shee-lowfen]

ski instructor (man/woman) der Skilehrer [**shee**-lairer]/die Skilehrerin

ski-lift der Skilift [**shee**lift]

skin die Haut [howt]

skinny dünn [d**oo**nn]

ski-pants die Skihose [**shee**-hohz-uh]

ski-pass der Skipaß [**shee**pas]

ski pole der Skistock [**shee**shtock]

skirt der Rock

ski run die Skipiste [**shee**-pist-uh]

ski slope die Skipiste [**shee**-pist-uh]

ski wax das Skiwachs [**shee**vacks]

sky der Himmel

sleep schlafen [**shlah**fen]
did you sleep well? haben Sie gut geschlafen? [**hah**ben zee goot geshl**ah**fen]

I need a good sleep ich muß mich mal richtig ausschlafen [rishtish **owss**-shlahfen]

sleeper (on train) der Schlafwagen [shl**ah**fvahgen]

sleeping bag der Schlafsack [shl**ah**fzack]

sleeping car der Schlafwagen [shl**ah**fvahgen]

sleeping pill die Schlaftablette [shl**ah**f-tablett-uh]

sleepy: I'm feeling sleepy ich bin müde [ish bin m**oo**d-uh]

sleeve der Ärmel [**air**mel]

slide (photographic) das Dia [**dee**-ah]

slip (under dress) der Unterrock [**oo**nter-rock]

slippery glatt

Slovak (adj) slowakisch [slov**ah**kish]

Slovak Republic die Slowakische Republik [slov**ah**kish-uh rep**oo**bleek]

slow langsam [**lang**zahm]

slow down! etwas langsamer bitte [**et**vass]

slowly langsam [**lang**zahm]

could you say it slowly? könnten Sie das etwas langsamer sagen? [**kurn**ten zee dass **et**vass langz**ah**mer z**ah**gen]

very slowly ganz langsam [**g**ants]

small klein [k**line**]

smell: it smells es stinkt [sht**inkt**]

smile (verb) lächeln [**les**heln]

smoke der Rauch [rowKH]

do you mind if I smoke? macht es Ihnen etwas aus, wenn ich rauche? [m**ak**Ht ess **ee**n-en **et**vass owss venn ish row**KH**-uh]

I don't smoke ich bin Nichtraucher [**ni**shtrowKHer]

do you smoke? rauchen Sie? [**row**KHen zee]

snack: I'd just like a snack ich möchte nur eine Kleinigkeit [ish m**ur**sht-uh n**oo**r **ine**-uh kl**y**nish-kite]

sneeze (verb) niesen [**nee**zen]

snorkel der Schnorchel [shn**or**shel]

snow der Schnee [shnay]

it's snowing es schneit [shn**ite**]

so: it's so good es ist so gut [zo g**oo**t]

not so fast nicht so schnell

so am I ich auch [ish owKH]

so do I ich auch

so-so einigermaßen [ine-iger-m**ah**ssen]

soaking solution (for contact lenses) die Aufbewahrungslösung [**owf**bevahroongs-lurzoong]

soap die Seife [z**y**f-uh]

soap powder das Waschpulver [**va**shpoolver]

sober nüchtern [n**oo**shtern]

sock die Socke [z**ock**-uh]

socket (electrical) die Steckdose [sht**eck**-dohz-uh]

soda (water) das Sodawasser [z**oh**da-vasser]

sofa das Sofa [**zoh**fa]

soft (material etc) weich [vysh]

soft-boiled egg das weichgekochte Ei [**vysh**-gekoKHt-uh ī]

soft drink das alkoholfreie Getränk [alkoho**hl**fry-uh getrenk], der Soft drink

soft lenses die weichen Kontaktlinsen [**vy**shen kontakt-linzen]

sole die Sohle [**zoh**l-uh]

could you put new soles on these? können Sie diese Schuhe neu besohlen? [**ku**rnen zee dee**z**-uh sh**oo**-uh noy bez**oh**len]

some: can I have some water/rolls? kann ich etwas Wasser/ein paar Brötchen haben? [**et**vass **va**sser/ine pahr br**ur**t-shen **ha**hben]

can I have some of those? kann ich ein paar davon haben? [da-**fon**]

somebody, someone jemand [**yay**mant]

something etwas [**et**vass]

something to drink etwas zu trinken

sometimes manchmal [**mansh**mahl]

somewhere irgendwo [**eer**gentvo]

son der Sohn [zohn]

song das Lied [leet]

son-in-law der Schwiegersohn [shv**ee**ger-zohn]

soon bald [balt]

I'll be back soon ich bin bald zurück [ish bin balt tsoor**oo**ck]

as soon as possible so bald wie möglich [vee m**u**rglish]

sore: it's sore es tut weh [t**oo**t vay]

sore throat die Halsschmerzen pl [hals-shmairtsen]

sorry: (I'm) sorry tut mir leid [t**oo**t meer lite]

sorry? (didn't understand) wie bitte? [vee bitt-uh]

sort: what sort of ...? welche Art von ...? [**velsh**-uh art fon]

soup die Suppe [**zoo**p-uh]

sour (taste) sauer [**zow**er]

south der Süden [z**oo**den]

in the south im Süden

to the south nach Süden

South Africa Südafrika [z**oo**t-afrika]

South African (adj) südafrikanisch [z**oo**t-afrik**ah**nish]

I'm South African (man/woman) ich bin Südafrikaner [z**oo**t-afrik**ah**ner]/Südafrikanerin

southeast der Südosten [z**oo**t-osten]

southwest der Südwesten [z**oo**t-v**e**sten]

souvenir das Souvenir

spa der Kurort [k**oo**r-ort]

spanner der Schraubenschlüssel [shr**ow**ben-shl**oo**sel]

spare part das Ersatzteil

[airz**a**ts-tile]

spare tyre der Ersatzreifen
[airz**a**ts-ryfen]

spark plug die Zündkerze
[ts**oo**nt-kairts-uh]

speak: do you speak English?
sprechen Sie Englisch?
[shpr**e**shen zee **e**ng-lish]

I don't speak ... ich spreche
kein ... [ish shpr**e**sh-uh kine]

dialogue

can I speak to Wolfgang?
kann ich Wolfgang
sprechen?

who's calling? wer spricht
bitte? [vair shprisht b**i**tt-uh]

it's Patricia Patricia

**I'm sorry, he's not in, can I
take a message?** tut mir
leid, er ist nicht da, kann
ich etwas ausrichten? [t**oo**t
meer lite, air ist nisht da, kann ish
etvass **ow**ss-rishten]

**no thanks, I'll call back
later** nein danke, ich rufe
später nochmal an [nine
d**a**nk-uh, ish r**oo**f-uh shp**ay**ter
n**o**KHmahl an]

please tell him I called
bitte sagen Sie ihm, daß
ich angerufen habe
[z**a**hgen zee eem, dass ish an-
ger**oo**fen h**a**hb-uh]

speciality die Spezialität
[shpets-yalit**ayt**]

spectacles die Brille [br**i**ll-uh]

speed die Geschwindigkeit
[geshv**i**ndish-kite]

speed limit die Geschwindigkeitsbeschränkung
[geshv**i**ndishkites-beshr**e**nkoong]

Speed limits are 50 km/h
(31 mph) in towns and
100 km/h (62 mph) out of
town, except on motorways
(**Autobahnen**). There is still no
nationwide speed limit on German
motorways, although relatively few
stretches are without any
restrictions at all.

speedometer der Tachometer
[taKHom**ay**ter]

spell: how do you spell it? wie
schreibt man das? [vee shrypt
man dass]
see **alphabet**

spend ausgeben
[**ow**ssgayben](time) verbringen
[fairbr**i**ng-en]

spider die Spinne [shp**i**nn-uh]

spin-dryer die Schleuder
[shl**oy**der]

splinter der Splitter [shpl**i**tter]

spoke (in wheel) die Speiche
[shp**y**sh-uh]

spoon der Löffel [l**u**rfel]

sport der Sport [shport]

sprain: I've sprained my ... ich
habe mein ... verstaucht [ish
h**a**hb-uh mine ... fair-sht**ow**KHt]

spring (season) der Frühling
[fr**oo**ling]
(of car, seat) die Feder [f**ay**der]

square (in town) der Platz
[plats]
stairs die Treppe [trepp-uh]
stale (bread) alt
(drink) abgestanden [ap-geshtanden]
stall: the engine keeps stalling
der Motor geht dauernd aus
[dair **moh**tohr gayt **dow**ernt owss]
stamp die Briefmarke
[**breef**mark-uh]

Stamps can be bought at post offices, from yellow vending machines (at post offices, stations, airports) and at some newspaper kiosks.

dialogue

a stamp for England, please eine Marke nach England bitte [**ine**-uh mark-uh naKH]
what are you sending? was möchten Sie senden?
[vass **mur**shten zee **zen**den]
this postcard diese Postkarte [**deez**-uh **posst**kart-uh]

standby: standby ticket das Standby-Ticket
star der Stern [shtairn]
(in film) der Star
start der Anfang [**an**fang]
(verb) anfangen
when does it start? wann fängt es an? [van fengt ess an]

the car won't start das Auto springt nicht an [dass **ow**to shpringt nisht an]
starter (of car) der Anlasser
(food) die Vorspeise [**for**-shpize-uh]
state (in country) das Land [lant]
the States (USA) die USA
[oo-ess-**ah**]
station der Bahnhof
[**bahn**hohf]
statue die Statue [shtah-too-uh]
stay: where are you staying?
wo wohnen Sie? [vo **voh**nen zee]
I'm staying at ... ich wohne in ... [ish **vohn**-uh]
I'd like to stay another two nights ich möchte gern noch zwei Tage bleiben
[**mur**sht-uh gairn noKH – **tahg**-uh **bly**ben]
steak das Steak
steal stehlen [**shtay**len]
my bag has been stolen
meine Tasche ist gestohlen worden [ge**shtoh**len **vor**den]
steep (hill) steil [shtile]
steering die Lenkung
[**len**koong]
step: on the steps auf den Stufen [owf dayn **shtoo**fen]
stereo die Stereoanlage
[**shtay**ray-oh-**an**lahg-uh]
sterling das Pfund Sterling
[pfoont]
steward (on plane) der Steward
stewardess die Stewardeß
sticking plaster das

Heftpflaster

still: I'm still waiting ich warte immer noch [vart-uh – noKH]

is he still there? ist er noch da?

keep still! stillhalten! [shtill-halten]

sting: I've been stung ich bin gestochen worden [geshtoKHen vorden]

stockings die Strümpfe [shtroompf-uh]

stomach der Magen [mahgen]

stomach ache die Magenschmerzen [mahgen-shmairtsen]

stone (rock) der Stein [shtine]

stop (verb) anhalten

please, stop here (to taxi driver etc) bitte halten Sie hier [bitt-uh hal-ten zee heer]

do you stop near ...? halten Sie in der Nähe von ...? [nay-uh]

stop doing that! hören Sie auf damit! [hur-ren zee owf damit]

stopover die Zwischenstation [tsvishen-shtats-yohn]

storm der Sturm [shtoorm]

straight: it's straight ahead es ist geradeaus [gerahd-uh-owss]

a straight whisky ein Whisky pur [poor]

straightaway sofort [zofort]

strange (odd) seltsam [zeltzahm]

stranger (man/woman) der/die Fremde [fremd-uh]

I'm a stranger here ich bin hier fremd [heer fremt]

strap (on watch) das Band [bant]

(on dress) der Träger [trayger]

(on suitcase) der Riemen [reemen]

strawberry die Erdbeere [airtbair-uh]

stream der Bach [baKH]

street die Straße [shtrahss-uh]

on the street auf der Straße [owf dair]

streetmap der Stadtplan [shtattplahn]

string die Schnur [shnoor]

strong (person, drink) stark [shtark]

(taste) kräftig [kreftish]

stuck: the key's stuck der Schlüssel steckt fest [shteckt]

student (male/female) der Student [shtoodent]/die Studentin

stupid dumm [doomm]

suburb die Vorstadt [for-shtatt]

subway (US) die U-Bahn [oo-bahn]

suddenly plötzlich [plurtslish]

suede das Wildleder [vilt-layder]

sugar der Zucker [tsoocker]

suit der Anzug [antsook]

it doesn't suit me (jacket etc) es steht mir nicht [shtayt meer nisht]

it suits you es steht Ihnen [eenen]

suitcase der Koffer

summer der Sommer
[**zo**mmer]
in the summer im Sommer
sun die Sonne [**zo**nn-uh]
in the sun in der Sonne
out of the sun im Schatten
[**sh**atten]
sunbathe sonnenbaden
[**zo**nnen-bahden]
sunblock (cream) die Sun-
Block-Creme [-kraym]
sunburn der Sonnenbrand
[**zo**nnen-brant]
sunburnt: to get sunburnt
einen Sonnenbrand
bekommen [**ine**-en **zo**nnen-
brant]
Sunday Sonntag [**zo**nntahk]
sunglasses die Sonnenbrille
[**zo**nnen-brill-uh]
sun lounger der Ruhesessel
[**r00**-uh-zessel]
sunny: it's sunny die Sonne
scheint [dee **zo**nn-uh shynt]
sun roof (in car) das
Schiebedach [**shee**b-uh-daKH]
sunset der Sonnenuntergang
[**zo**nnen-oontergang]
sunshade der Sonnenschirm
[**zo**nnen-sheerm]
sunshine der Sonnenschein
[**zo**nnen-shine]
sunstroke der Sonnenstich
[**zo**nnen-shtish]
suntan die Sonnenbräune
[**zo**nnen-broyn-uh]
suntan lotion die
Sonnenmilch [**zo**nnen-milsh]
suntanned braungebrannt

[br**ow**n-gebrannt]
suntan oil das Sonnenöl
[**zo**nnen-url]
super fantastisch [fant**a**stish]
supermarket der Supermarkt
[**z00**permarkt]
supper das Abendessen
[**ah**bent-essen]
supplement (extra charge) der
Zuschlag [ts**00**shlahk]
sure: are you sure? bist
du/sind Sie sicher? [bist
d00/zint zee **zi**sher]
sure! klar!
surname der Nachname
[**na**KHnahm-uh]
swearword der Kraftausdruck
[kr**a**ft-owssdroock]
sweater der Pullover
[pool**oh**ver]
sweatshirt das Sweatshirt
Sweden Schweden [shv**ay**den]
Swedish schwedisch
[shv**ay**dish]
sweet (taste) süß [z**00**ss]
(noun: dessert) der Nachtisch
[**na**KHtish]
sweets die Süßigkeiten
[z**00**ssish-kyten]
swelling die Schwellung
[shv**e**lloong]
swim (verb) schwimmen
[shv**i**mmen]
I'm going for a swim ich
gehe schwimmen [**gay**-uh]
let's go for a swim gehen wir
schwimmen [**gay**-en veer]
swimming costume der
Badeanzug [**bah**d-uh-antsook]

swimming pool das Schwimmbad [shvimmbaht]

swimming trunks die Badehose [bahd-uh-hohz-uh]

Swiss (man/woman) der Schweizer [shvytser]/die Schweizerin

(adj) schweizerisch [shvytserish]

the Swiss die Schweizer

Swiss Alps die Schweizer Alpen [shvytser]

switch der Schalter [shalter]

switch off (TV, lights) ausschalten [owss-shalten]

(engine) abstellen [ap-shtellen]

switch on (TV, lights) einschalten [ine-shalten]

(engine) anlassen

Switzerland die Schweiz [shvites]

swollen geschwollen [geshvollen]

T

table der Tisch [tish]

a table for two ein Tisch für zwei Personen [foor tsvy pairzohnen]

tablecloth das Tischtuch [tishtOOKH]

table tennis das Tischtennis [tishtennis]

table wine der Tafelwein [tahfelvine]

tailback (of traffic) der Rückstau [rOOck-shtow]

tailor der Schneider [shnyder]

take (lead) bringen

(accept) nehmen [naymen]

can you take me to the airport? können Sie mich zum Flughafen bringen? [kurnen zee mish tsoom]

do you take credit cards? nehmen Sie Kreditkarten?

fine, I'll take it gut, ich nehme es [gOOt, ish naym-uh ess]

can I take this? (leaflet etc) kann ich das mitnehmen? [mitnaymen]

how long does it take? wie lange dauert es? [vee lang-uh dowert ess]

it takes three hours es dauert drei Stunden

is this seat taken? ist dieser Platz besetzt? [deezer plats bezetst]

hamburger to take away Hamburger zum Mitnehmen [tsoom]

can you take a little off here? (to hairdresser) können Sie hier etwas kürzen? [kurnen zee heer etvass kOOrtsen]

talcum powder der Körperpuder [kurper-pOOder]

talk (verb) sprechen [shpreshen]

tall (person) groß [grohss]

(building) hoch [hohKH]

tampons die Tampons

tan die Bräune [broyn-uh]

to get a tan braun werden [brown vairden]

tank (of car) der Tank
tap der Wasserhahn
[**v**asserhahn]
tape (for cassette) das Band
[bant]
(sticky) das Klebeband [**k**layb-uh-bant]
tape measure das Bandmaß
[**b**antmahss]
tape recorder der
Kassettenrecorder
taste der Geschmack
[ge**sh**mack]
can I taste it? kann ich es
probieren? [prob**ee**ren]
taxi das Taxi
will you get me a taxi?
können Sie mir ein Taxi
bestellen? [**kur**nen zee meer]
where can I find a taxi? wo
bekomme ich ein Taxi? [vo
bek**omm**-uh ish]

Taxis have a sign on the
roof which is illuminated
when the taxi is free. You
can hail them in the street, but
Germans tend to wait at taxi ranks
(always to be found at train stations
and near big hotels) or to phone.

dialogue

to the airport/to Hotel ...
please zum
Flughafen/zum Hotel ...
bitte [tsoom]
how much will it be? was
kostet das?

thirty euros dreißig Euro
that's fine right here thanks
bis hierhin, danke [heer-hin]

taxi-driver der Taxifahrer
taxi rank der Taxistand [**t**aksi-shtant]
tea (drink) der Tee [tay]
tea for one/two please Tee
für eine Person/zwei
Personen bitte [für **ine**-uh
pair**zohn**/tsvy pair**zoh**nen bitt-uh]
teabag der Teebeutel
[**t**ayboytel]
teach: could you teach me?
könnten Sie es mir
beibringen? [**kur**nten zee ess
meer b**y**bringen]
teacher (man/woman) der
Lehrer [**l**airer]/die Lehrerin
team das Team
teaspoon der Teelöffel [**t**ay-lurfel]
tea towel das Geschirrtuch
[ge**sh**eer-tookH]
teenager der Teenager
telegram das Telegramm
telephone das Telefon
[telef**ohn**]
see phone
television das Fernsehen
[**f**airn-zay-en]
tell: could you tell him ...?
können Sie ihm sagen ...?
[**kur**nen zee eem **zah**gen]
temperature (weather) die
Temperatur [temperat**oor**]
(fever) das Fieber [**f**eeber]

tennis das Tennis
tennis ball der Tennisball
[**ten**nis-bal]
tennis court der Tennisplatz
[**ten**nis-plats]
tennis racket der Tennis-
schläger [**ten**nis-shlayger]
tent das Zelt [tselt]
term (at school) das Halbjahr
[**halp**-yar]
(at university) das Semester
[ze**mes**ter]
terminus (rail) die Endstation
[**ent**-shtats-yohn]
terrible furchtbar [**foor**shtbar]
terrific sagenhaft [**zah**genhaft]
than* als [alss]
smaller than kleiner als
thanks, thank you danke
[**dank**-uh]
thank you very much vielen
Dank [**feel**en]
thanks for the lift danke fürs
Mitnehmen [f00rs **mit**naymen]
no thanks nein danke [nine]

dialogue

> **thanks** danke
> **that's OK, don't mention it**
> bitte [**bitt**-uh]

that: that man dieser Mann
[**deez**er]
that woman diese Frau [**deez**-
uh]
that one das da
I hope that ... ich hoffe, daß
... [dass]

that's nice das ist schön
is that ...? ist das ...?
that's it (that's right) genau
[ge**now**]
the* (singular) der/die/das
[dair/dee/dass]
(plural) die [dee]
theatre das Theater [tay**ah**ter]
their* ihr/ihre [eer/**eer**-uh]
theirs* ihrer [**eer**-er]
them* sie [zee]
for them für sie [f00r]
with them mit ihnen [**een**-en]
I gave it to them ich habe es
ihnen gegeben [**hahb**-uh]
then (at that time) damals
[**dah**malss]
(after that) dann
there da, dort
over there dort drüben
[**dr00**ben]
up there da oben
is there ...? gibt es ...? [geept]
are there ...? gibt es ...?
there is ... es gibt ...
there are ... es gibt ...
there you are (giving something)
bitte [**bitt**-uh]
thermometer das
Thermometer [tairmo-**may**ter]
thermos flask die
Thermosflasche [**tair**moss-
flash-uh]
these*: these men diese
Männer [**deez**-uh]
these women diese Frauen
can I have these? kann ich
diese hier haben? [heer]
they* sie [zee]

thick dick
 (stupid) blöd [blurt]
thief der Dieb [deep]
thigh der Schenkel [shenkel]
thin dünn [dœn]
thing das Ding
 my things meine Sachen
 [mine-uh zaKHen]
think denken
 I think so ich glaube ja
 [glowb-uh ya]
 I don't think so ich glaube
 nicht [nisht]
 I'll think about it ich werde
 darüber nachdenken [vaird-
 uh darœber naKHdenken]
third party insurance die
 Haftpflichtversicherung
 [haft-pflisht-fairzisheroong]
thirsty: I'm thirsty ich habe
 Durst [hahb-uh doorst]
this: this man dieser Mann
 [deezer]
 this woman diese Frau [deez-
 uh]
 this one dieser/diese/dieses
 [deezess]
 this is my wife das ist meine
 Frau [mine-uh frow]
 is this ...? ist das ...?
those: those men diese
 Männer [deez-uh]
 those women diese Frauen
 which ones? – those welche?
 – diese [velsh-uh]
thread der Faden [fahden]
throat der Hals [halss]
throat pastilles die
 Halstabletten [halss-tabletten]

through durch [doorsh]
 does it go through ...? (train,
 bus) fährt er über ...? [fairt air
 œber]
throw (verb) werfen [vairfen]
throw away (verb) wegwerfen
 [vekvairfen]
thumb der Daumen [dowmen]
thunderstorm das Gewitter
 [gevitter]
Thursday Donnerstag
 [donnerstahk]
ticket (train, bus, boat) die
 Fahrkarte [fahrkart-uh]
 (plane) das Ticket
 (theatre, cinema) die
 Eintrittskarte [ine-trittskart-uh]
 (cloakroom) die
 Garderobenmarke
 [garderohben-mark-uh]

dialogue

a return ticket to
Heidelberg eine
Rückfahrkarte nach
Heidelberg
coming back when? wann
soll die Rückfahrt sein?
[rœck-fahrt]
today/next Tuesday
heute/nächsten
Dienstag
that will be ninety euros
das macht neunzig Euro

ticket office (bus, rail) der
 Fahrkartenschalter
 [fahrkarten-shalter]

tide: high tide die Flut [floot]
 low tide die Ebbe [ebb-uh]
tie (necktie) die Krawatte
 [kravatt-uh]
tight (clothes etc) eng
 it's too tight es ist zu eng
 [ts00]
tights die Strumpfhose
 [shtroompf-hohz-uh]
till (cash desk) die Kasse [kass-
 uh]
time* die Zeit [tsite]
 what's the time? wie spät ist
 es? [vee shpayt ist ess]
 this time diesmal [deessmahl]
 last time letztes Mal [letstess
 mahl]
 next time nächstes Mal
 [naykstess]
 four times viermal [feermahl]
timetable der Fahrplan
 [fahrplahn]
tin (can) die Dose [dohz-uh]
tinfoil die Alufolie [ahloo-fohl-
 yuh]
tin opener der Dosenöffner
 [dohzen-urfner]
tiny winzig [vintsish]
tip (to waiter etc) das Trinkgeld
 [trinkgelt]

 Prices in pubs and
restaurants usually
include a service charge,
but it is still customary to leave a tip
of around 5-10% if you are happy
with the service received.

tired müde [mood-uh]

I'm tired ich bin müde
tissues die Papiertücher
 [papeer-toosher]
to: to Freiburg/London nach
 Freiburg/London [naкн]
 to Germany/England nach
 Deutschland/England
 to the post office zum
 Postamt [tsoom]
 to the bank zur Bank [ts00r]
toast (bread) der Toast
today heute [hoyt-uh]
toe der Zeh [tsay]
together zusammen
 [tsoozammen]
 we're together (in shop etc)
 wir sind zusammen [veer zint]
 can we pay together?
 können wir zusammen
 bezahlen? [kurnen veer –
 betsahlen]
toilet die Toilette [twalett-uh]
 where is the toilet? wo ist die
 Toilette? [vo]
 I have to go to the toilet ich
 muß zur Toilette [ts00r]

 The signs on toilets are **H**
(= **Herren**) for men and **D**
(= **Damen**) for women.
Public conveniences are not
especially numerous.

toilet paper das
 Toilettenpapier [twaletten-
 papeer]
tomato die Tomate [tomaht-uh]
tomato juice der Tomatensaft
 [tomahtenzaft]

tomato ketchup der Tomatenketchup

tomorrow morgen

tomorrow morning morgen früh [frω]

the day after tomorrow übermorgen [**oo**bermorgen]

toner (cosmetic) die Tönungslotion [**tur**noongs-lohts-yohn]

tongue die Zunge [ts**oo**ng-uh]

tonic (water) das Tonic

tonight heute abend [**hoy**t-uh **ah**bent]

tonsillitis die Mandel-entzündung [**m**andel-ent-ts**oo**ndoong]

too (excessively) zu [ts**oo**]

(also) auch [owкн]

too hot zu heiß [hice]

too much zuviel [tsoof**eel**]

me too ich auch [ish]

tooth der Zahn [tsahn]

toothache die Zahnschmerzen [ts**ahn**-shmairtsen]

toothbrush die Zahnbürste [ts**ahn**-b**oo**rst-uh]

toothpaste die Zahnpasta [ts**ahn**pasta]

top: on top of ... oben auf... [**oh**ben owf]

at the top oben

top floor der oberste Stock [**oh**berst-uh shtock]

topless oben ohne [**oh**ben **oh**n-uh]

torch die Taschenlampe [t**a**shenlamp-uh]

total die Endsumme [**ent**zoom-uh]

what's the total? was macht das zusammen? [vass makнt dass tsooz**a**mmen]

tour (journey) die Reise [**rize**-uh]

is there a tour of ...? gibt es eine Führung durch...? [geept ess **ine**-uh f**oo**roong doorsh]

tour guide der Reiseleiter [**rize**-uh-lyter]

tourist (man/woman) der Tourist [t**oo**rist]/die Touristin

tourist information office das Fremdenverkehrsbüro [fremden-fairkairs-b**oo**r**oh**]

tour operator der Reiseveranstalter [**rize**-uh-fair**a**nshtalter]

towards nach [naкн]

towel das Handtuch [hant-t**oo**кн]

town die Stadt [shtatt]

in town in der Stadt [dair]

just out of town am Stadtrand [sht**a**ttrant]

town centre die Innenstadt [**inn**en-shtatt]

town hall das Rathaus [**raht**-howss]

toy das Spielzeug [shpeel-tsoyk]

track (US: at train station) der Bahnsteig [**bahn**shtike]

tracksuit der Trainingsanzug [**trainings**-antsook]

traditional traditionell [tradits-yohn**ell**]

traffic der Verkehr [fair**k**air]
traffic jam der Stau [shtow]
traffic lights die **A**mpel
trailer (for carrying tent etc) der
 Anhänger [**anh**eng-er]
 (US: caravan) der Wohnwagen
 [**voh**nvahgen]
trailer park (US) der
 Wohnwagenplatz
 [**voh**nvahgen-plats]
train der Zug [ts00k]
 by train mit dem Zug [daym]

dialogue

is this the train for ...?
fährt dieser Zug nach ...?
[fairt d**ee**zer ts00k naкн]
sure ja [yah]
**no, you want that platform
there** nein, gehen Sie zu
dem Bahnsteig da [nine,
gay-en zee ts00 daym
bahnshtike]

trainers (shoes) die
 Turnschuhe [**toor**nsh00-uh]
train station der Bahnhof
 [**bah**nhohf]
tram die Straßenbahn
 [shtr**ah**ssen-bahn]
translate übersetzen [ơber-
 zetsen]
 could you translate that?
 könnten Sie das übersetzen?
 [**kur**nten zee]
translation die Übersetzung
 [ơber-z**et**soong]
translator (man/woman) der

Übersetzer [ơber-**zet**ser]/die
 Übersetzerin
trash (waste) der Abfall [**ap**-fal]
 (poor quality goods) der Mist
trashcan (US) die Mülltonne
 [m**ooll**tonn-uh]
travel reisen [**ry**zen]
 we're travelling around wir
 machen eine Rundreise
 [veer ma**k**нen **ine**-uh r**oo**nt-rize-uh]
travel agent's das Reisebüro
 [**rize**-uh-b0ro]
traveller's cheque der
 Reisescheck [**rize**-uh-sheck]
tray das Tablett
tree der Baum [bowm]
tremendous fantastisch
 [fant**a**stish]
trendy schick [shick]
trim: just a trim please (to
 hairdresser) nur etwas kürzen,
 bitte [n00r etvass k**oor**tsen b**it**t-uh]
trip (excursion) der Ausflug
 [**ows**sfl00k]
 I'd like to go on a trip to ...
 ich möchte gern eine Reise
 nach ... machen [**mur**sht-uh
 gairn **ine**-uh **rize**-uh naкн ...
 ma**k**нen]
trolley (in supermarket) der
 Einkaufswagen [**ine**-kowfs-
 vahgen]
 (in station) der Kofferkuli
 [**koff**er-k00lee]
trouble die Schwierigkeiten
 [shv**ee**rish-kyten]
 I'm having trouble with ... ich
 habe Schwierigkeiten mit ...
 [**hahb**-uh]

sorry to trouble you tut mir
leid, Sie zu belästigen [toot
meer lite zee tsoo belestigen]
trousers die Hose [hohz-uh]
true wahr [vahr]
  that's not true das stimmt
  nicht [shtimmt nisht]
trunk (US: of car) der
Kofferraum [koffer-rowm]
trunks (swimming) die
Badehose [bahd-uh-hohz-uh]
try (verb) versuchen
[fairzooKHen]
  can I have a try? kann ich es
  versuchen?
try on: can I try it on? kann
ich es anprobieren? [an-
probeeren]
T-shirt das T-Shirt
Tuesday Dienstag [deenstahk]
tuna der Thunfisch [toonfish]
tunnel der Tunnel [toonnel]
Turkey die Türkei [toork-ī]
Turkish (adj) türkisch [toorkish]
  (language) Türkisch
turn: turn left/right biegen Sie
links/rechts ab [beegen zee
links/reshts ap]
turn off: where do I turn off?
wo muß ich abbiegen? [vo
mooss ish ap-beegen]
  can you turn the heating off?
  können Sie die Heizung
  abstellen? [kurnen zee dee
  hytsoong ap-shtellen]
**turn on: can you turn the
heating on?** können Sie die
Heizung anstellen? [kurnen
zee dee hytsoong an-shtellen]

turning (in road) die
Abzweigung [ap-tsvygoong]
TV das Fernsehen [fairnzay-en]
tweezers die Pinzette [pin-
tsett-uh]
twice zweimal [tsvymahl]
  twice as much zweimal
  soviel [zofeel]
twin beds zwei Einzelbetten
[tsvy ine-tsel-betten]
twin room das
Zweibettzimmer [tsvybett-
tsimmer]
twist: I've twisted my ankle
ich habe mir den Fuß
vertreten [ish hahb-uh meer dayn
fooss fairtrayten]
type die Art
  a different type of ... eine
  andere Art von ... [ine-uh
  ander-uh]
typical typisch [toopish]
tyre der Reifen [ryfen]

U

ugly häßlich [hesslish]
UK das Vereinigte Königreich
[fair-ine-isht-uh kurnish-rysh]
ulcer das Geschwür [geshvoor]
umbrella der Schirm [sheerm]
uncle der Onkel
unconscious bewußtlos
[bevoost-lohss]
under unter [oonter]
underdone (meat) nicht gar
[nisht]
underground (railway) die U-

Bahn [**oo**-bahn]

underpants die Unterhose [**oo**nter-hohz-uh]

understand: I understand ich verstehe [ish fairsh**tay**-uh]

I don't understand das verstehe ich nicht [nisht]

do you understand? verstehen Sie? [fairsh**tay**-en zee]

unemployed arbeitslos [**ar**bites-lohss]

United States die Vereinigten Staaten [fair-**ine**-ishten sh**tah**ten]

university die Universität [**oo**nivairzi-**tayt**]

unleaded petrol das bleifreie Benzin [**bly**-fry-uh bent**see**n]

unlimited mileage ohne Kilometerbeschränkung [**ohn**-uh keelo-**mayt**er-beshr**enk**oong]

unlock aufschließen [**owf**-shleessen]

unpack auspacken [**owss**-packen]

until bis [biss]

unusual ungewöhnlich [**oo**n-gevurnlish]

up oben [**ohb**en]

up there da oben

he's not up yet (not out of bed) er ist noch nicht auf [noKH nisht owf]

what's up? (what's wrong?) was ist los? [vass ist lohss]

upmarket (restaurant, hotel, goods etc) anspruchsvoll [**an**shprooKHsfoll]

upset stomach die Magenverstimmung [**mah**gen-fairsht**imm**oong]

upside down verkehrt herum [fairk**air**t hair**oo**m]

upstairs oben [**ohb**en]

urgent dringend [dring-ent]

us* uns [oonss]

with us mit uns

for us für uns [f**oo**r]

USA die USA [00-ess-**ah**]

use (verb) benutzen [ben**oo**tsen]

may I use ...? kann ich ... benutzen?

useful nützlich [n**oo**tslish]

usual üblich [**oo**plish]

the usual (drink etc) dasselbe wie immer [dass**el**b-uh vee]

V

vacancy: do you have any vacancies? (hotel) haben Sie Zimmer frei? [**hah**ben zee tsimmer fry]

vacation der Urlaub [**oo**rlowp] (from university) die Semesterferien [zem**est**er-fairee-en]

vaccination die Impfung [**imp**foong]

vacuum cleaner der Staubsauger [sht**owp**-zowger]

valid (ticket etc) gültig [g**oo**ltish]

how long is it valid for? wie lange ist es gültig? [vee lang-uh]

valley das Tal [**tahl**]
valuable (adj) wertvoll [**vair**tfol]
 can I leave my valuables
 here? kann ich meine
 Wertsachen hierlassen?
 [**mine**-uh **vair**tzakнen **heer**lassen]
value der Wert [vairt]
van der Lieferwagen
 [**lee**fervahgen]
vanilla die Vanille [vanill-uh]
 a vanilla ice cream ein
 Vanilleeis [vanill-uh-ice]
vary: it varies es ist
 unterschiedlich [**oon**ter-
 sheetlish]
vase die Vase [**vah**z-uh]
veal das Kalbfleisch [kalp-flysh]
vegetables das Gemüse
 [gem**oo**z-uh]
vegetarian (man/woman) der
 Vegetarier [vegay**tah**ree-
 er]/die Vegetarierin
vending machine der
 Automat [owtom**aht**]
very sehr [zair]
 very little for me nur eine
 Kleinigkeit für mich [n**oo**r
 ine-uh k**line**-ishkite f**oo**r mish]
 I like it very much ich mag es
 sehr gern [gairn]
vest (under shirt) das
 Unterhemd [**oon**terhemt]
via über [**oo**ber]
video (film) das Video
 (recorder) der Videorecorder
Vienna Wien [veen]
view der Blick
villa die Villa
village das Dorf

vinegar der Essig [**ess**ish]
vineyard der Weinberg [**vine**-
 bairk]
visa das Visum [**vee**zoom]
visit (verb) besuchen
 [bez**oo**кнen]
 I'd like to visit ... ich möchte
 ... besuchen [**mur**sht-uh]
vital: it's vital that ... es ist
 unbedingt notwendig,
 daß ... [**oon**-bedingt **noht**vendish
 dass]
vodka der Wodka [**vod**ka]
voice die Stimme [shtimm-uh]
voltage die Spannung
 [shp**ann**oong]

 The voltage is 240V. All
sockets are for plugs with
two round pins so a travel
plug is useful.

vomit erbrechen [airbr**e**shen]

W

waist die Taille [tal-yuh]
waistcoat die Weste [**vest**-uh]
wait warten [**var**ten]
 wait for me warten Sie auf
 mich [zee owf mish]
 don't wait for me warten Sie
 nicht auf mich [nisht]
 can I wait until my
 wife/partner gets here? (eg as
 said to waiter) kann ich
 warten, bis meine
 Frau/Partnerin kommt?

can you do it while I wait?
kann ich darauf warten?
[dar**owf**]

could you wait here for me?
(eg as said to taxi driver) können
Sie hier warten? [**kur**nen zee
heer]

waiter der Ober [**oh**ber]
waiter! Herr Ober! [hair]

waitress die Kellnerin
waitress! Fräulein! [**froy**line]

**wake: can you wake me up at
5.30?** können Sie mich um
5.30 Uhr wecken? [**kur**nen
zee mish oom – **ve**cken]

wake-up call der Weckanruf
[**veck**-anroof]

Wales Wales

walk: is it a long walk? geht
man lange dorthin? [gayt man
lang-uh]

it's only a short walk es ist
nicht weit zu gehen [nisht vite
tsoo g**ay**-en]

I'll walk ich gehe zu Fuß
[**gay**-uh tsoo f**oo**ss]

I'm going for a walk ich gehe
spazieren [shpats**ee**ren]

Walkman® der Walkman

wall die Wand [vant]
(external) die Mauer [**mow**er]

wallet die Brieftasche
[**bree**ftash-uh]

**wander: I like just wandering
around** ich wandere gern
einfach so durch die
Gegend [ish **va**nder-uh gairn **ine**-
faкН zo doorsh dee **gay**gent]

want: I want a ... ich möchte

ein(e)... [ish m**ur**sht-uh ine(-uh)]
I don't want any ... ich
möchte keinen ... [**kine**-en]
I want to go home ich will
nach Hause [vill]
I don't want to ich will nicht
[nisht]
he wants to ... er will ...
what do you want? was
wollen Sie? [vass **v**ollen zee]

ward (in hospital) die Station
[shtats-y**ohn**]

warm warm [varm]
I'm so warm mir ist so warm
[meer]

was*: it was ... es war ... [ess
vahr]

wash (verb) waschen [**va**shen]
can you wash these?
können Sie die für mich
waschen? [**kur**nen zee]

washer (for bolt etc) die
Dichtung [**di**shtoong]

washhand basin das
Handwaschbecken [**h**antvash-
becken]

washing (clothes) die Wäsche
[**ve**sh-uh]

washing machine die
Waschmaschine
[**va**shmasheen-uh]

washing powder das
Waschpulver [**va**shpoolver]

washing-up liquid das
Spülmittel [shp**oo**lmittel]

wasp die Wespe [**ve**sp-uh]

watch (wristwatch) die
Armbanduhr [**a**rmbant-oor]
will you watch my things for

me? könnten Sie auf meine Sachen aufpassen? [**kur**nten zee owf m**ine**-uh za**kh**en **owf**passen]

watch out! passen Sie auf!

watch strap das Uhrarmband [**oor**-armbant]

water das Wasser [**va**sser]

may I have some water? kann ich etwas Wasser haben? [**et**vass – **hah**ben]

waterproof (adj) wasserfest [**va**sserfest]

waterskiing Wasserskilaufen [**va**ssershee-lowfen]

wave (in sea) die Welle [**vell**-uh]

way: it's this way es ist hier entlang [heer]

it's that way es ist dort entlang

is it a long way to ...? ist es weit bis nach ...? [vite biss na**kh**]

no way! auf keinen Fall! [owf **kine**-en fal]

dialogue

could you tell me the way to ...? können Sie mir sagen, wie ich nach ... komme? [**kur**nen zee meer **zah**gen vee ish na**kh** ... **komm**-uh]

go straight on until you reach the traffic lights fahren Sie geradeaus bis zur **A**mpel [ge**rah**d-uh-owss]

turn left biegen Sie links

ab [**bee**gen]

take the first on the right nehmen Sie die erste Straße rechts [**nay**men zee dee **airst**-uh shtra**hss**-uh reshts]

see also **where**

we* wir [veer]

weak schwach [shva**kh**]

weather das Wetter [**vett**er]

dialogue

what's the weather forecast? wie ist die Wettervorhersage? [vee ist dee **vett**er-forh**air**zahg-uh]

it's going to be fine es gibt schönes Wetter [geept sh**ur**ness]

it's going to rain es gibt Regen [**ray**gen]

it'll brighten up later es wird sich später aufklären [veert zish shp**ayt**er owf-kl**air**en]

wedding die Hochzeit [**ho**kh-tsite]

wedding ring der Ehering [**ay**-uh-ring]

Wednesday Mittwoch [**mitt**vo**kh**]

week die Woche [**vo**kh-uh]

a week (from) today heute in einer Woche [**hoy**t-uh in **ine**-er]

a week (from) tomorrow morgen in einer Woche

weekend das Wochenende [**vo**kh-en-end-uh]

at the weekend am Wochenende

weight das Gewicht [gevisht]

weird seltsam [zeltzahm]

weirdo der Verrückte [fair-rookt-uh]

welcome: welcome to ... willkommen in ... [villkommen]

you're welcome (don't mention it) keine Ursache [kine-uh oorzakH-uh]

well: I don't feel well ich fühle mich nicht wohl [ish fool-uh mish nisht vohl]

she's not well sie fühlt sich nicht wohl [zee]

you speak English very well Sie sprechen sehr gut Englisch [shpreshen zair goot eng-lish]

well done! gut gemacht! [gemakHt]

this one as well diesen auch [deezen owkH]

well well! (surprise) na so was! [zo vass]

dialogue

how are you? wie geht es dir? [vee gayt ess deer]
very well, thanks sehr gut, danke [zair goot dank-uh]
and you? und dir? [oont deer]

well-done (meat) gut durchgebraten [goot doorsh-gebrahten]

Welsh walisisch [val-eezish]

I'm Welsh (man/woman) ich bin Waliser [valleezer]/Waliserin

were*: I/you were ich war [var]/du warst [varst]

we/they were wir/sie waren [vahren]

west der Westen [vesten]

in the west im Westen

West Indian (adj) westindisch [vestindish]

wet naß [nass]

what? was? [vass]

what's that? was ist das?

what should I do? was soll ich tun? [zoll ish toon]

what a view! was für ein Blick! [vass foor ine]

what bus is it? welcher Bus ist das? [velsher]

wheel das Rad [raht]

wheelchair der Rollstuhl [rol-shtool]

when? wann? [van]

when's the train/ferry? wann fährt der Zug/die Fähre? [van fairt dair tsook/dee fair-uh]

when we get back wenn wir zurückkommen [ven veer tsoorock-kommen]

when we got back als wir zurückkamen [alss]

where? wo? [vo]

I don't know where it is ich weiß nicht, wo es ist [vice nisht]

dialogue

where is the cathedral?
wo ist der Dom?
it's over there er ist dort
drüben [**dr**ooben]
**could you show me where
it is on the map?** können
Sie ihn mir auf der Karte
zeigen? [**kur**nen zee een meer
– **tsy**gen]
it's just here er ist da
see also way

which: which bus? welcher
Bus? [**vel**sher]
which house? welches Haus?
which bar? welche Bar?

dialogue

which one? welcher?
that one dieser [**dee**zer]
this one? dieser?
no, that one nein, dieser
[nine]

while: while I'm here während
ich hier bin [**vair**ent ish heer]
whisky der Whisky
white weiß [vice]
white wine der Weißwein
[**vice**-vine]
who? wer? [vair]
who is it? (reply to knock at door
etc) wer ist da?
the man who ... der Mann,
der ... [dair]
whole: the whole week die

ganze Woche [dee **g**ants-uh
voKH-uh]
the whole lot das Ganze
whose: whose is this? wem
gehört das? [vaym geh**urt**]
why? warum? [vah**room**]
why not? warum nicht?
[nisht]
wide breit [brite]
wife: my wife meine Frau
[**mine**-uh frow]
will*: will you do it for me?
können Sie es für mich tun?
[**kur**nen zee ess foor mish toon]
wind der Wind [vint]
window das Fenster
near the window am Fenster
in the window (of shop) im
Schaufenster [**show**-fenster]
window seat der Fensterplatz
windscreen die
Windschutzscheibe [**vint**-
shoots-shybuh]
windscreen wiper der
Scheibenwischer [**shy**ben-
visher]
windsurfing das Windsurfen
[**vint**zurfen]
windy: it's so windy es ist so
windig [zo **vin**dish]
wine der Wein [vine]
**can we have some more
wine?** können wir noch
etwas Wein haben? [**kur**nen
veer noKH **et**vass – **hah**ben]

The vast majority of
German wine is white.
Like most EC wine,

German wine is divided into two broad categories: **Tafelwein** [tah-fel-vine] (table wine) and **Qualitätswein** [kvalitayts-vine] (quality wine). **Landwein** is a superior Tafelwein. There are two basic subdivisions of **Qualitätswein: QbA (Qualitätswein beson-derer Anbaugebiete)** and **QmP (Qualitätswein mit Prädikat)**. QbA wines come from eleven delimited regions and must pass an official tasting and analysis. QmP wines are further divided into six grades:

Kabinett: the first and lightest style.
Spätlese [shpayt-layz-uh]: must come from a late grape harvest, which gives riper flavours.
Auslese [owss-layz-uh]: made from a selected bunch of grapes, making a concentrated medium-sweet wine.
Beerenauslese [bairen-owss-layz-uh]: wine made from late-harvested grapes; a rare wine, made only in the very best years, and extremely sweet.
Trockenbeerenauslese [trocken-bairen-owss-layz-uh]: a very rare wine which is intensely sweet and concentrated.
Eiswein [ice-vine]: literally 'ice wine'; a hard frost freezes the water content of the grape, concentrating the juice; the flavour of an Eiswein is remarkably fresh-tasting, due to its high acidity.

Some useful wine terms:
trocken dry
halbtrocken [halptrocken] semi-dry
lieblich [leeplish] mellow
süß [zOOss] sweet
herb [hairp] very dry

If you are keen to try a local wine, ask for '**einen hiesigen Wein**' [**ine**-en **hee**zigen vine].

wine list die Weinkarte [**vine**-kart-uh]
winter der Winter [**vin**ter]
  in the winter im Winter
winter holiday der Winterurlaub [**vin**ter-OOrlowp]
wire die Draht
  (electric) die Leitung [**ly**toong]
wish: best wishes mit besten Wünschen [**vOO**nshen]
with mit
  I'm staying with ... ich wohne bei... [**voh**n-uh by]
without ohne [**ohn**-uh]
witness (man/woman) der Zeuge [**tsoyg**-uh]/die Zeugin
  will you be a witness for me? würden Sie für mich als Zeuge zur Verfügung stehen? [**vOOr**den zee fOOr mish – tsOOr fairfOOgoong sht**ay**-en]
woman die Frau [frow]
wonderful wundervoll [**voo**nder-fol]
won't*: it won't start es will nicht anspringen [vill nisht **an**-shpringen]

wood (material) das Holz [holts]

woods (forest) der Wald [valt]

wool die Wolle [voll-uh]

word das Wort [vort]

work die Arbeit [arbite]

it's not working es funktioniert nicht [foonkts-yohneert nisht]

I work in ... ich arbeite in ... [arbite-uh]

world die Welt [velt]

worry: I'm worried ich mache mir Sorgen [ish makH-uh meer zorgen]

worse: it's worse es ist schlimmer [shlimmer]

worst am schlimmsten [shlimmsten]

worth: is it worth a visit? lohnt sich ein Besuch dort? [zish ine bezookH dort]

would: would you give this to ...? könnten Sie dies ... geben? [kurnten zee – gayben]

wrap: could you wrap it up? können Sie es einpacken? [kurnen zee ess ine-packen]

wrapping paper das Packpapier [pack-papeer]

wrist das Handgelenk [hantgelenk]

write schreiben [shryben]

could you write it down? könnten Sie es aufschreiben? [kurnten zee ess owf-shryben]

how do you write it? wie schreibt man das? [vee shrypt]

writing paper das Schreibpapier [shripe-papeer]

wrong: it's the wrong key es ist der falsche Schlüssel [dair falsh-uh]

this is the wrong train dies ist der falsche Zug

the bill's wrong in der Rechnung ist ein Fehler [dair reshnoong ist ine fayler]

sorry, wrong number tut mir leid, falsch verbunden [toot meer lite falsh fairboonden]

sorry, wrong room tut mir leid, ich habe mich im Zimmer geirrt [ish hahb-uh mish im tsimmer guh-eerrt]

there's something wrong with ... mit ... stimmt etwas nicht [shtimmt etvass nisht]

what's wrong? was ist los? [vass ist lohss]

X

X-ray die Röntgenaufnahme [rurntgen-owfnahm-uh]

Y

yacht die Jacht [yakHt]

yard* das Yard [yahr]

year das Jahr [yahr]

yellow gelb [gelp]

yes ja [yah]

you don't smoke, do you? – yes Sie rauchen nicht, oder? – doch [zee rowkHen nisht ohder

– doKH]
yesterday gestern
yesterday morning gestern morgen
the day before yesterday vorgestern [**fo**rgestern]
yet noch [noKH]

dialogue

is he here yet? ist er schon hier? [air shohn heer]
no, not yet nein, noch nicht [nine noKH nisht]
you'll have to wait a little longer yet Sie müssen noch etwas warten [zee **mOO**ssen]

yoghurt der Joghurt [y**oh**g-hoort]
you* (familiar: singular) du [doo]
(plural) ihr [eer]
(polite) Sie [zee]
this is for you das ist für dich/euch [oych]/Sie
with you mit dir/euch/ Ihnen [**ee**nen]
young jung [yoong]
your* (familiar: singular) dein [dine]
(plural) euer [**oy**er]
(polite) Ihr [eer]
your camera deine/Ihre Kamera [**dine**-uh/**eer**-uh]
yours* (familiar: singular) deiner [**dine**-er]
(plural) eurer [**oy**rer]
(polite) Ihrer [**eer**er]

youth hostel die Jugendherberge [y**oo**gent-hairbairg-uh]

Z

zero null [nooll]
zip der Reißverschluß [rice-fairshlooss]
could you put a new zip on? könnten Sie einen neuen Reißverschluß anbringen? [**kur**nten zee **ine**-en n**oy**-en]
zoo der Zoo [tsoh]

German → English

Colloquialisms

The following are words you might well hear. You shouldn't be tempted to use any of the stronger ones unless you are sure of your audience.

Arschloch n [arshloKH] arsehole
aufs Kreuz legen to screw, to lay; to take for a ride
blau [blow] pissed, smashed
Bulle m [bool-uh] cop
bumsen [boomss-en] to bonk
Bumslokal n [boomss-lohkahl] dive
das ist Jacke wie Hose [yack-uh vee hohz-uh] it doesn't make any difference
das ist mir scheißegal [meer shice-aygahl] I couldn't give a shit
du kannst mich mal fuck off, go to hell
du spinnst ja you're off your head
einen Scheißdreck werd' ich tun [ine-en shice-dreck vaird ish toon] no fucking way
ficken to fuck
geil [gile] brilliant; horny
kotzen to puke
leck mich am Arsch fuck off; fuck it
Mensch! [mensh] wow!, hey!
Mist m crap, rubbish
Nutte f [noot-uh] hooker, whore
Puff m [poof] brothel
Scheißdreck m [shice-dreck] shit
Scheiße f [shice-uh] shit
Scheißkerl m [shice-kairl] bastard, son-of-a-bitch
scheißvornehm [shice-fornaym] bloody posh, swanky
Spinner m [shpinner] crazy guy, nutcase
stark [shtark] great
verdammte Scheiße [fairdammt-uh shice-uh] bloody hell, fucking hell
verdammt noch mal bloody hell
verpiß dich [fairpiss] piss off, fuck off

A

ab [ap] from; off; down

abbiegen [ap-beegen] to turn off

Abblendlicht n [ap-blent-lisht] dipped/dimmed headlights

Abend m [ahbent] evening
zu Abend essen to have dinner

Abendessen n [ahbent-essen] dinner

Abendkleid n [ahbent-klite] evening dress

abends [ahbents] in the evening

aber [ahber] but

Abf. (Abfahrt) dept, departure

Abfahrt f [ap-fahrt] departure(s)

Abfall m [ap-fal] litter; rubbish, garbage

Abfälle litter

Abfalleimer m [apfal-ime-er] rubbish bin, trashcan

Abfertigung f [ap-fairtigoong] check-in

Abflug m [ap-flook] departure(s)

Abführmittel n [ap-foor-mittel] laxative

abgefüllt in ... bottled in ...

abgezähltes Geld [ap-getsayltess gelt] exact fare

abheben [ap-hayben] to take off; to withdraw

Abhebung f [ap-hayboong] withdrawal

abholen [ap-hohlen] to pick up

Abkürzung f [ap-koortsoong] abbreviation; shortcut

ablehnen [ap-laynen] to refuse

abnehmen [ap-naymen] to lift (the receiver); to remove; to lose weight

abreisen [ap-rize-en] to leave

abschließen [ap-shleessen] to lock

Absender m [ap-zender] sender

absichtlich [ap-zishtlish] deliberately

absolutes Halteverbot waiting strictly prohibited

absolutes Parkverbot parking strictly prohibited

absolutes Rauchverbot smoking strictly prohibited

Abstand m [ap-shtant] distance

Abtei f [ap-ti] abbey

Abteil n [ap-tile] compartment

Abteilung f [ap-tyloong] department

Abtreibung f [ap-tryboong] abortion

abtrocknen [ap-trocknen] to dry the dishes

Abwasch m [ap-vash] washing-up

abwaschen [ap-vashen] to do the dishes

Achse f [aks-uh] axle

ach so! [aKH zo] I see

acht [aKHt] eight

Achtung! [aKHtoong] look out!; attention

Achtung! Straßenbahn beware of trams

achtzehn [aKH-tsayn] eighteen

achtzig [aKH-tsish] eighty

ADAC (Allgemeiner Deutscher Automobil-Club) [ah-day-ah-tsay] German motoring organization

Adreßbuch n [adressbooKH] address book

Affe m [aff-uh] monkey

Agentur f [agentoor] agency

ähneln [ayneln] to look like

ähnlich [aynlish] similar

Aktentasche f [akten-tash-uh] briefcase

Aktie f [aktsee-uh] share

Akzent m [aktsent] accent

akzeptieren [aktsepteeren] to accept

albern silly

alle [al-uh] all; everybody; finished, all gone

allein [aline] alone

alle Kassen all health insurance schemes accepted

alle Rechte vorbehalten all rights reserved

Allergie f [alairgee] allergy

allergisch gegen [alairgish gaygen] allergic to

Allerheiligen n [allerhyligen] All Saints' Day (1 November)

alles [al-ess] everything

alles Gute [al-ess goot-uh] best wishes; all the best

alles klar! [al-ess klar] fine!, great!

allgemein [al-gemine] general; generally

Alpen Alps

als [alss] when; than; as

also [alzo] therefore

als ob [alss op] as if

alt [alt] old

Altbau m [altbow] old building

Altenheim n [alten-hime] old people's home

Alter n [alter] age

Altersheim n [alters-hime] old people's home

altmodisch [alt-mohdish] old-fashioned

Altstadt f [alt-shtatt] old (part of) town

Alufolie f [ahloo-fohlee-uh] silver foil

a.M. (am Main) on the Main

am at the; on (the)

am schnellsten (the) fastest

am Apparat [am apparaht] speaking

Ambulanz f [amboolants] out-patients

Ameise f [ahmize-uh] ant

Amerikaner m [amairee-kahner], **Amerikanerin f** American

amerikanisch [amairee-kahnish] American

Ampel f traffic lights

amüsieren: sich amüsieren [zish amoozeeren] to have fun

an at; to; on

anbieten [anbeeten] to offer

Andenken n souvenir

andere [ander-uh] other(s)

andere Orte other destinations

anderthalb [andert-halp] one and a half

Änderung f [enderoong]

change; alteration
Anfall m [**an**fal] attack; fit
Anfang m beginning
anfangen to begin
Anfänger m [**an**fenger],
Anfängerin f beginner
Anfassen der Waren verboten
do not touch the
merchandise
Angeklagte m/f [**an**-geklahkt-uh]
defendant
Angeln m [**ang**-eln] fishing
Angeln verboten no fishing
angenehm [**an**-genaym]
pleasant; pleased to meet
you
Angestellte m/f [**an**-geshtellt-uh]
employee
Angst f fear
anhalten to stop
Anhalter: per Anhalter fahren
to hitchhike
Anhänger m [**an**henger] trailer;
pendant; follower
Ank. (Ankunft) arr, arrival
Ankauf ... we buy ...
ankommen to arrive
ankreuzen [**an**kroytsen] to cross
Ankunft f [**an**koonft] arrival(s)
Ankunftshalle f [**an**koonfts-hal-
uh] arrivals (area)
Anlieger frei residents only
Anmeldung f [**an**-meldoong]
reception
anprobieren [**an**probeeren] to
try on
Anruf m [**an**roof] call
anrufen [**an**roofen] to phone,
to ring

ans [anss] to the
anschalten [**an**-shalten] to
switch on
Anschluß m [**an**-shlooss]
connection
Anschluß an ... connects
with ...
Anschrift f [**an**-shrift] address
ansehen [**an**zay-en] to look
(at)
Ansicht f [**an**zisht] view;
opinion
Ansichtskarte f [**an**zishts-kart-
uh] picture postcard
anstatt [**an**-shtatt] instead of
ansteckend [**an**-shteckent]
contagious
Antenne f [ant**enn**-uh] aerial;
antenna
Antiquitäten [anti-kvit**ay**ten]
antiques
Antwort f [**an**tvort] answer
antworten [**an**tvorten] to
answer
Anwalt m [**an**valt], **Anwältin**
[**an**veltin] f lawyer
Anwohner frei residents only
Anzahlung f [**an**-tsahloong]
deposit
anziehen [**an**tsee-en] to dress
sich anziehen [zish] to get
dressed
Anzug m [**an**tsook] suit
anzünden [**an**-ts∞nden] to light
AOK (Allgemeine
Ortskrankenkasse) [ah-oh-k**ah**]
German health insurance
scheme
Apotheke f [apot**ayk**-uh]

chemist's, pharmacy

Apparat m [appar**aht**] telephone; apparatus

Appetit m [appet**eet**] appetite

a.R. (am Rhein) on the Rhine

Arbeit f [**a**rbite] work; job

arbeiten [**a**rbite-en] to work

Arbeiter m [**a**rbyter], **Arbeiterin** f worker

arbeitslos [**a**rbites-lohss] unemployed

ARD (Arbeitsgemeinschaft der Rundfunkanstalten Deutschlands) [ah-air-d**a**y] first German television channel

Ärger m [**a**irger] annoyance; trouble; hassle

ärgerlich [**a**irgerlish] annoying

ärgern: sich ärgern [zish **a**irgern] to be/get annoyed

arm poor

Arm m arm

Armaturenbrett n [armat**oo**renbrett] dashboard

Armband n [**a**rmbant] bracelet

Armbanduhr f [**a**rmbant-**oo**r] watch

Arschloch! [**a**rshlokH] bastard!

Art f sort, kind

Arzt m [**a**rtst] doctor

Ärztin f [**a**irtstin] doctor

Ärztlicher Notdienst m [**a**irtstlisher n**oh**t-deenst] emergency medical service

Asche f [**a**sh-uh] ash

Aschenbecher m [**a**shenbesher] ashtray

Aschermittwoch m [asher-mittvokH] Ash Wednesday

aß [ahss], **aßen** [**ah**ssen], **aßt** [ahsst] ate

atmen [**ah**t-men] to breathe

Attentat n [atten-taht] assassination

Attest n certificate

auch [owkH] too, also

auf [owf] on; to; open

auf deutsch in German

Aufbewahrungslösung f [owf-bevahroongs-l**ur**zoong] soaking solution

Aufenthalt m [owf-ent-halt] stay

Aufenthaltsraum m [owf-ent-halts-rowm] lounge

Aufführung f [owf-f**oo**roong] performance

aufgeben [owf-gayben] to give up; to post, to mail

aufhören [owf-hur-ren] to stop

aufpassen [owf-passen] to pay attention

aufpassen auf [owf] to take care of; to watch out for

aufregend [owf-raygent] exciting

aufs [owfs] on the; onto the

Aufsicht f [owf-zisht] supervision

aufstehen [owf-shtay-en] to get up

aufwachen [owf-vakHen] to wake up

Aufzug m [owf-ts**oo**k] lift, elevator

Auge n [owg-uh] eye

Augenarzt m [owgen-artst] ophthalmologist, optician

Augenblick m [owgenblick**]** moment

Augenbraue f [owgen-brow-uh**]** eyebrow

Augenoptiker m [owgen-optiker**]** optician

Augenzeuge m [owgen-tsoyg-uh**], Augenzeugin f** eye witness

aus [owss**]** from; off; out; out of; made of; finished

Ausfahrt f [owssfahrt**]** exit

Ausfahrt freihalten keep exit clear

Ausfahrt Tag und Nacht freihalten keep exit clear day and night

Ausflug m [owssfl00k**]** trip

ausfüllen [owssf0llen**]** to fill in

Ausgang m [owssgang**]** exit, way out; gate; departure

ausgeben [owssgayben**]** to spend

ausgenommen [owss-genommen**]** except

ausgezeichnet [owss-getsy**shnet]** excellent

Auskunft f [owsskoonft**]** information; information desk; directory enquiries

Ausland n [owsslant**]** international; overseas, abroad

Ausländer m [owsslender**], Ausländerin f** foreigner

ausländisch [owsslendish**]** foreign

ausländisches Erzeugnis foreign produce

ausländische Währungen fpl [owsslendish-uh **vai**roongen**]** foreign currencies

Ausland: im/ins Ausland [owsslant**]** abroad

Auslandsflüge international departures

Auslandsgespräche international calls

Auslandsporto n [owssslants-porto**]** overseas postage

Ausnahme f [owssnahm-uh**]** exception

auspacken [owsspacken**]** to unpack

Auspuff m [owsspooff**]** exhaust

ausruhen: sich ausruhen [zish **ow**ssr00-en**]** to relax; to take a rest

ausschalten [owss-shalten**]** to switch off

ausschl. (ausschließlich) excl., exclusive

aussehen [owss-zay-en**]** to look

Aussehen n look; appearance

außen [owssen**]** outside

außer [owsser**]** except

außer Betrieb out of order

außerhalb [owsser-halp**]** outside (of)

äußerlich anzuwenden not to be taken internally

außer sonntags Sundays excepted

Aussicht f [owss-zisht**]** view

Aussichtspunkt m [owss-zishts-poonkt**]** viewpoint

aussprechen [owss-shpreshen**]**

to pronounce

aussteigen [owss-shtygen**]** to get off

Ausstellung f [owss-shtelloong**]** exhibition

Australien n [owstra**h**lee-en**]** Australia

australisch [owstra**h**lish**]** Australian

Ausverkauf m [owss-fairk**owf]** sale

ausverkauft [owss-fairk**owft]** sold out

Auswahl f [owssvahl**]** choice; selection

Ausweis m [owssvice**]** pass, identity card; identification

Auszahlungen withdrawals; cash desk, cashier

ausziehen: sich ausziehen [zish **ow**ss-tsee-en**]** to undress

Auto n [owto**]** car

   mit dem Auto by car

Autobahn f [owto-bahn**]** motorway, highway, freeway

Autobahndreieck motorway junction; motorways merge

Autobahnkreuz motorway junction

Autobahnraststätte service station

Autobus m [owtobooss**]** bus

Autofähre f [owto-fair-uh**]** car-ferry

Autofahrer m [owtofahrer**], Autofahrerin f** car driver, motorist

Automat m vending machine

   dieser Automat nimmt

folgende Banknoten an this machine will accept the following banknotes/bills

automatisch [owtoma**h**tish**]** automatic

Autoradio n [owto-rahdee-o**]** car radio

Autoreparaturen auto repairs

Autotelefon n [owto-telefo**h**n**]** car phone

Autounfall m [owto-oonfal**]** car accident

Autovermietung f [owto-fairm**ee**toong**]** car rental

Autowäsche f [owtovesh-uh**]** car wash

B

Babyartikel babywear, items for babies

Bach m [bakH**]** stream

Bäcker m [becker**]** baker

Bäckerei f [becker-**ī]** baker's, bakery

Bad n [baht**]** bath; bathroom

Badeanzug m [bahd-uh-ants**oo**k**]** swimming costume

Badehose f [bahd-uh-hohz-uh**]** swimming trunks

Bademantel m [bahd-uh-mantel**]** dressing gown

baden [bah**den]** to have a bath

Badesalz n [bahd-uh-zalts**]** bath salts

Badewanne f [bahd-uh-vann-uh**]** bathtub

Badezimmer n [bahd-uh-tsimmer] bathroom

Badezimmerartikel bathroom furniture and fittings

Badezimmerbedarf for the bathroom

Bahnhof m [bahn-hohf] station

Bahnhofsmission f [bahnhohfs-miss-**yohn**] office providing help for travellers in difficulty

Bahnhofspolizei railway police

Bahnkilometer kilometres by rail

Bahnsteig m [bahn-shtike] platform, (US) track

Bahnsteigkarte f [bahn-shtike-kart-uh] platform ticket

Bahnübergang m [bahn- oobergang] level crossing

bald [balt] soon

Balkangrill m [balkahn-grill] restaurant serving dishes from Balkan countries

Balkon m [balkohn] balcony

Band n [bant] tape

Bank f bank; bench

Bankkonto n bank account

Bankleitzahl f [banklite-tsahl] sort code

Bankomat m [bankomaht] cash dispenser, automatic teller

bar zahlen [tsahlen] to pay cash

Bardame f [bardahm-uh] barmaid

Bargeld n [bargelt] cash

Barmann m [barmann] barkeeper

Bart m beard

Basel n [bahzel] Basle

bat [baht], **baten** [bahten] asked

Bauch m [bowKH] stomach; belly

Bauer m [bower] farmer

Bauernhof m [bowern-hohf] farm

Baum m [bowm] tree

Baumwolle f [bowmvoll-uh] cotton

Baustelle f building site; roadworks

Baustellenausfahrt works exit; building site exit

Bayern [by-ern] Bavaria

bayrisch [by-rish] Bavarian

Beamter m [buh-amter], **Beamtin f** [buh-amtin] official

Bedarf m needs, requirements; demand

bedeuten [bedoyten] to mean

bedeutend [bedoytent] important

bedienen [bedeenen] to serve

bedienen Sie sich! [zee zish] help yourself

Bedienung f [bedeenoong] service (charge)

Bedienung inbegriffen service included

Bedienungsanleitung instructions for use

Bedingung f [bedingoong] condition

beeilen: sich beeilen [zish buh-ilen] to hurry

beeilen Sie sich! [zee zish] hurry up!

beenden [buh-**en**den] to finish

Beerdigung f [buh-**air**digoong] funeral

Beerdigungsunternehmen undertaker, mortician

befehlen [be**fay**len] to order

Beginn der Vorstellung um ... [dair **for**shtelloong oom] performance begins at ...

begleiten [be**gly**ten] to accompany

behalten [be**hal**ten] to keep

behandeln to treat

Behandlung f [be**han**tloong] treatment

behaupten [be**how**pten] to claim

Behauptung f [be**how**ptoong] claim

behindert [be**hin**dert] disabled

Behinderte m/f [be**hin**dert-uh] handicapped person

bei [by] by; at; next to; near

bei Peter at Peter's

beide [**bide**-uh] both (of them)

Bei Frost Glatteisgefahr icy in cold weather

beim at the

Bein n [bine] leg

Beinbruch m [**bine**-brookH] broken leg

Beispiel n [**by**-shpeel] example

zum Beispiel [tsoom] for example

Bei Störung Taste drücken press key in case of technical fault

bekannt known

Bekannte m/f [be**kannt**-uh] acquaintance

Bekleidung f [be**kly**doong] clothing

bekloppt [be**kloppt**] crazy

bekommen to get

belegt [be**laykt**] occupied, busy; no vacancies; full

beleidigen [be**ly**digen] to offend

Beleuchtung f [be**loysh**toong] lights

Beleuchtungsartikel lamps and lighting

Belgien n [**bel**gee-en] Belgium

belgisch [**bel**gish] Belgian

Belichtungsmesser m [be**lish**toongs-messer] light meter

bellen to bark

Belohnung f [be**loh**noong] reward

bemerken [be**mair**ken] to notice; to remark

Bemerkung f [be**mair**koong] remark

Benehmen n [be**nay**men] behaviour

benehmen: sich benehmen [zish be**nay**men] to behave

Benutzung f [be**noot**soong] use

Benutzung auf eigene Gefahr use at own risk

Benzin n [bent**seen**] petrol, gas(oline)

Benzinkanister m [bent**seen**-kanister] petrol/gasoline can

Benzinuhr f [bent**seen**-oor] fuel

gauge

beobachten [buh-**oh**baKHten] to watch

bequem [bekv**ay**m] comfortable

bereit [be**rite**] ready

Bereitschaftsdienst m [be**rite**-shaftsdeenst] duty doctor; duty pharmacy

Berg m [bairk] mountain

Bergsteigen n [**bai**rk-shtygen] mountaineering

Bergwacht f [**bai**rk-vaKHt] mountain rescue

Bericht m [be**ri**sht] report

beruhigen: sich beruhigen [zish ber**00**-igen] to calm down

Beruhigungsmittel n [ber**00**-igoongs-mittel] tranquillizer

berühmt [ber**00**mt] famous

berühren [ber**00**ren] to touch

Berühren der Waren verboten do not touch

Besatzung f [bez**a**tsoong] crew

beschädigen [besh**ay**digen] to damage

Bescheid m [besh**ite**] information

Bescheid sagen to tell

Bescheid wissen to know

Bescheinigung f [besh**y**nigoong] certificate

bescheuert [besh**oy**ert] crazy, daft

beschreiben [besh**ry**ben] to describe

Beschreibung f description

beschweren: sich beschweren [zish beshv**ai**ren] to complain

besetzt [bez**etst**] busy; engaged, occupied

Besetztzeichen n [bes**etst**-tsyshen] engaged tone

Besichtigung f [bez**i**shtigoong] tour

Besitzer m [bez**i**tser] owner

besoffen [bez**o**ffen] pissed, smashed

besonders [bez**o**nders] especially

besorgt [bez**or**kt] worried

besser better

Bestandteile ingredients; component parts

bestätigen [besht**ay**tigen] to confirm

Bestattungen funeral director's

beste [b**e**st-uh] best

Bestechung f [besht**e**shoong] bribery

Besteck n [besht**e**ck] cutlery

bestellen [besht**e**llen] to order

Bestellung f [besht**e**lloong] order

Bestimmungsort m [beshtim-moongs-ort] destination

bestrafen [besht**ra**hfen] to punish

Besuch m [bez**00**KH] visit

besuchen [bez**00**KHen] to visit

Besuchszeit f [bez**00**KHs-tsite] visiting time

Besuchszeiten fpl [bez**00**KHs-tsyten] visiting hours

Betäubung f [bet**oy**boong] anaesthetic

Beton m [b**ay**tong] concrete

Betrag m [betr**ah**k] amount
Betreten auf eigene Gefahr enter at own risk, keep off/out
Betreten der Baustelle verboten no admission to building site
Betreten der Eisfläche verboten keep off the ice
Betreten des Rasens nicht gestattet keep off the grass
Betreten verboten keep out
Betrieb m [betr**ee**p] company, firm; operation, running; bustle
   außer Betrieb out of order
betriebsbereit ready to use
Betriebsferien [betr**ee**ps-fairee-en] works' holidays/vacation
Betrug m [betr**oo**k] fraud
betrunken [betr**oo**nken] drunk
Bett n bed
Bettdecken bedding
Betteln und Hausieren verboten no beggars, no hawkers
Bettwäsche f [b**ett**vesh-uh] bed linen
Bettzeug n [b**ett**-tsoyk] bedding
Be- und Entladen erlaubt loading and off-loading permitted
bevor [bef**or**] before
bewegen: sich bewegen [zish be-v**ay**gen] to move
Beweis m [bev**ice**] proof
Bewohner m [bev**oh**ner], **Bewohnerin** f inhabitant
bewölkt [bev**url**kt] cloudy

bezahlen [bets**ah**len] to pay
Bezahlung f [bets**ah**loong] payment
Bezahlung mit Kreditkarte möglich credit cards welcome
beziehungsweise or
Bf. (Bahnhof) station
BH (Büstenhalter) m [bay-h**ah**] bra
Bierkeller m [b**eer**-keller] beer cellar
Bild n [bilt] picture
billig [b**ill**ish] cheap, inexpensive
Billigpreise reduced prices
bin am
Bindemittel starch
Bio-Laden m [b**ee**-oh-lahden] health food shop
biologisch abbaubar biodegradable
Birne f [b**eer**n-uh] light bulb; pear
bis until; by
   bis morgen see you tomorrow
   bis später [shp**ay**ter] see you later
Biß m [bis] bite
bißchen: ein bißchen [ine b**iss**-shen] a little bit (of)
bist are
bitte [b**itt**uh] please; you're welcome
bitte? pardon (me)?; can I help you?
bitte anschnallen fasten seat belt

bitte einordnen get in lane
bitte eintreten ohne zu läuten please enter without ringing
bitte einzeln eintreten please enter one at a time
bitte entwerten please stamp your ticket
bitte Karte einführen please insert card
bitte klingeln please ring
bitte klopfen please knock
bitten to ask
bitte nicht ... please do not ...
bitte nicht stören please do not disturb
bitte schließen please close the door
bitte schön/sehr [bitt-uh shurn/zair] here you are; you're welcome
bitte schön/sehr? what will it be?; can I help you?
bitte Schuhe abtreten please wipe your shoes
bitte warten please wait
Blase f [blahz-uh] bladder; blister
blaß [blass] pale
Blatt n leaf
blau [blow] blue
blauer Fleck m [blower] bruise
Blei n [bly] lead
bleiben [blyben] to stay, to remain
bleiben Sie am Apparat [zee am apparaht] hold the line
Bleichmittel n [blysh-mittel] bleach
bleifrei [blyfry] unleaded

Bleistift m [bly-shtift] pencil
Blick m look; view
mit Blick auf ... [owf] overlooking ...
blieb [bleep], **bliebst, blieben** stayed
Blinddarmentzündung f [blint-darm-ent-tsoondoong] appendicitis
blinder Passagier m [blinnder passaJeer] stowaway
Blinker m indicator
Blitz m [blits] flash; lightning
blockiert [blockeert] blocked
Blödmann m [blurtmann] twit
Blödsinn m [blurt-zinn] nonsense, rubbish
Blume f [bloom-uh] flower
Blumenhandlung f [bloomen-hantloong] florist
Bluse f [blooz-uh] blouse
Blut n [bloot] blood
Blutdruck m [bloot-droock] blood pressure
bluten [blooten] to bleed
Blutgruppe f [bloot-groopp-uh] blood group
Blutübertragung f [bloot-oobertrahgoong] blood transfusion
BLZ (Bankleitzahl) sort code
Boden m [bohden] bottom; floor
Bodenpersonal n [bohden-pairzonahl] ground crew
Bodensee: der Bodensee [bohdenzay] Lake Constance
Bohrer m drill
Boje f [boh-yuh] buoy

Bolzen m [boltsen] bolt
Boot n [boht] boat
Bootsverleih m [bohts-fairlī] boat hire/rental
Bordkarte f [bortkart-uh] boarding card
böse [burz-uh] angry
Botschaft f [bohtshaft] embassy
brachte [braKHt-uh], brachtest, brachten brought
Branchenverzeichnis n [brangshen-fairtsyshniss] yellow pages
Brand m [brant] fire
Brandstiftung f [brant-shtiftoong] arson
Bratpfanne f [braht-pfann-uh] frying pan
Bräu n [broy] brew
Brauch m [browKH] custom
brauchen [browKHen] to need
Brauerei f brewery
Brauereiabfüllung bottled in the brewery
braun [brown] brown
braungebrannt [brown-gebrannt] tanned

BRD (Bundesrepublik Deutschland) [bay-air-day] FRG (Federal Republic of Germany)
breit [brite] wide
Breite f [bryt-uh] width
Bremse f [bremz-uh] brake
bremsen [bremzen] to brake
Bremsflüssigkeit f [brems-flōssishkite] brake fluid
brennbar combustible
brennen to burn

Brief m [breef] letter
Brieffreund m [breef-froynt], Brieffreundin f pen pal
Briefkasten m [breefkasten] letterbox, mailbox
Briefmarke f [breefmark-uh] stamp
Brieftasche f [breeftash-uh] wallet
Briefträger m [breeftrayger] postman
Briefträgerin f [breeftraygerin] postwoman
Brille f [brill-uh] glasses, eyeglasses
bringen to bring
Brosche f [brosh-uh] brooch
Broschüre f [broshōr-uh] brochure
Bruch m [brooKH] fracture
Brücke f [brōck-uh] bridge
Bruder m [brooder] brother
Brunnen m [broonnen] fountain
Brust f [broost] breast; chest
Buch n [booKH] book
buchen [booKHen] to book
Bücherei f [boosher-ī] library
Bücher und Zeitschriften books and magazines
Buchhandlung f [booKH-hantloong] bookshop, bookstore
Bucht f [booKHt] bay
Bügeleisen n [boogel-īzen] iron
Bügelfalte f [boogel-falt-uh] crease
bügeln [boogeln] to iron
Bühne f [boon-uh] stage
Bundesautobahn federal

motorway/highway

Bundesgesundheitsminister m
German Minister of Health
Der
Bundesgesundheitsminister:
Rauchen gefährdet Ihre
Gesundheit government
warning: smoking can
damage your health

Bundeskanzler m [**boo**ndess-
kantsler] chancellor

Bundesrepublik Deutschland f
[**boo**ndess-rep**oo**bleek **doy**tchlant]
Federal Republic of
Germany

Bundesstraße f [**boo**ndess-
shtrahss-uh] major road, A-
road

Bundestag m [**boo**ndess-tahk]
German parliament

Burg f [boork] castle

Bürgersteig m [b**oo**rger-shtike]
pavement, sidewalk

Büro n [b**oo**ro] office

Büroartikel office supplies

Bürste f [b**oo**rst-uh] brush

Busbahnhof m [**boo**ss-bahnhohf]
bus station

Bushaltestelle f [**boo**ss-halt-uh-
sht**e**ll-uh] bus stop

bzw. (beziehungsweise) or

C

Café n [k**a**ffay] café, serving
mainly cakes, coffee and tea
etc

Campingbedarf camping

equipment

Campingliege f [k**e**mping-leeg-
uh] campbed

Campingplatz m [k**e**mpingplats]
campsite; caravan site, trailer
park

CD-Spieler m [tsay-d**a**y-shpeeler]
CD player

Charterflug m [charter-fl**oo**k]
charter flight

Chauvi m [sh**oh**vee] male
chauvinist pig

Chef m [shef], **Chefin f** boss

chemische Reinigung f
[sh**a**ymish-uh r**y**nigoong] dry
cleaner's

Chinarestaurant n [sh**ee**na-
restor**ong**] Chinese restaurant

chinesisch [sheen**a**yzish]
Chinese

Chirurg m [sheer**oo**rk],
Chirurgin f surgeon

Coiffeur m [kwaff**ur**] hairdresser

D

da there; as; since

Dach n [da**KH**] roof

Dachboden m [da**KH**bohden]
attic

Dachgepäckträger m [da**KH**-
gepeck-trayger] roof rack

dafür [daf**oo**r] for that; on that;
in that; in favour; then again;
considering

daher [dah**air**] from there;
that's why

Dame f [d**ah**m-uh] lady

Damen ladies' (toilet), ladies' room

Damenbinde f [**dah**menbind-uh] sanitary towel/napkin

Damenkleidung f [**dah**men-**kly**doong] ladies' clothing

Damenmoden ladies' fashions

Damensalon m [**dah**men-zalong] ladies' hairdresser's

Damentoilette f [**dah**men-twalett-uh] ladies' (toilet), ladies' room

Damenunterwäsche f [**dah**men-oontervesh-uh] lingerie

damit so that; with it

Dampfer m steamer

danach [dana**KH**] after that; accordingly

Dänemark n [**day**n-uh-mark] Denmark

dänisch [**day**nish] Danish

dankbar grateful

danke [dank-uh] thank you, thanks

danke gleichfalls [**gly**shfals] the same to you

danken to thank

dann then

darf am allowed to; is allowed to; may

darfst are allowed to; may

Darlehen n [**dah**rlay-en] loan

darum [da**room**] about it; that's why

das the; who; that; which

daß [dass] that

Datum n [**dah**toom] date

Dauerwelle f [**dow**ervell-uh] perm

Daumen m [**dow**men] thumb

davon from there; of it; of them; from it; from them

DB (Deutsche (Bundes)bahn) German Railways

Decke f [**deck**-uh] blanket; ceiling

Deckel m lid

defekt out of order; faulty

dein(e) [**dine**(-uh)] your

denken to think

Denkmal n [**denk**mahl] monument

denn for, because; than

deprimiert [deprim**eert**] depressed

der [dair] the; who; that

deshalb [dess-halp] therefore

Desinfektionsmittel n [desinfekts-**yohns**-mittel] disinfectant

deutsch [doytch] German

Deutsche m/f [**doy**tch-uh] German

deutsches Erzeugnis made in Germany

Deutschland n [**doy**tchlant] Germany

Deutschlandlied n [**doy**tchlant-leet] German national anthem

d.h. (das heißt) i.e.

Dia n [**dee**-ah] slide

Diabetiker m [dee-ah-**bay**tiker], **Diabetikerin f** diabetic

Diamant m [dee-ah-**mant**] diamond

Diät f [dee-**ayt**] diet

dich [dish] you

Dichter m [dishter] poet

dick fat; thick

die [dee] the; who; that; which

Dieb m [deep] thief

Diebstahl m [deep-shtahl] theft

Dienstag m [deenstahk] Tuesday

dienstbereit [deenst-berite] on duty

dies [deess] this (one); that (one)

diese [deez-uh] this (one); that (one); these (ones); those (ones)

dieser [deezer] this (one); that (one)

dieses [deezess] this (one); that (one)

diesseits [deess-zites] on this side (of)

Ding n thing

dir [deer] (to) you

Direktflug m [deerekt-flook] non-stop flight

diskutieren [disk00teeren] to discuss

DJH (Deutsche Jugendherberge) German Youth Hostel Association

DLRG (Deutsche Lebensrettungsgesellschaft) [day-el-air-gay] German lifeguards association

DM (Deutsche Mark) DM, German mark

doch! [doKH] oh yes it is!; oh yes I am! etc

Dolmetscher m [dolmetcher],

Dolmetscherin f interpreter

Dom m [dohm] cathedral

Donau f [dohnow] Danube

Donner m thunder

Donnerstag m [donnerstahk] Thursday

doof [dohf] stupid

Doppelbett n double bed

doppelt double

Doppelzimmer n [doppel-tsimmer] double room

Dorf n village

dort there

dort drüben [drooben] over there; up there

dort oben [ohben] over there; up there

Dose f [dohz-uh] can

Dosenöffner m [dohzen-urfner] tin opener

Dragees npl [draJayss] sugar-coated tablets

Draht m wire

Drahtseilbahn f [drahtzilebahn] cable car

Dreck m dirt

drehen [dray-en] to turn

drei [dry] three

dreimal täglich einzunehmen to be taken three times a day

dreißig [dryssish] thirty

dreizehn [dry-tsayn] thirteen

dringend [dring-ent] urgent

dritte(r,s) [dritt-uh,-er,-ess] third

Droge f [drohg-uh] drug

Drogerie f [drohgeree] chemist's, toiletries shop

Druck m [droock] pressure

drücken [droocken] to push

Drucker m [dr**oo**cker] printer

Drucksache f printed matter

DSD (Duales System Deutschland) recycling scheme

du [d**oo**] you

du lieber Gott! [l**ee**ber gott] good God!

du liebe Zeit! [l**ee**b-uh tsite] struth!

Duft m [dooft] smell; fragrance

dumm [doomm] stupid

Dummheit f [d**oo**mmhite] stupidity

Dummkopf m [d**oo**mmkopf] idiot

Dünen fpl [d**œœ**nen] sand dunes

dunkel [d**oo**nkel] dark

Dunkelheit f [d**oo**nkelhite] darkness

dünn [d**œœ**nn] thin; skinny

durch [doorsh] through; by; well-done

Durcheinander n [doorsh-ine-ander] mess

Durchfall m [doorshfal] diarrhoea

Durchgang m [doorshgang] passage

Durchgangsverkehr through traffic

durchgehend geöffnet open 24 hours

Durchschnitt m [doorsh-shnitt] average

durchstreichen [doorsh-shtryshen] to cross out, to delete

Durchsuchung f [doorsh-zooKHoong] search

Durchwahl direct dialling

dürfen [d**œœ**rfen] to be allowed to

Durst m [doorst] thirst

Durst haben [h**ah**ben] to be thirsty

Dusche f [d**oo**sh-uh] shower

duschen [d**oo**shen] to have a shower

Düsenflugzeug n [d**œœ**zen-fl**oo**ktsoyk] jet plane

Dutzend n [d**oo**tsent] dozen

duzen: sich duzen [zish d**oo**tsen] to use the familiar 'du' form

D-Zug [d**ay**-ts**oo**k] express train

E

Ebbe f [**e**bb-uh] low tide

echt [esht] genuine

Ecke f [**e**ck-uh] corner

Edelstein m [**ay**del-shtine] precious stone

EG (Europäische Gemeinschaft) [ay-g**ay**] EC, European Community

ehe [**ay**-uh] before

Ehe f [**ay**-uh] marriage

Ehefrau f [**ay**-uh-frow] wife

Ehemann m [**ay**-uh-man] husband

ehrlich [**air**lish] honest; sincere

Ehrlichkeit f [**air**lishkite] honesty

Eiche f [**ī**sh-uh] oak

Eieruhr f [**ī**er-oor] egg timer

eifersüchtig [ī̄ferzOOshtish] jealous

eigen [ī̄gen] own

eigenartig [ī̄gen-artish] strange

eigentlich [ī̄gentlish] actual; actually

Eigentümer m [ī̄gentOOmer], Eigentümerin f owner

Eilzug m [ile-tsOOk] fast local train

Eimer m [ime-er] bucket

ein(e) [ine(-uh)] a; one

Einbahnstraße f [ine-bahn-shtrahss-uh] one-way street

Einbrecher m [ine-bresher] burglar

Einbruch m [ine-brooKH] burglary

einchecken [ine-checken] to check in

Eindruck m [ine-droock] impression

eine [ine-uh] a

einfach [ine-faKH] simple; single

einfache Fahrt one-way journey; single; one way

Einfahrt f [ine-fahrt] entrance, way in

Einfahrt freihalten keep entrance clear

Eingang m [ine-gang] entrance, way in

Eingang um die Ecke entrance round corner

eingeschränktes Halteverbot restricted parking

eingetragenes Warenzeichen registered trademark

Einheit f [ine-hite] unit

Einheitspreis flat rate

einige [ine-ig-uh] a few; some

Einkauf m [ine-kowf] shopping

einkaufen: einkaufen gehen [ine-kowfen gay-en] to go shopping

Einkaufskorb m [ine-kowfss-korp] shopping basket

Einkaufstasche f [ine-kowfss-tash-uh] shopping bag

Einkaufswagen m [ine-kowfss-vahgen] shopping trolley

Einkaufszentrum n [ine-kowfss-tsentroom] shopping centre

einladen [ine-lahden] to invite

Einladung f [ine-lahdoong] invitation

Einlaß m [ine-lass] admission

einmal [ine-mahl] once
nicht einmal not even

einmalig [ine-mahlish] unique

einpacken [ine-packen] to wrap

einreiben [ine-ryben] to rub in

Einrichtung f [ine-rishtoong] furnishing; organization

eins [ine-ss] one

einsam [ine-zahm] lonely

einschalten [ine-shalten] to switch on

einschenken [ine-shenken] to pour

einschlafen [ine-shlahfen] to fall asleep

einschl. (einschließlich) incl., inclusive

einschließlich 15% Bedienung 15% service charge included

Einschreiben n [ine-shryben] registered letter

Einschreibsendungen registered mail

einsteigen [ine-shtygen] to get in

Einstieg hinten enter at the rear

Einstieg nur mit Fahrausweis obtain a ticket before boarding

Einstieg vorn enter at the front

eintreten in [ine-trayten] to enter

Eintritt m [ine-tritt] entry

Eintritt frei admission free

Eintrittskarte f [ine-tritts-kart-uh] ticket

Eintrittspreise admission

einverstanden! [ine-fair-shtanden] OK!; agreed

einwerfen [ine-vairfen] to insert

Einzahlungen deposits

Einzelbett n [ine-tselbett] single bed

Einzelfahrkarte f [ine-tsel-fahrkart-uh] single/one-way ticket

Einzelhändler m [ine-tsel-hentler] retailer

Einzelheit f [ine-tselhite] detail

Einzelpreis m [ine-tsel-price] (unit) price

Einzelzimmer n [ine-tsel-tsimmer] single room

Eiscafé n [ice-kaffay] ice cream parlour (also serves coffee and liqueurs)

Eisenbahn f [izenbahn] railway

Eisenwarenhandlung f [izenvahren-hantloong] hardware store

Eisstadion n [ice-shtahdee-on] ice rink

Eiter m [ite-er] pus

Elektriker m [aylektriker] electrician

Elektrizität f [aylektritsitayt] electricity

Elektroartikel mpl [aylektro-arteekel] electrical goods

Elektrogeräte npl [aylektro-gerayt-uh] electrical equipment

elf eleven

Elfmeter m [elfmayter] penalty

Ellbogen m [ell-bohgen] elbow

Eltern parents

Eltern haften für ihre Kinder parents are responsible for their children

Empfang m reception

Empfänger m [emp-fenger] addressee

empfehlen [emp-faylen] to recommend

Ende der Autobahn end of motorway/highway

Ende der Vorfahrtsstraße end of priority

endlich [entlish] at last; finally

Endstation f [ent-shtats-yohn] terminus

eng narrow; tight

Engländer m [eng-lender] Englishman

Engländerin f [eng-lenderin]

English girl/woman

englisch [eng-lish] English; rare (meat)

Enkel m grandson

Enkelin f granddaughter

entdecken to discover

entfernt [entfairnt] away; distant

Entfernung f [entfairnoong] distance

entführen [entfooren] to kidnap, to abduct

Entgleisung f [ent-glyzoong] derailment

enthält ... contains ...

entlang along(side)

entscheiden [ent-shyden] to decide

entschlossen [ent-shlossen] determined

entschuldigen: sich entschuldigen [zish entshooldigen] to apologize

entschuldigen Sie bitte [zee bitt-uh] excuse me

Entschuldigung [entshooldigoong] sorry, excuse me

entsetzlich [entzetslish] appalling

enttäuscht [ent-toysht] disappointed

Enttäuschung f [ent-toyshoong] disappointment

entweder ... oder ... [entvayder ohder] either ... or ...

Entwerter m [entvairter] ticket-stamping machine

entwickeln [entvickeln] to develop

Entzündung f [ent-tsoondoong] infection

er [air] he

Erde f [aird-uh] earth

Erdgeschoß n [airt-geshoss] ground floor, (US) first floor

Erfahrung f [airfahroong] experience

Erfolg m [airfollk] success

Erfrischung f [airfrishoong] refreshment

ergibt die doppelte/dreifache Menge makes twice/three times as much

erhalten [airhalten] to receive

erholen: sich erholen [zish airhohlen] to recover

Erholungsgebiet n [airhohloongs-gebeet] recreational area

erinnern: sich erinnern an [zish air-innern] to remember

Erinnerung f [air-inneroong] memory

erkälten: sich erkälten [zish airkelten] to catch cold

erkältet: erkältet sein [airkeltet] to have a cold

Erkältung f [airkeltoong] cold

erkennen [airkennen] to recognize

erklären [airklairen] to explain

erlauben [airlowben] to allow

Erlaubnis f [airlowpniss] permission

Erlebnis n [airlaypniss] experience

Ermäßigte Preise reduced

prices

Ermäßigungen reductions; concessions

ermorden [airmorden] to murder

ernst [airnst] serious

Ersatzreifen m [airzatz-ryfen] spare tyre

Ersatzteile npl [airzatz-tile-uh] spare parts

erschießen [airsheessen] to shoot (and kill)

Ersparnisse fpl [airshpahrniss-uh] savings

erst [airst] only just; only

erstatten [airshtatten] to refund

erstaunlich [airshtownlich] astonishing

erste(r,s) [airst-uh, -er, -es] first

Erste Hilfe f [airst-uh hilf-uh] first aid

erste Klasse [airst-uh klass-uh] first class

erstens [airstens] first; firstly

erster Stock m [airster shtock] first floor, (US) second floor

ersticken [airshticken] to suffocate

ertrinken [airtrinken] to drown

Erwachsene m/f [airvaksen-uh] adult

erwähnen [airvaynen] to mention

es [ess] it

eßbar [essbar] edible

essen to eat

Essen n food

Eßlöffel m [ess-lurffel] tablespoon

Etage f [aytahJ-uh] floor, storey

Etagenbett n [aytahJen-bett] bunk beds

Etat m [aytah] budget

Etikett n label

etwa [etvah] about; perhaps

etwas [etvass] something; some; somewhat

etwas anderes [anderess] something else

euch [oysh] you

euer [oyer] your

eure [oyr-uh] your

europäisch [oyro-pay-ish] European

Euroscheck m [oyrosheck] Eurocheque

ev. (evangelisch) Protestant

evangelisch [evangaylish] Protestant

Explosionsgefahr f [eksplohz-yohns-gefahr] danger of explosion

F

Fabrik f [fabreek] factory

Fach n [faкн] subject; pigeonhole

Facharzt m: Facharzt für ... [faкнartst foor] specialist for ...

Fachmann m [faкнmann] specialist

Faden m [fahden] string; thread

Fahne f [fahn-uh] flag

Fahrausweis m [fahr-owssvice]

ticket

Fahrausweise sind auf Verlangen vorzuzeigen tickets must be displayed on request

Fahrbahn f roadway

Fähre f [fair-uh] ferry

fahren to drive; to go

Fahrer m driver

Fahrgäste passengers

Fahrkarte f [fahrkart-uh] ticket

Fahrkartenautomat m [fahrkarten-owtomaht] ticket machine

Fahrkartenschalter m [fahrkarten-shalter] ticket office

Fahrplan m [fahrplahn] timetable, (US) schedule

Fahrpreise mpl [fahrprize-uh] fares

Fahrrad n [fahr-raht] bicycle

Fahrräder bicycles

Fahrradkarte f [fahr-rahtkart-uh] bicycle ticket

Fahrradverleih m [fahr-raht-fairlī] bicycles for hire/to rent

Fahrradweg m [fahr-raht-vayk] cycle path

Fahrschein m [fahr-shine] ticket

Fahrscheinkauf nur beim Fahrer buy your ticket from the driver

Fahrstuhl m [fahr-shtool] lift, elevator

Fahrt f journey

Fahrtziele destinations

Fahrzeug n [fahr-tsoyk] vehicle

Fall m [fal] fall; case

fallen [fal-en] to fall

fallenlassen [fal-en-lassen] to drop

falls [falss] if

falsch [falsh] wrong; false

falten to fold

Familie f [fameelee-yuh] family

Familienpackung f family pack

fand [fant], fanden found

fangen to catch

Farbe f [farb-uh] colour; paint

Farben und Lacke paints

Farbfilm m [farpfilm] colour film

Fasching m [fashing] annual carnival held in the pre-Lent period with fancy-dress processions and general celebrating

Fasse dich kurz! keep it brief!

fast [fasst] almost, nearly

faul [fowl] lazy; rotten

Feder f [fayder] feather; spring

Federbett n [fayderbett] quilt

Fehler m [fayler] mistake; defect

fehlerhaft [fayler-haft] faulty

Feierabend m [fy-erahbent] closing time; time to stop

Feiertag m [fy-ertahk] public holiday

Feinkostgeschäft n [fine-kost-gesheft] delicatessen

Feinschmecker m [fine-shmecker], Feinschmeckerin f gourmet

Feld n [felt] field

Felsen m [felzen] rock

Fenster n window

Fensterläden mpl [fenster-

layden] shutters

Ferien fpl [fairee-en] holidays, vacation

Ferienwohnung f [fairee-en-vohnoong] holiday home

Ferngespräch n [fairn-geshpraysh] long-distance call

Fernlicht n [fairn-lisht] full beam

Fernschreiben n [fairn-shryben] telex

Fernsehen n [fairnzay-en] television

Fernsprecher m telephone

Ferse f [fairz-uh] heel

fertig [fairtish] ready; finished

fest fixed; firm; definite

festnehmen [festnaymen] to arrest

Fete f [fayt-uh] party

fett greasy

Fett n fat

Fettgehalt fat content

feucht [foysht] damp

Feuchtigkeitscreme f [foyshtish-kites-kraym] moisturizer; cold cream

Feuer n [foyer] fire

Feuergefahr f [foyer-gefahr] fire hazard

Feuerlöscher m [foyerlursher] fire extinguisher

Feuertreppe f [foyertrepp-uh] fire escape

Feuerwehr f [foyervair] fire brigade

Feuerwehrausfahrt fire brigade exit

Feuerwerk n [foyervairk] fireworks

Feuerzeug n [foyer-tsoyk] lighter

Fieber n [feeber] fever

Filmmusik f [film-moozeek] soundtrack

Filzstift m [filts-shtift] felt-tip pen

finden [fin-den] to find

Fingernagel m [fing-er-nahgel] fingernail

Firma f [feermah] company

Fischgeschäft n [fish-gesheft] fishmonger's

FKK [ef-kah-kah] nudism

flach [flakH] flat

Flasche f [flash-uh] bottle

Flaschenöffner m [flashen-urfner] bottle-opener

Fleck m stain; spot

Fleischerei f [flysher-I] butcher's

Fliege f [fleeg-uh] fly; bow tie

fliegen [fleegen] to fly

fließend [fleessent] fluent

Flitterwochen fpl [flittervokHen] honeymoon

Flucht f [flookHt] escape

flüchten [flooshten] to escape

Flug m [flook] flight

Flugdauer f [flook-dower] flight time

Flügel m [floogel] wing

Fluggast m [flook-gast] air passenger

Fluggeschwindigkeit f [flook-geshwindish-kite] flight speed

Fluggesellschaft f [flook-gezellshafft] airline

Flughafen m [flook-hahfen]
airport

Flughafenbus m [flook-hahfen-booss] airport bus

Flughöhe f [flook-hur-uh]
altitude

Flugkarte f [flook-kart-uh] flight
ticket

Fluglinie f [flook-leen-yuh]
airline

Fluglotse m [flook-lohts-uh] air
traffic controller

Flugplan m [flookplahn]
timetable, (US) schedule

Flugsteig m [flook-shtike] gate

Flugzeug n [flook-tsoyk]
(aero)plane

Flugzeugabsturz m [flooktsoyk-apshtoorts] plane crash

Flur m [floor] corridor

Fluß m [flooss] river

Flut f [floot] high tide

fl.W. (fließendes Wasser)
running water

folgen [fol-gen] to follow

folgende [folgend-uh] next

Fön® m [furn] hair dryer

fönen: sich fönen lassen [zish furnen] to have a blow-dry

fordern to demand

Formular n [formoolahr] form

Foto n [foto] photo(graph)

Fotoartikel mpl [foto-arteekel]
photographic equipment

Fotograf m [fotograhf]
photographer

fotografieren [foto-grafeeren] to
photograph

Fotografin f [fotograhfin]

photographer

Fr. (Frau) Mrs; Ms

Frage f [frahg-uh] question

fragen [frahgen] to ask

Frankreich n [frank-rysh]
France

Franzose m [frantsohz-uh]
Frenchman

Französin f [frantsurzin] French
girl; French woman

französisch [frantsurzish]
French

Frau f [frow] woman; wife;
Mrs; Ms

Frauenarzt m [frowen-artst]
gynaecologist

Fräulein n [froyline] Miss

frech [fresh] cheeky

frei [fry] free, vacant

frei von Konservierungsstoffen
contains no preservatives

**frei von künstlichen
Aromastoffen** contains no
artificial flavouring

Freibad n [frybaht] outdoor
swimming pool

freigegeben ab ... Jahren
suitable for those over ...
years of age

Freikörperkultur f [fry-kurper-kooltoor] nudism

Freitag m [frytahk] Friday

freiwillig [fry-villish] voluntary;
voluntarily

Freizeichen n [fry-tsyshen]
ringing tone

Freizeit f [fry-tsite] spare time;
leisure

Freizeitzentrum n [fry-tsitetsentroom] leisure centre

fremd [fremt] strange; foreign

Fremde m/f [fremd-uh] stranger; foreigner

Fremdenzimmer npl [fremden-tsimmer] room(s) to let/rent

freuen: sich freuen [zish froyen] to be happy

Freund m [froynt] friend; boyfriend

Freundin f [froyndin] friend; girlfriend

freundlich [froyntlish] kind; friendly

freut mich! [froyt mish] pleased to meet you!

Frieden m [freeden] peace

Friedhof m [freet-hohf] cemetery

frisch [frish] fresh

frisch gestrichen wet paint

Frischhaltepackung f airtight pack

Friseur m [frizzur] barber; hairdresser

Frisur f [frizzoor] hairstyle

Frittenbude f [fritten-bood-uh] chip shop

Frl. (Fräulein) Miss

froh glad

frohes neues Jahr [froh-ess noy-ess yahr] happy New Year!

frohe Weihnachten! [froh-uh vynaKHten] happy Christmas!

Frostschaden m [frost-shahden] frost damage

Frostschutzmittel n [frost-shoots-mittel] antifreeze

früh [froo] early

Frühling m [frooling] spring

Frühstück n [frooshtoock] breakfast

frühstücken [frooshtoocken] to have breakfast

fühlen: (sich) fühlen [(zish) foolen] to feel

fuhr [foor], **fuhren** drove; went; travelled

führen [fooren] to lead

wir führen ... we stock ...

Führer m [foorer] guide; guidebook

Führerin f [foorerin] guide

Führerschein m [foorer-shine] driving licence

fuhrst [foorst] drove; went

Führung f [fooroong] guided tour

füllen [foollen] to fill

Fundbüro n [foont-booro] lost property office

fünf [foonf] five

fünfzehn [foonf-tsayn] fifteen

fünfzig [foonf-tsish] fifty

Fünfzigmarkschein m [foonftsish-mark-shine] fifty-mark note/bill

Funktaxi n [foonk-taksee] radio taxi

funktionieren [foonkts-yohneeren] to work

für [foor] for

Furcht f [foorsht] fear

furchtbar [foorshtbar] terrible

fürchten: sich fürchten [zish foorshten] to be afraid

fürs [foorss] for the

Fuß m [fooss] foot
  zu Fuß on foot
Fußball m [foossbal] football
Fußballplatz m [foossbal-plats]
  football ground
Fußballstadion n [foossbal-
  shtahdee-on] football stadium
Fußgänger m [fooss-geng-er],
  Fußgängerin f pedestrian
Fußgänger bitte andere
  Straßenseite benutzen
  pedestrians please use other
  side of road
Fußgängerüberweg m
  [foossgeng-er-oobervayk]
  pedestrian crossing
Fußgängerzone f [foossgeng-er-
  tsohn-uh] pedestrian precinct

G

gab [gahp] gave
Gabel f [gahbel] fork; hook
gaben [gahben], **gabst** [gahpst]
  gave
gähnen [gaynen] to yawn
Gang m corridor; gear; walk;
  course
ganz [gants] whole; quite;
  very
  den ganzen Tag all day
  ganz gut [goot] pretty good
Garderobe f [garderohb-uh]
  cloakroom
  für Garderobe wird nicht
  gehaftet the management
  accepts no liability for items
  left here

Garten m garden
Gaspedal n [gahss-pedahl]
  accelerator
Gast m guest
Gastarbeiter m [gast-arbyter],
  Gastarbeiterin f foreign
  worker
Gästebuch n [gest-uh-bookh]
  visitors' register
Gastfreundschaft f [gastfroynt-
  shafft] hospitality
Gastgeber m [gast-gayber] host
Gastgeberin f [gast-gayberin]
  hostess
Gasthaus n [gast-howss] inn
Gasthof m [gast-hohf]
  restaurant, inn
Gaststätte f [gast-shtett-uh]
  restaurant; pub; inn
Gastwirtschaft f [gast-veert-
  shafft] pub
geb. (geboren) born, née
Gebäude n [geboyd-uh]
  building
geben [gayben] to give
Gebiß n [gebiss] dentures
geblieben [gebleeben] stayed
geboren: geboren sein
  [gebohren zine] to be born
gebracht [gebrakht] brought
Gebrauch m [gebrowkh] use;
  custom
  vor Gebrauch schütteln shake
  before using
gebrauchen [gebrowkhen] to
  use
Gebrauchsanleitung
  instructions for use
Gebrauchsanweisung

beachten follow instructions for use

gebraucht [gebrowKHt] second-hand

gebrochen [gebroKHen] broken

gebt [gaypt] give

Gebühren fpl [gebʊren] charges

gebührenpflichtig liable to charge

Geburt f [geboort] birth

Geburtsort m [geboorts-ort] place of birth

Geburtstag m [geboorts-tahk] birthday

Gedächtnis n [gedeshtnis] memory

Gedanke m [gedank-uh] thought

Gefahr f [gefahr] danger

gefahren travelled; gone; driven

gefährlich [gefairlish] dangerous

Gefährliche Einmündung dangerous junction; danger: concealed exit

Gefährliche Kurve dangerous bend

gefallen: das gefällt mir [dass gefellt meer] I like it

Gefangene m/f [gefangen-uh] prisoner

Gefängnis n [gefengniss] prison

Gefriertruhe f [gefreer-troo-uh] freezer

gefroren [gefrohren] frozen

Gefühl n [gefool] feeling

gefunden [gefoonden] found

gegangen [gegang-en] gone

gegeben [gegayben] given

gegen [gaygen] against

Gegenanzeige contra-indications

Gegend f [gaygent] area

Gegenstand m [gaygenshtant] object

Gegenteil n [gaygen-tile] opposite

gegenüber [gaygen-ʊber] opposite

Gegenverkehr hat Vorfahrt oncoming traffic has right of way

gegessen eaten

Gegner m [gaykner], **Gegnerin f** opponent

gehabt [gehapt] had

geheim [gehime] secret

Geheimnis n [gehymnis] secret

Geheimzahl eingeben enter personal number

gehen [gay-en] to go; to walk

geht das? is that OK?

das geht nicht that's not on

Gehirn n [geheern] brain

Gehirnerschütterung f [geheern-airshʊtteroong] concussion

Gehör n [gehur] hearing

gehören [ge-hur-ren] to belong (to)

Geisel f [gyzel] hostage

Geistlicher m [gystlisher] priest

gekommen come

gekonnt been able to; masterly

gekühlt haltbar bis ... if chilled

will keep until ...

gelassen relaxed; left

gelb [gelp] yellow

Gelbe Seiten [gelb-uh zyten] yellow pages

Geld n [gelt] money

Geldautomat m [gelt-owtomaht] cash dispenser, automatic teller

Geld einwerfen insert money

Geldeinwurf insert money

Geldrückgabe returned coins

Geldschein m [geltshine] banknote, (US) bill

Geldstrafe f [geltshtrahf-uh] fine

Geldwechsel m [geltveksel] bureau de change

Gelegenheitskauf m [gelaygen-hites-kowf] bargain

Gelenk n [gelenk] joint

Gemälde n [gemayld-uh] painting

gemocht [gemoкнt] liked

Gemüsehändler m [gem@z-uh-hentler] greengrocer

gemußt [gemoosst] had to

genau [genow] exact; exactly

Genf [genf] Geneva

genommen taken

genug [gen00k] enough

genug haben (von) to be fed up (with)

geöffnet [guh-urfnet] open; opened

geöffnet von ... bis ... open from ... to ...

Gepäck n [gepeck] luggage, baggage

Gepäckaufbewahrung f

[gepeck-owf-bevahroong] left luggage, (US) baggage check

Gepäckausgabe f [gepeck-owssgahb-uh] baggage claim

Gepäckkontrolle f [gepeck-kontrol-uh] baggage check

Gepäckschließfach n [gepeck-shleessfaкн] luggage locker

Gepäckträger m [gepeck-trayger] porter

gepflegt [gepflaykt] well looked after; refined

gerade [gerahd-uh] just; straight

geradeaus [gerahd-uh-owss] straight on

Gerät n [gerayt] device

gerecht [geresht] fair

Gericht n [gerisht] court; dish

gern(e) [gairn(uh)] gladly

etwas gern(e) tun to like doing something

Geruch m [ger00кн] smell

Gesamtpreis m [gezamt-price] total

Geschäft n [gesheft] shop; business

Geschäftsfrau f [gesheftsfrow] businesswoman

Geschäftsführer m [geshefts-f00rer] manager

Geschäftsführerin f [geshefts-f00rerin] manageress

Geschäftsmann m [gesheftsmann] businessman

Geschäftsreise f [geshefts-rize-uh] business trip

Geschäftszeiten hours of business

geschehen [gesh**ay**-en] to happen

Geschenk n [gesh**e**nk] present, gift

Geschenkartikel gifts

Geschichte f [gesh**i**sht-uh] story; history

geschieden [gesh**ee**den] divorced

Geschirr n [gesh**ee**rr] crockery

Geschirrtuch n [gesh**ee**rr-tOOKH] tea towel

Geschlecht n [gesh**le**sht] sex

Geschlechtskrankheit f [gesh**le**shts-krank-hite] VD

geschlossen closed

geschlossen von ... bis ... closed from ... to ...

Geschmack m [gesh**ma**ck] taste; flavour

geschrieben [gesh**ree**ben] written

Geschwindigkeit f [gesh**vi**ndish-kite] speed

Geschwindigkeitsbeschränkung f [gesh**vi**ndish-kites-beshr**e**nkoong] speed limit

Geschwindigkeitsbeschränkung beachten observe speed limit

geschwollen [gesh**vo**llen] swollen

gesehen [gez**ay**-en] seen

Gesellschaft f [gez**e**llshafft] society; company

Gesetz n [gez**e**ts] law

Gesicht n [gez**i**sht] face

Gesichtscreme f [gez**i**shts-kraym] face cream

gesperrt closed; no entry

Gesperrt für Fahrzeuge aller Art closed to all vehicles

Gespräch n [gesh**pray**sh] call; conversation

Gestalt f [gesh**ta**lt] figure

gestattet [gesh**ta**ttet] allowed

gestern [g**e**stern] yesterday

gestorben [gesh**to**rben] died

gesund [gez**oo**nt] healthy

Gesundheit f [gez**oo**nt-hite] health

Gesundheit! bless you!

getan [get**ah**n] done

Getränkekarte f [getr**e**nk-uh-kart-uh] drinks list

getrennt [getr**e**nnt] separate; separately

Getriebe n [getr**ee**b-uh] gearbox

getrunken [getr**oo**nken] drunk

Gewehr n [gev**ai**r] gun

gewesen [gev**ay**zen] been

Gewicht n [gev**i**sht] weight

Gewichtsverlust durch Erhitzen weight loss through heating

Gewinn m [gev**i**nn] prize; profit

gewinnen [gev**i**nnen] to win

Gewitter n [gev**i**tter] thunderstorm

Gewohnheit f [gev**o**hnhite] habit

gewöhnlich [gev**ur**nlish] usual; usually

geworden [gev**o**rden] become

gewünschten Betrag wählen select required amount

gewünschte Rufnummer wählen dial number required

gewußt [gev**oo**sst] known

Gezeiten [getsyten] tides
gibst [geepst] give
gibt [geept] gives
 gibt es ...? is/are there ...?
 es gibt ... there is/are ...
Gift n poison
giftig [giftish] poisonous
ging, gingen [ging-en], gingst went
Gips m plaster (of Paris)
Gipsverband m [gips-fairbant] plastercast
Girokonto n [Jeero-konto] current account
Giroverkehr m [Jeero-fairkair] giro transactions
Gitarre f [gitarr-uh] guitar
Glas n [glahss] glass
glatt slippery; smooth
Glatteis n [glatt-ice] black ice
Glatteisgefahr black ice
Glatze f [glats-uh] bald head
glauben [glowben] to believe
gleich [glysh] equal; same; in a moment
Gleis n [glice] platform, (US) track
 zu den Gleisen to the platforms/tracks
Glocke f [glock-uh] bell
Glück n [glOOck] luck; happiness
 zum Glück [tsoom] fortunately
glücklich [glOOcklish] lucky; happy
Glücksbringer m [glOOcks-bring-er] lucky charm
Glühbirne f [glOObeern-uh] light

bulb
GmbH (Gesellschaft mit beschränkter Haftung) [gay-em-bay-hah] Ltd, limited company
Gott n God
Gottesdienst m [gottes-deenst] church service; mass
Grab n [grahp] grave
Grammatik f grammar
Gras n [grahss] grass
gratis [grahtiss] free
grau [grow] grey
grausam [growzahm] cruel
Grenze f [grents-uh] border
Grenzkontrolle f [grents-kontroll-uh] border checkpoint
Griechenland n [greeshenlant] Greece
griechisch [greeshish] Greek
Griff m handle
grinsen [grinzen] to grin
Grippe f [gripp-uh] flu
Groschen m [groshen] 10 pfennig piece
groß [grohss] big, large; tall
Großbritannien n [grohss-britannee-en] Great Britain
Größe f [grurss-uh] size
Großmutter f [grohss-mootter] grandmother
Großpackung f [grohss-packoong] large size
Großvater m [grohss-fahter] grandfather
grün [grOOn] green
 der grüne Punkt suitable for recycling
Grund m [groont] cause

Grundierungscreme f
[groond**ee**roongs-kraym]
foundation cream

Grundschule f [gr**oo**nt-shool-uh]
primary school

Gruppe f [gr**oo**pp-uh] group;
party

Gruppenreise f [gr**oo**ppen-rize-
uh] group excursion

Gruß m [gr**oo**ss] greeting
schöne Grüße an ... [sh**u**rn-uh
gr**oo**ss-uh] give my regards
to ...

grüßen [gr**oo**ssen] to greet; to
say hello to

grüß Gott [gr**oo**ss] hello (South
German)

gültig [g**oo**ltish] valid

Gummi n [g**oo**mmee] rubber

Gummiband n [g**oo**mmeebant]
rubber band

günstig [g**oo**nstish] favourable;
convenient; inexpensive

Gürtel m [g**oo**rtel] belt

gut [g**oo**t] good; well

gutaussehend [g**oo**t-owss-zay-
ent] handsome; good-
looking

gute Besserung! [g**oo**t-uh
besseroong] get well soon!

guten Abend [g**oo**ten **ah**bent]
good evening

gute Nacht [g**oo**t-uh naкнt]
good night

guten Appetit! [g**oo**ten appeteet]
enjoy your meal!

guten Morgen [g**oo**ten] good
morning

guten Tag [g**oo**ten tahk] hello

guten Tag, freut mich [g**oo**ten
tahk froyt mish] how do you
do, nice to meet you

gute Reise [g**oo**t-uh rize-uh]
have a good trip

Güterzug m [g**oo**ter-tsook] goods
train

gutmütig [g**oo**tmootish] good-
natured

Gutschein m [g**oo**t-shine]
voucher

Gymnasium n [g**oo**m-n**ah**zee-
oom] secondary school

H

H (Haltestelle) bus/tram stop

Haar n [hahr] hair

Haarfestiger m [h**ah**rfestiger]
conditioner

Haarschnitt m [h**ah**rshnitt]
haircut

Haarstudio n [hahr-sht**oo**dee-oh]
hairdressing studio

haben [h**ah**ben] to have

Hafen m [h**ah**fen] harbour, port

Hafenpolizei f [h**ah**fen-polits-ī]
harbour police

Hafenrundfahrt f [h**ah**fen-
roontfahrt] boat trip round the
harbour

Haft f custody

Häftling m [h**e**ftling] prisoner

Hagel m [h**ah**gel] hail

Haken m [h**ah**ken] hook

halb [halp] half

halbe Stunde f [halb-uh sht**oo**nd-
uh] half an hour

Halbpension f [halp-pangz-**yohn**] half board

Hälfte f [**helf**t-uh] half

Hallenbad n [**hallen**baht] indoor swimming pool

Hals n [halss] neck

Halskette f [**halss**kett-uh] necklace

Hals-Nasen-Ohren-Arzt m [halss-**nah**zen-**ohr**en-artst] ear, nose and throat specialist

Halsschmerzen [halss-**shmair**tsen] sore throat

Halstabletten fpl [halss-**tabletten**] throat pastilles

halt! [hallt] stop!

Haltbar bis ... best before ...

Haltbarkeitsdatum best before date

Halte deine Stadt sauber keep your city clean

halten to hold; to stop

Haltestelle f [**hallt**-uh-shtell-uh] stop

Halteverbot no stopping; no waiting

hält nicht in ... does not stop in ...

Handarbeit f [**hant**-arbite] needlework

Handbremse f [**hant**bremz-uh] handbrake

Handel m deal; commerce

Handelsgesellschaft f (trading) company

Handelsbank f merchant bank

Handgelenk n [**hant**-gelenk] wrist

Handgepäck n [**hant**-gepeck] hand luggage/baggage

Handlung f [**hant**loong] shop; action

Handschuhe mpl [**hant**-shoo-uh] gloves

Handtasche f [**hant**-tash-uh] handbag, (US) purse

Handtuch n [**hant**-tooKH] towel

Handwerk n [**hant**vairk] crafts

Handzettel m [**hant**-tsettel] leaflet

Hansaplast® n [**hanza**plast] Elastoplast®, (US) Band-Aid

hart hard

Hase m [**hah**z-uh] hare; rabbit

Haß m [hass] hatred

hassen to hate

häßlich [**hess**lish] ugly

hast have

hat has

hatte [**hatt**-uh] had

hätte [**hett**-uh] would have; had

hatten, hattest had

Haupt- [howpt] main

Hauptbahnhof m [**howpt**-bahnhohf] central station

Hauptpost f [**howpt**-posst] main post office

Hauptprogramm n [**howpt**-programm] main feature

Hauptsaison f [**howpt**-zaysong] high season

Hauptstraße f [**howpt**-shtrahss-uh] main road; high street

Haus n [howss] house

zu Hause [tsoo **howz**-uh] at home

nach Hause gehen [naKH –

gay-en] to go home

Haushaltsgeräte npl [howss-hallts-gerayt-uh] household equipment

Haushaltwaren [howss-hallt-vahren] household goods

Hausmeister m [howss-myster] caretaker, janitor

Hausnummer f [howss-noommer] street number

Hausordnung f [howss-ortnoong] house rules

Hausschuhe [howss-shoo-uh] slippers

Haustier n [howsteer] pet

Hauswirt m [howssveert] landlord

Hauswirtin f [howss-veertin] landlady

Haut f [howt] skin

Hautreiniger m [howt-ryniger] skin cleanser

Hbf (Hauptbahnhof) central station

Heft n exercise book

Heftzwecke f [heft-tsveck-uh] drawing pin

Heißlufttrockner m [hice-looft-trockner] hot-air hand-drier

heilen [hylen] to cure

Heiligabend m [hylish-ahbent] Christmas Eve

Heimwerkerbedarf DIY supplies

Heirat f [hyraht] marriage

heiraten [hyrahten] to get married

heiß [hice] hot

heißen [hyssen] to be called

wie heißen Sie? [vee] what's your name?

Heißwachs m [hice-vaks] hot wax

Heizdecke f [hites-deck-uh] electric blanket

Heizgerät n [hites-gerayt] heater

Heizung f [hytsoong] heating

helfen to help

hell light; bright

Hemd n [hemt] shirt

herabgesetzt reduced

zu stark herabgesetzten Preisen prices slashed

Herbergsmutter f [hairbairks-mootter] warden

Herbergsvater m [hairbairks-fahter] warden

Herbst m [hairpst] autumn, (US) fall

herein! [hair-ine] come in!

hergestellt in ... made in ...

Herr m [hair] Mr; gentleman

Herren gents' (toilet), men's room

Herrenkleidung f [hairen-klydoong] menswear

Herrenmoden men's fashions

Herrensalon m [hairen-zalong] men's hairdresser

Herrentoilette f [hairen-twalett-uh] gents' (toilet), men's room

herrlich [hairlish] lovely

Hersteller m manufacturer

Herz n [hairts] heart

Herzinfarkt m [hairts-infarkt] heart attack

herzlich willkommen [hairtslish

villkommen] welcome
herzlichen Glückwunsch!
[**hair**tslishen gl**oo**ckvoonsh]
congratulations!; happy
birthday!; happy anniversary!
Heufieber n [**hoy**feeber] hay
fever
heute [**hoy**t-uh] today
heute abend [**ah**bent] tonight
heute geschlossen closed
today
hier [heer] here
hier abreißen tear off here
hier abschneiden cut off here
hier einreißen tear off here
hier einsteigen enter here
hierher [**heer**hair] here
hierhin here
hier öffnen open here
hier Parkschein lösen buy
parking permit here
Hilfe f [**hilf**-uh] help
Himmel m sky; heaven
hinlegen: sich hinlegen [zish
hinlaygen] to lie down
hinsichtlich [**hin**zishtlish] with
regard to
hinten at the back
hinter behind
Hintergrund m [**hin**tergroont]
background
Hinterhof m [**hin**terhohf] back
yard
Hintern m bottom
Hinterrad n [**hin**ter-raht] back
wheel
Hirsch m [heersh] stag
Hitzewelle f [**hits**-uh-vell-uh]
heat wave

hoch [hohKH] high
Hochschule f [**hoh**KH-shOOl-uh]
college; university
höchste [**hurk**st-uh] highest
Höchstgeschwindigkeit
maximum speed
Hochzeit f [**ho**KH-tsite] wedding
Hochzeitstag m [**ho**KH-tsites-
tahk] wedding anniversary
hoffen to hope
hoffentlich [**hoff**entlish]
hopefully
Hoffnung f [**hoff**noong] hope
höflich [**hur**flish] polite
Höhe f [**hur**-uh] height
höher [**hur**-er] higher
höhere Schule f [**hur**er-uh shOOl-
uh] secondary school
Höhle f [**hurl**-uh] cave
holen [**hoh**len] to fetch, to get
holländisch [**holl**endish] Dutch
Holz n [holts] wood
hören [**hur**-ren] to hear
Hörer m [**hur**-rer] receiver;
listener
Hörer abnehmen lift receiver
Hörer einhängen replace
receiver
Hörerin f [**hur**-rerin] listener
Hörgerät n [**hur**-gerayt] hearing
aid
Höschen n [**hur**ss-shen] panties
Hose f [**hoh**z-uh] trousers, (US)
pants
Hr. (Herr) Mr
hübsch [h**oo**psh] pretty
Hubschrauber m [**hoo**p-
shrowber] helicopter
Hüfte f [h**oo**ft-uh] hip

Hügel m [hoogel] hill
Hund m [hoont] dog
Hunde bitte anleinen dogs
  must be kept on a lead
hundert [hoondert] hundred
Hundertmarkschein m
  [hoondert-mark-shine] hundred-
  mark note/bill
Hunde sind an der Leine zu
  führen dogs must be kept on
  a lead
Hunger: Hunger haben [hoong-
  er hahben] to be hungry
Hupe f [hoop-uh] horn
Hupen verboten sounding
  horn forbidden
Husten m [hoosten] cough
Hut f [hoot] hat
Hypothek f [hoopotayk]
  mortgage

I

i.A. (im Auftrag) pp
ich [ish] I; me
Idee f [eeday] idea
i.d.T. (in der Trockenmasse)
  dry measure
ihm [eem] him; to him
ihn [een] him
ihnen them; to them
Ihnen [eenen] you; to you
ihr [eer] you; her; to her; their
Ihr [eer] your
ihre [eer-uh] her; their
Ihre [eer-uh] your
Illustrierte f [illoostreert-uh]
  magazine

im in (the)
immer always
Immobilienmakler m [immobeel-
  yen-mahkler] estate agent
Impfung f [impfoong]
  vaccination
indem [indaym] as; by
Industriegebiet n [indoostree-
  gebeet] industrial zone
infolge [in-folg-uh] as a result of
Infopostsendung f [info-posst-
  zendoong] printed matter
Informationsschalter m
  [informats-yohns-shalter]
  information desk
Inh. (Inhaber) proprietor
Inhalt contents
Initialen fpl [inits-yahlen] initials
Inland domestic
Inlandsflüge domestic flights
Inlandsgespräch n [inlants-
  gespraysh] inland call
Inlandsporto n [inlants-porto]
  inland postage
innen (im/in) inside
innerhalb [inner-halp] within
ins into the; to the
Insektenschutzmittel n
  [inzekten-shoots-mittel] insect
  repellent
Insel f [inzel] island
insgesamt altogether
Installateur m [inshtalatur]
  plumber
Intensivstation f [intenzeef-
  shtats-yohn] intensive care
  unit
interessant interesting
Interesse n [interess-uh] interest

Hu

irgend etwas [**eer**gent **et**vass] something; anything

irgend jemand [**eer**gent **yay**mant] somebody; anybody

irgendwo [**eer**gent-vo] somewhere

irisch [**eer**ish] Irish

ißt [isst] eat; eats

ist is

Italien n [i**tah**lee-en] Italy

italienisch [ital-**yay**nish] Italian

J

ja [yah] yes

Jacht f [ya**KH**t] yacht

Jachthafen m [ya**KH**t-hahfen] marina

Jacke f [**yack**-uh] jacket; cardigan

Jahr n [yahr] year

Jahreszeit f [**yah**ress-tsite] season

Jahrhundert n [yahr-**hoo**ndert] century

Jahrmarkt m [**yah**rmarkt] fair

Jalousie f [Jal**oo**zee] Venetian blind

Jausenstation f [**yow**zen-shtats-yohn] snack bar

je [yay] ever

jede [**yay**d-uh] each; every

jeden Tag [**yay**den tahk] every day

jeder [**yay**der] everyone; each

jedes [**yay**dess] each

jedesmal [**yay**dessmahl] every time

je ... desto ... [yay **des**to] the ... the ...

jemals [**yay**mahlss] ever

jemand [**yay**mant] somebody

jenseits [**yayn**-zites] on the other side (of); beyond

jetzt [yetst] now

JH (Jugendherberge) youth hostel

joggen: joggen gehen [dJoggen **gay**-en] to go jogging

Jucken n [**yoo**cken] itch

jüdisch [**yoo**dish] Jewish

Jugendherberge f [**yoo**gent-hairbairg-uh] youth hostel

Jugendklub m [**yoo**gent-kloop] youth club

Jugendliche: für Jugendliche ab ... Jahren for young people over the age of ...

Juli m [**yoo**lee] July

jung [yoong] young

Junge m [**yoo**ng-uh] boy

junge Leute [**yoo**ng-uh **loyt**-uh] young people

Junge Mode fashions for the young

Junggeselle m [**yoo**ng-gezell-uh] bachelor

Juni m [**yoo**nee] June

Juwel m [**yoo**vayl] jewel

Juwelier m [**yoov**-uh-**leer**] jeweller's

K

Kabel n [**kah**bel] cable

Kabine f [ka**been**-uh] cabin

Kaffeefilter m [kaffay-filter] coffee filter

Kaffeehaus n [kaffay-howss] café

kahl bald

Kai m [kī] quay

Kalender m calendar; diary

kalt cold

kam [kahm], **kamen** came

Kamin m [kameen] chimney; fireplace

Kamm m comb

Kampf m fight

kämpfen [kempfen] to fight

kamst [kahmst] came

Kanadier m [kanahdee-er], **Kanadierin** f Canadian

kanadisch [kanahdish] Canadian

Kanal m [kanahl] canal; Channel

Kaninchen n [kaneenshen] rabbit

kann can

Kännchen n [kennshen] pot

Kanne f [kann-uh] (tea/coffee) pot

kannst can

Kanu n [kahnoo] canoe

Kapitän m [kapitayn] captain

Kappe f [kapp-uh] cap

kaputt [kapoott] broken

Karfreitag m [karfrytahk] Good Friday

Karneval m [karn-uh-val] annual carnival held in the pre-Lent period with fancy-dress processions and general celebrating

Karte f [kart-uh] card; ticket

Karten tickets

Kartenleser m [karten-layzer] card reader

Kartenspiel n [kartenshpeel] card game

Kartentelefon n [karten-telefohn] cardphone

Kasse f [kass-uh] cashdesk, till, cashier; box office

Katalysator m [kataloozahtohr] catalytic converter

Kater m [kahter] hangover; tomcat

kath. (katholisch) Catholic

Katze f [kats-uh] cat

kaufen [kowfen] to buy

Kaufhaus n [kowfhowss] department store

kaum [kowm] hardly

Kaution f [kowts-yohn] deposit

Kehle f [kayl-uh] throat

Keilriemen m [kile-reemen] fan belt

kein(e) ... [kine(-uh)] no ...; not ...

keine Ahnung [kine-uh ahnoong] no idea

ich habe keine [ish hahb-uh kine-uh] I don't have any

keine ... mehr [kine-uh mair] no more ...

kein ... mehr [kine mair] no more ...

kein Ausstieg no exit

keine heiße Asche einfüllen do not put hot ashes in this container

kein Einstieg no entry

keine Selbstbedienung no self-service

keine Zufahrt no entry

kein Trinkwasser not drinking water

kein Verkauf an Jugendliche unter ... Jahren sales forbidden to minors under the age of ...

kein Zugang no entry

kein Zutritt no admittance; no entrance

kein Zutritt fur Jugendliche unter ... Jahren no admission to minors under the age of ...

Keller m cellar

Kellner m waiter

Kellnerin f waitress

kennen to know

Keramik f [kairahmik] china

Kerze f [kairts-uh] candle

Kette f [kett-uh] chain

Keuchhusten m [koysh-hoosten] whooping cough

Kiefer m [keefer] jaw; pine

Kind n [kint] child

Kinder npl children

für Kinder ab ... Jahren for children from the age of ...

Kinderarzt m [kinder-artst], **Kinderärztin f** pediatrician

Kinderbett n cot

Kinderkleidung f [kinder-klydoong] children's clothing

Kindermoden children's fashions

Kindersitz m [kinder-zits] child seat

Kinderspielplatz m [kinder-shpeelplats] children's playground

Kindervorstellung f [kinder-forshtelloong] children's performance

Kinderwagen m [kindervahgen] pram

Kinn n chin

Kino n [keeno] cinema, movie theater

Kinocenter n [keeno-senter] multiplex cinema/movie theater

Kirche f [keersh-uh] church

Klang m sound

klar clear; OK, sure

Klasse f [klass-uh] class

klebrig [klaybrish] sticky

Kleid n [klite] dress

Kleider [klyder] clothes

Kleiderbügel m [klyder-boogel] (coat)hanger

klein [kline] small

Kleinbus m [kline-booss] van

Kleingeld n [kline-gelt] change

Klempner m plumber

Klima n [kleemah] climate

Klimaanlage f [kleemah-anlahg-uh] air-conditioning

klimatisiert [klimateezeert] air-conditioned

Klingel f bell

klingeln to ring

Klippe f [klipp-uh] cliff

Klo n loo

Kloster n [klohster] convent; monastery

klug [klook] clever

KI

Kneipe f [k-nipe-uh] pub, bar
Knie n [k-nee] knee
Knöchel m [k-nurshel] ankle
Knochen m [k-noKHen] bone
Knopf m [k-nopf] button
Knoten m [k-nohten] knot
Koch m [koKH] cook
Kochgeschirr n [koKH-gesheerr] cooking utensils
Köchin f [kurshin] cook
Kochnische f [koKHneesh-uh] kitchenette
Kochtopf m [koKHtopf] saucepan
Koffer m [koffer] bag; suitcase
Kofferkuli m [kofferkoolee] luggage/baggage trolley
Kofferraum m [koffer-rowm] boot, (US) trunk
Kohle f [kohl-uh] coal
Kollege m [kollayg-uh], **Kollegin** f colleague
Köln [kurln] Cologne
Kölnisch Wasser [kurlnish vasser] eau de Cologne
komisch [kohmish] funny
kommen to come
  das kommt darauf an [dahrowf] it depends
Komödie f [komurdee-uh] comedy
kompliziert [komplitseert] complicated
Konditorei f [kondeetor-ī] cake shop
Kondom n [kondohm] condom
König m [kurnish] king
Königin f [kurnigin] queen
Konkurrenz f [konkoorents] competition

können [kurnen] to be able to; can
können Sie ...? [zee] can you ...?
könnte [kurnt-uh], **könnten**, **könntest** could
konnte [konnt-uh], **konnten**, **konntest** could
Konservierungsstoffe preservatives
Konsulat n [konzoolaht] consulate
Kontaktlinsen fpl [kontakt-linzen] contact lenses
Konto n account
Kontrolle f [kontrol-uh] control
kontrollieren [kontrolleeren] to control
Konzert n [kontsairt] concert
Kopf m head
Kopfkissen n pillow
Kopfschmerzmittel n [kopfshmairts-mittel] aspirin
Kopfstütze f [kopf-shtœts-uh] headrest
Kopftuch n [kopftooKH] scarf
Kopfweh n [kopf-vay] headache
Kopie f [kopee] copy
kopieren [kopeeren] to copy
Korb m [korp] basket
Korkenzieher m [korken-tsee-er] corkscrew
Körper m [kurper] body
Körperpuder m [kurper-pooder] talcum powder
Kosmetika npl [kosmaytikah] cosmetics
kostbar [kost-bar] precious

kosten to cost

kostenlos [**ko**sten-lohss] free of charge

köstlich [**kur**stlish] delicious

Kostüm n [kost**oo**m] ladies' suit

Kragen m [**krah**gen] collar

Krampf m cramp

krank ill, sick

Kranke m/f [**krank**-uh] sick person

Krankenhaus n [**kra**nken-howss] hospital

Krankenkasse f [**kra**nkenkass-uh] medical insurance

Krankenpfleger m [**kra**nken-pflayger] male nurse

Krankenschein m [**kra**nken-shine] health insurance certificate

Krankenschein nicht vergessen don't forget your health insurance certificate

Krankenschwester f [**kra**nken-shvester] nurse

Krankenwagen m [**kra**nkenvahgen] ambulance

Krankheit f [**krank**-hite] disease

Krawatte f [krav**att**-uh] tie, necktie

Krebs m [**krayps**] cancer

Kreditabteilung accounts department

Kredite [kray**deet**-uh] loans

Kreditkarte f [kray**deet**kart-uh] credit card

Kreis m [**krice**] circle

Kreisverkehr m [**krice**-fairkair] roundabout

Kreuz n [**kroyts**] cross

Kreuzfahrt f [**kroy**tsfahrt] cruise

Kreuzung f [**kroy**tsoong] junction; crossroads, intersection

Kreuzworträtsel n [**kroy**tsvort-raytsel] crossword puzzle

Kriechspur crawler lane

Krieg m [**kreek**] war

kriegen [**kree**egen] to get

Krücken fpl [kr**oo**cken] crutches

Krug m [kr**oo**k] jug

Küche f [k**oo**sh-uh] cooking, cuisine; kitchen

Küchenbedarf for the kitchen

Kugel f [k**oo**gel] ball

Kugelschreiber m [k**oo**gelshryber] biro®

Kuh f [k**oo**] cow

kühl [k**oo**l] cool

Kühler m [k**oo**ler] radiator (on car)

kühl lagern keep in a cool place

Kühlschrank m [k**oo**l-shrank] fridge

kühl servieren serve chilled

Kultur f [koolt**oo**r] culture

Kulturbeutel m [koolt**oo**r-boytel] toilet bag

Kumpel m [k**oo**mpel] pal

Kunde m [k**oo**nd-uh], **Kundin** f customer

Der Kunde ist König the customer is always right

Kundenparkplatz customer car park/parking lot

Kunst f [k**oo**nst] art

Kunstgalerie f [k**oo**nst-galer**ee**] art gallery

Kunsthalle f [koonst-hal-uh] art gallery
Künstler m [koonstler], **Künstlerin** f artist
künstlich [koonstlish] artificial
Kupplung f [kooploong] clutch
Kurbelwelle f [koorbel-vell-uh] crankshaft
Kurort m [koor-ort] spa
Kurs m [koorss] rate; exchange rate; course
Kurswagen m [koors-vahgen] through coach
Kurve f [koorv-uh] bend
Kurvenreiche Strecke bends
kurz [koorts] short
  kurz nach [naкн] just after
  kurz vor [for] just before
kurzsichtig [koorts-zishtish] shortsighted
Kurzstrecke f [koorts-shtreck-uh] short journey
Kurzwaren fpl [koortsvahren] haberdashery
Kusine f [koozeen-uh] cousin
Kuß m [kooss] kiss
küssen [koossen] to kiss
Küste f [koost-uh] coast
Küstenwacht f [koosten-vaкнt] coastguard

L

l (Liter) litre
Labor n [labohr] laboratory
lächeln [lesheln] to smile
Lächeln n smile
lachen [laкнen] to laugh

lächerlich [lesherlish] ridiculous
Laden m [lahden] shop
Ladenstraße f [lahdenshtrahss-uh] shopping street
Laken n [lahken] sheet
Lampe f [lamp-uh] lamp
Land n [lant] country
landen to land
Länder npl [lender] administrative districts of Germany, each with its own parliament
Landeskennzahl f [landess-kenntsahl] country dialling code
Landkarte f [lantkart-uh] map
Landschaft f [lantshafft] countryside; landscape; scenery
Landstraße f [lant-shtrahss-uh] country road
Landtag m [lant-tahk] regional parliament
Land- und forstwirtschaftlicher Verkehr frei agricultural and forestry vehicles only
lang long
lange [lang-uh] for a long time
Länge f [leng-uh] length
langsam [langzahm] slow; slowly
Langsam fahren drive slowly
langweilig [langvile-ish] boring
Lärm m [lairm] noise
lassen to let; to leave
lässig [lessish] relaxed
Laster m lorry, truck

Lastwagen m [lasst-vahgen] lorry, truck

Latzhose f [lats-hohz-uh] dungarees

laufen [lowfen] to run

Läufer m [loyfer] runner; rug

laut [lowt] loud; noisy

lauwarm [low-varm] lukewarm

Lawine f [laveen-uh] avalanche

Lawinengefahr danger of avalanches

Leben n [layben] life

leben to live

lebendig [lebendish] alive

Lebensgefahr f [laybens-gefahr] danger

Lebenshaltungskosten pl [laybens-haltoongs-kosten] cost of living

Lebenslauf m [laybens-lowf] CV, résumé

Lebensmittel npl [laybens-mittel] groceries

Lebensmittelhandlung f [laybensmittel-hantloong] grocer's

Lebensmittelvergiftung f [laybensmittel-fairgiftoong] food poisoning

Leber f [layber] liver

Leck n leak

lecker tasty

Leder n [layder] leather

Lederwaren leather goods

ledig [laydish] single

leer [lair] empty

Leerung f [lairoong] collection

Nächste Leerung next collection

legen [laygen] to put

Lehrer m [lairer], Lehrerin f teacher; instructor

leicht [lysht] easy; light

leicht verderblich will not keep, perishable

leiden [lyden] to suffer

leider [lyder] unfortunately

leid: tut mir leid [toot meer lite] I'm sorry

leihen [ly-en] to borrow; to lend

Leihgebühr f [ly-geboor] rental

Leim m [lime] glue

Leiter f [lyter] ladder

Leiter m, Leiterin f leader; manager

Lenkrad n [lenkraht] steering wheel

Lenkung f [lenkoong] steering

lernen [lairnen] to learn

lesen [layzen] to read

Leser m [layzer], Leserin f reader

letzte(r,s) [letst-uh,-er,-ess] last

Leute pl [loyt-uh] people

Licht n [lisht] light

Licht einschalten turn on lights

Lichtspiele cinema, movie theater

Lidschatten m [leet-shatten] eye shadow

Liebe f [leeb-uh] love

lieben [leeben] to love

lieber [leeber] rather

Liebhaber m [leep-hahber], Liebhaberin f lover

Lieblings- [leeplings] favourite

Lied n [leet] song

Lieferant m [leeferant] supplier

liefern to deliver

liegen [leegen] to lie; to be situated

Liegestuhl f [leeg-uh-shtool] deckchair

Liegewagen f [leeg-uh-vahgen] couchette

lila [leelah] purple

Limousine f [limoozeen-uh] saloon car

Linie f [leen-yuh] line; airline

Linienflug m [leen-yen-flook] scheduled flight

links left

links (von) [fon] on the left (of)

Linksabbieger left filter

Links halten keep left

linkshändig [links-hendish] left-handed

Linse f [linz-uh] lens

Lippe f [lipp-uh] lip

Lippenstift m [lippen-shtift] lipstick

Liste f [list-uh] list

Lkw m [el-kah-vay] lorry, truck; heavy goods vehicle, HGV

Loch n [loKH] hole

Locke f [lock-uh] curl

Lockenwickler m [locken-vickler] curler

Löffel m [lurfel] spoon

los [lohss] loose

los! come on!

was ist los? what's up?

Löwe m [lurv-uh] lion

Lücke f [lück-uh] gap

Luft f [looft] air

luftdicht verpackt airtight pack

Luftdruck m [looft-droock] air pressure

Luftkissenboot n [looftkissen-boht] hovercraft

Luftpost: per Luftpost [pair looftposst] by airmail

Luftpostsendungen airmail

lügen [lügen] to lie

Lunge f [loong-uh] lung

Lungenentzündung f [loongen-ent-tsoondoong] pneumonia

Lust haben auf [loost hahben owf] to feel like

Luxus m [looksoos] luxury

M

machen [maKHen] to make; to do

mach schon! [maKH shohn] get on with it!

mach's gut [goot] take care

Mädchen n [mayt-shen] girl

Mädchenname m [mayt-shen-nahm-uh] maiden name

mag [mahk] like; likes; may

Magen m [mahgen] stomach

Magenschmerzen mpl [mahgen-shmairtsen] stomach ache

Magenverstimmung f [mahgen-fairshtimmoong] indigestion

magst [mahkst] like

Mahlzeit f [mahl-tsite] meal

nach den Mahlzeiten

einzunehmen to be taken after meals

vor den Mahlzeiten einzunehmen to be taken before meals

Mai m [my] May

Mal n [mahl] time

zum ersten Mal [tsoom airsten] for the first time

malen [mahlen] to paint

man one; you

man spricht Englisch English spoken

manchmal [manshmahl] sometimes

Mandelentzündung f [mandel-ent-tsœndoong] tonsillitis

Mandeln fpl tonsils

Mangel m shortage

Mann m man; husband

Mann! boy!

männlich [mennlish] male

Mannschaft f [mannshafft] team; crew

Mantel m coat

Markt m market

Markthalle f [markt-hal-uh] indoor market

März m [mairts] March

Masern [mahzern] measles

Massenmedien npl [massen-mayd-yen] mass media

Matratze f [matrats-uh] mattress

Mauer f [mower] wall

Maus f [mowss] mouse

maximale Belastbarkeit maximum load

Mechaniker m [meshahneeker] mechanic

Medikament n medicine

Meer n [mair] sea

mehr [mair] more

mehrere [mairer-uh] several

Mehrfachstecker m [mairfaкн-shtecker] adaptor

Mehrfahrtenkarte f [mairfahrten-kart-uh] multi-journey ticket

Mehrheit f [mairhite] majority

Mehrwertsteuer f [mairvairt-shtoyer] Value Added Tax, VAT

mein [mine], **meine** [mine-uh] my

Meinung f [mynoong] opinion

meiste: das meiste (von) [myst-uh (fon)] most (of)

Melone f [melohn-uh] melon; bowler hat

Menge f [meng-uh] crowd

Mensch m [mensh] person

Mensch! wow!

Menschen people

menschlich [menshlish] human

Messe f [mess-uh] (trade) fair

Messegelände n [messuh-gelenduh] fair (site)

Messer n knife

Meter m [mayter] metre

Metzger m [metsger] butcher

Metzgerei f [metsger-ī] butcher's

mich [mish] me

Mietauto n [meet-owto] hire car, rental car

Miete f [meet-uh] rent

mieten [meeten] to rent

Mietkauf m [meetkowf] lease purchase

Militärisches Sperrgebiet keep off: military zone
Milliardär m [mill-yard**air**], **Milliardärin f** billionaire
Millionär m [mill-yon**air**], **Millionärin f** millionaire
min. (Minute) minute
Minderheit f [**minder**hite] minority
mindestens at least
Mindestens haltbar bis ... will keep at least until ...
Mineralölsteuer f [miner**ahl**-url-sht**oy**er] oil tax
Minirock m miniskirt
mir [meer] me; to me
　mir geht's gut [gayts g**oo**t] I'm OK
Mischung f [**mish**oong] mixture
Mißbrauch strafbar penalty for misuse
Mißgeschick n [**miss**-geshick] mishap
Mißverständnis n [miss-fairsht**entnis**] misunderstanding
Mist! bugger!, shit!
Miststück n [mist-sht**oo**ck] bitch
mit with
Mitbringen von Hunden nicht gestattet no dogs allowed
Mitfahrzentrale f [mitfahr-tsentr**ahl**-uh] agency for arranging lifts
Mitleid n [**mit**-lite] pity
mitnehmen [**mit**-naymen] to take; to give a lift to
　zum Mitnehmen to take away, (US) to go

Mittag m [**mit**tahk] midday
Mittagessen n [**mit**tahk-essen] lunch
mittags [**mit**tahks] at midday
mittags geschlossen closed at lunchtime
Mitte f [**mit**t-uh] middle
Mitteilung f [mit-ty**loong**] message
Mittel n means
Mittelalter n [**mit**tel-alter] Middle Ages
mittelgroß [**mit**tel-grohss] medium-sized
Mittelmeer n [**mit**tel-mair] Mediterranean
Mitternacht f [**mit**terna**KHt**] midnight
Mittwoch m [**mit**tvo**KH**] Wednesday
Möbel pl [**mur**bel] furniture
möbliert [mur-bl**ee**rt] furnished
möchte [**mur**sht-uh] would like to
　ich möchte gern [gairn] I would like
Mode f [**moh**d-uh] fashion
Modeartikel fashions
modisch [**moh**dish] fashionable
Mofa n [**moh**fah] small moped
mögen [**mur**gen] to like
möglich [**mur**klish] possible
Möglichkeit f [**mur**klishkite] possibility
Monat m [**moh**naht] month
Monatskarte f [**moh**nats-kart-uh] monthly ticket
Monatsraten [**moh**nahts-rahten] monthly instalments

Mond m [mohnt] moon
Montag m [mohntahk] Monday
Mord m [mort] murder
Mörder m [murder], **Mörderin f** murderer
morgen tomorrow
Morgen m morning
morgens in the morning
Motor abstellen switch off engine
Motorboot n [mohtorboht] motorboat
Motorhaube f [mohtohr-howb-uh] bonnet, (US) hood
Motorrad n [motohr-raht] motorbike
Möwe f [murv-uh] seagull
müde [mood-uh] tired
Mühe f [moo-uh] trouble
Müll abladen verboten no tipping (rubbish/garbage)
Mülltonne f [mooll-tonn-uh] dustbin, trashcan
München [moonshen] Munich
Mund m [moont] mouth
Münzeinwurf insert coin here
Münzen f [moontsen] coins
Münztank m [moonts-tank] coin-operated pump
Muschel f [mooshel] shell; mussel
Muskel m [mooskel] muscle
muß [mooss] must
müssen [moossen] to have to
mußt [moosst], **müßt** [moosst] must
mußte [moosst-uh], **mußten**, **mußtest** had to
Muster n [mooster] pattern; specimen

mutig [mootish] brave
Mutter f [mootter] mother; nut
Mutti f [mootee] mum
Mütze f [moots-uh] cap
MWSt (Mehrwertsteuer) VAT

N

nach [nakH] after; to; according to
Nachbar m [nakHbar], **Nachbarin f** neighbour
nachdem [nakHdaym] after; afterwards
nachher [nakH-hair] afterwards
Nachmittag m [nakHmittahk] afternoon
Nachmittags geschlossen closed in the afternoons
Nachname m [nakHnahm-uh] surname
Nachricht f [nakHrisht] message
Nachrichten fpl [nakHrishten] news
nachsenden [nakHzenden] to forward
nächste [naykst-uh] next; nearest
  nächstes Jahr next year
Nacht f [nakHt] night
Nachtdienst m [nakHt-deenst] late night chemist's/pharmacy
Nachteil m [nakHtile] disadvantage
Nachthemd n [nakHt-hemt] nightdress

Nachtportier m [**naKHt**-port-yay] night porter

Nachtruhe f [**naKHt**roo-uh] sleep

nachts [**naKHts**] at night

Nacken m nape of the neck

nackt naked

Nadel f [**nah**del] needle; pin

Nagel m [**nah**gel] nail

Nagelfeile f [**nah**gelfile-uh] nailfile

Nagellack m [**nah**gel-lack] nail polish

Nagellackentferner m [**nah**gel-lack-entf**ai**rner] nail polish remover

Nagelschere f [**nah**gel-shair-uh] nail clippers

nah(e) [**nah**(-uh)] near

Nähe: in der Nähe [in dair **nay**-uh] near here

nähen [**nay**-en] to sew

nahm, nahmen, nahmst took

Nahschnellverkehrszug m [**nah**-shnell-fairkairs-ts**oo**k] local train

Nahverkehrszug m local train

Narkose f [nark**oh**z-uh] anaesthetic

Nase f [**nah**z-uh] nose

Nasenbluten n [**nah**zenbl**oo**ten] nosebleed

naß [nass] wet

natürlich [nat**oo**rlish] natural; of course

Naturprodukt m natural produce

Nebel m [**nay**bel] fog

Nebelschlußleuchte f [**nay**bel-shl**oo**ss-loysht-uh] rear fog light

neben [**nay**ben] next to

Nebenstraße f [**nay**ben-shtrahss-uh] minor road

nee [nay] nope

Neffe m [**neff**-uh] nephew

nehmen [**nay**men] to take

Neid m [nite] envy

neidisch [**ny**dish] envious

nein [nine] no

Nerven mpl [**nair**fen] nerves

Nervenzusammenbruch m [**nair**fen-ts**oo**zammenbroo**KH**] nervous breakdown

nervös [nairv**u**rss] nervous

nett nice

Nettogewicht n net weight

Nettoinhalt m net contents

Netz n [nets] net; network

Netzkarte f [**nets**kart-uh] travelcard, runabout ticket

neu [noy] new

Neubau m [**noy**bow] new building

Neujahr n [**noy**-yar] New Year

neulich [**noy**lish] recently; the other day

neun [noyn] nine

neunzehn [**noyn**-tsayn] nineteen

neunzig [**noyn**-tsish] ninety

nicht [nisht] not

nicht ... do not ...

nicht berühren do not touch

nicht betriebsbereit not ready

nicht bügeln do not iron

Nichte f [**nisht**-uh] niece

Nichtgefallen: bei Nichtgefallen Geld zurück money back if not satisfied nicht hinauslehnen do not lean out

nicht hupen sounding horn forbidden

nicht in der Maschine waschen do not machine wash

nicht rauchen no smoking

Nichtraucher non-smokers

Nichtraucherabteil n [nishtrowkHer-aptile] non-smoking compartment

nichts [nishts] nothing

nicht schleudern do not spin-dry

nicht stürzen fragile

nicht zur innerlichen Anwendung not for internal use

Nichtzutreffendes bitte streichen please delete as appropriate

nie [nee] never

Niederlage f [neederlahg-uh] defeat

Niederlande pl [needer-land-uh] Netherlands

niederländisch [needer-lendish] Dutch

niemals [neemalss] never

niemand [neemant] nobody

Niere f [neer-uh] kidney

niesen [neezen] to sneeze

nimmst take

nimmt takes

nirgends [neergents] nowhere

noch [noKH] still; even; more

noch ein(e) ... [ine(-uh)] another ...

noch nicht [nisht] not yet

nochmal [noKHmahl] again

Norden m north

Nordfriesische Inseln fpl [nortfreezish-uh inzeln] North Frisian Islands

nordirisch [nort-eerish] Northern Irish

Nordirland n [nort-eerlant] Northern Ireland

nördliche Stadtteile city north

nördlich von [nurtlish fon] north of

Nordsee f [nortzay] North Sea

Normal n [normahl] two-star petrol, regular gas

Norwegen n [norvaygen] Norway

norwegisch [norvaygish] Norwegian

Notarzt m [noht-artst] emergency doctor

Notaufnahme f [noht-owfnahm-uh] casualty department, A&E

Notausgang m [noht-owssgang] emergency exit

Notausstieg m [noht-owss-shteek] emergency exit

Notbremse f [nohtbremz-uh] emergency brake

Notfall m [nohtfal] emergency

im Notfall Scheibe einschlagen smash glass in case of emergency

Notfälle [noht-fell-uh] emergencies

nötig [nurtish] necessary

Notizbuch n [noteets-booKH]

notebook

Notruf m [**noh**t-roof]
emergency call

Notrufsäule f [**noh**t-roof-zoyl-uh]
emergency telephone

notwendig [noht**ven**dish] necessary

Nr. (Nummer) No., number

nüchtern einzunehmen to be taken on an empty stomach

null [nooll] zero

Nummer f [**noo**mmer] number

Nummernschild n [**noo**mmern-shilt] number plate

nun [noon] now

nur [noor] only; just

nur begrenzt haltbar will keep for a limited period only

nur für Anlieger access for residents only

nur für Bedienstete staff only

nur für Busse buses only

nur für Erwachsene adults only

nur für Gäste (hotel) patrons only

nur gegen Voranmeldung by appointment only

nur im Notfall benutzen emergency use only

nur mit der Hand waschen hand wash only

nur solange der Vorrat reicht only as long as stocks last

nur werktags weekdays only

nur zur äußerlichen Anwendung for external use only

nützlich [**noo**tslish] useful

O

ob [op] whether; if

oben [**oh**ben] top; at the top; upstairs

Obergeschoß n upper floor; top floor

Oberweite f bust measurement, chest measurement

Obst und Gemüse fruit and vegetables

obwohl [opv**oh**l] although

oder [**oh**der] or

oder? isn't it?; don't you?; aren't I? etc; OK?

offen open

offensichtlich [offen**zi**shtlish] obvious

öffentlich [**ur**fentlish] public

Öffentlichkeit f [**ur**fentlish-kite] public

öffnen [**ur**fnen] to open

Öffnung f [**ur**fnoong] opening

Nach Öffnung nur beschränkt haltbar will keep for a limited period only after opening

Öffnungszeiten [**ur**fnoongs-tsyten] opening times

oft often

ohne [**oh**n-uh] without

ohne Konservierungsstoffe no preservatives

ohne künstliche Aromastoffe no artificial flavouring

Ohnmacht: in Ohnmacht fallen [**oh**n-maкнt] to faint

Ohr n [ohr] ear
Oktoberfest n [oktohberfest] Munich beer festival (held in September)
Ölstand m [urlshtant] oil level
Ölwechsel sofort oil change while you wait
Oma f [ohmah] granny
Omnibus m [omneebooss] bus
Onkel m uncle
Opa m [ohpah] grandad
Oper f [ohper] opera
Operationssaal m [opairats-yohns-zahl] operating theatre
Opfer n victim
Optiker m optician
Ordner m [ortner] folder; steward
Ordnung f [ortnoong] order
in Ordnung all right
Ort m town; place
örtliche Betäubung f [urtlish-uh betoyboong] local anaesthetic
Ortsgespräch n [orts-geshpraysh] local call
Ortsnetz n [ortsnets] local network
Ortszeit f [orts-tsite] local time
Ossi m [ossee] East German
Osten m east
Ostern n [ohstern] Easter
Österreich n [urster-rysh] Austria
Österreicher m [urster-rysher] Austrian
Österreicherin f [urster-rysherin] Austrian (woman).
österreichisch [urster-ryshish] Austrian

Ostfriesische Inseln fpl [ostfreezish-uh inzeln] East Frisian Islands
östliche Stadtteile city east
östlich von [urstlish fon] east of
Ostsee f [ostzay] Baltic

P

Paar n [pahr] pair
paar: ein paar ... a few ...
Päckchen n(pl) [peckshen] small parcel(s)
packen to pack
Packung f [packoong] pack
Paket n [pakayt] parcel, package
Paketannahme f [pakayt-an-nahm-uh] parcels counter
Palast m palace
Panne f [pann-uh] breakdown
Pannendreieck n [pannen-dry-eck] emergency triangle
Pannenhilfe f [pannen-hilf-uh] breakdown services
Papier n [papeer] paper; litter
Papier(hand)tücher npl [papeer-(hant)tOOsher] paper handkerchiefs, tissues
Pappe f [papp-uh] cardboard
Parfüm n [parfOOm] perfume
Parkausweis m [park-owssvice] parking permit
Parkbucht f [parkbooKHt] parking space
Parkdauer parking allowed for ...
parken to park

Parken nur mit Parkscheibe parking disc holders only

Parken nur mit Parkschein parking only with parking permit

Parken verboten no parking

Parkett n stalls

Parkhaus n [parkhowss] multistorey car park/parking garage

Parkplatz m [parkplats] car park, parking lot

Parkscheinautomat m [parkshine-owtomaht] car park/parking lot ticket vending machine

Parkschein entnehmen take a ticket

Parkuhr f [park-oor] parking meter

Parkverbot no parking

Paß m [pas] passport; pass

Passagier m [passah-Jeer] passenger

Paßkontrolle f [pas-kontrol-uh] passport control

Pauschalreise f [powshahl-rize-uh] package tour

Pause f [powz-uh] interval, intermission; rest

Pech n [pesh] bad luck

peinlich [pine-lish] embarrassing

Pelz m [pelts] fur

Pelzmantel m [peltsmantel] fur coat

Pension f [pangz-yohn] guesthouse

Personalausweis m [pairzonahl-owssvice] identity card

Personaleingang m staff entrance

Personenzug m [pairzohnen-tsook] passenger train, stopping train

Perücke f [per**oo**ck-uh] wig

Pf. (Pfennig) pfennig

Pfandleihe f [pfant-ly-uh] pawnbroker

Pfanne f [pfann-uh] frying pan

Pfd. (Pfund) pound (German pound = 500g)

Pfeife f [pf**ife**-uh] pipe

Pferd n [pfairt] horse

Pferderennbahn f [pfaird-uh-rennbahn] race course

Pferdeschwanz m [pfaird-uh-shvants] ponytail

Pfingsten n Whitsun

Pflanze f [pflants-uh] plant

Pf. (Pfennig) pfennig (German unit of currency, 100 pf = DM 1)

Pfund n [pfoont] pound (German pound = 500g); pound (Sterling)

Phonoartikel hi-fi equipment

Pickel m spot

pikant savoury; spicy

Pille f [pill-uh] pill

Pinsel m [pinzel] paint brush

Pinzette f [pintsett-uh] tweezers

Pistole f [pist**oh**l-uh] gun

Pkw m [pay-kah-**vay**] private car

Plakat n [plakaht] poster

Plakate ankleben verboten stick no bills

Plastik n plastic

Plastiktüte f [plastik-tๅๅt-uh] plastic bag

platt flat

Plattenspieler m [platten-shpeeler] record player

Platz m [plats] seat; square; place; space

Platzanweiserin f [plats-anvyzerin] usherette

Platzkarte f [plats-kart-uh] seat reservation

pleite [plite-uh] broke

Plombe f [plomb-uh] filling

plötzlich [plurtslish] suddenly

PLZ (Postleitzahl) postcode, zip code

Pokal m [pohkahl] cup

Polen n [pohlen] Poland

Politik f [politeek] politics

Politiker m [poleeticker], **Politikerin f** politician

politisch [poleetish] political

Polizei f [polits-ī] police

Polizeipräsidium n [polits-ī-prayzeedee-oom] police headquarters

Polizeiwache f [polits-ī-vaкн-uh] police station

Polizist m [politsist] policeman

Polizistin f [politsistin] policewoman

polnisch [pol-nish] Polish

Pony m [ponnee] fringe

Portemonnaie n [port-monnay] purse

Portier m [port-yay] porter

Porto n postage

portugiesisch [portoo-geezish] Portuguese

Porzellan n [portsellahn] porcelain; china

Post f [posst] mail; post office

Postamt n [posst-amt] post office

Postanweisung f [posst-anvyzoong] postal/money order

Postanweisungen money orders

Postkarte f [posstkart-uh] postcard

postlagernd [posst-lahgernt] poste restante

postlagernde Sendungen poste restante

Postleitzahl f [posst-lite-tsahl] postcode, zip code

Postscheckkonto n [posst-sheck-konto] (post office) giro account

Postsparkasse f [posst-shparkass-uh] post office savings bank

Postwertzeichen n(pl) [posst-vairt-tsyshen] postage stamp(s)

Postwertzeichen in kl. Mengen stamps in small quantities

praktisch [praktish] practical

praktische Ärztin f [praktish-uh airtstin] GP

praktischer Arzt m [praktisher artst] GP

Präservativ n [prezairvateef] condom

Praxis f [praksis] doctor's surgery; practice

Preis m [price] price
zum halben Preis half price

preisgünstig [**price**-g**ꭢ**nstish] cheap; inexpensive

Preis reduziert price reduced

Preissenkung reduction

preiswert bargain price, inexpensive

prima! [**pree**mah] good!

Prinz m [prints] prince

Prinzessin f [prints**essin**] princess

Privateigentum private property

Privatgrundstück private property

Privatparkplatz private car park/parking lot

pro: pro Woche [**voKH**-uh] per week

Probe f [**prohb**-uh] rehearsal; sample

probieren [prob**eeren**] to taste; to try

Programmkino n [programm-**keeno**] arts cinema

Prospekt m brochure

prost! [prohst] cheers!

Prozent n [proh**tsent**] per cent

Prozeß m [proh-**tsess**] trial; process

prüfen [**prꭢfen**] to check

Publikum n [**poo**blikoom] audience

Puder m [**poo**der] powder

Pumpe f [**poomp**-uh] pump

Punkt m [**poonkt**] point; dot; full stop

pünktlich [**pꭢ**nktlish] punctual

Puppe f [**poopp**-uh] doll

putzen [**poot**sen] to clean

Putzfrau f [**poots**frow] cleaning lady

Q

Qualität f [kvalit**ayt**] quality

Qualitätsware quality goods

Qualle f [kvall-uh] jellyfish

Quatsch m [kvatsh] nonsense

Quelle f [kvell-uh] spring; source

Quittung f [kvittoong] receipt

R

Rabatt m reduction, discount

Rad n [raht] wheel

Radfahren n [**raht**-fahren] cycling

Radfahrer m [**raht**-fahrer] cyclist

Radfahrer frei cyclists only

Radfahrerin f [**raht**-fahrerin] cyclist

Radiergummi n [radeer-goommee] rubber, eraser

Radweg m [**raht**-vayk] cycle path

Radweg kreuzt cycle track crossing

Rand m [rant] edge; rim

Rang m row; stalls; grade

Rasen m [**rah**zen] lawn

Rasierapparat m [razeer-appar**aht**] razor

Rasiercreme f [razeer-kraym] shaving cream

rasieren: sich rasieren [zish

razeeren] to shave

Rasierklinge f [razeerkling-uh] razor blade

Rasierpinsel m [razeer-pinzel] shaving brush

Rasierseife f [razeerzife-uh] shaving foam

Rasierwasser n [razeervasser] aftershave

Raststätte f [rast-shtett-uh] services area

Rat m [raht] advice; council

Rate f [raht-uh] instalment; rate

raten [rahten] to guess; to advise

Ratenzahlung f [rahten-tsahloong] hire purchase, installment plan

Ratenzahlung möglich credit terms available

Rathaus n [raht-howss] town hall

Rätsel n [raytsel] puzzle

Ratskeller m [rahtskeller] restaurant and bar close to town hall

Ratte f [ratt-uh] rat

Rattengift n [rattengift] rat poison

Raub m [rowp] robbery

Raubüberfall m [rowp-ϖber-fal] armed robbery

Rauch m [rowKH] smoke

rauchen [rowKHen] to smoke

Rauchen einstellen no smoking

Rauchen und offenes Feuer verboten no smoking or naked lights

Rauchen verboten no smoking

Raucher smokers

Raucherabteil n [rowKHer-aptile] smoking compartment

rauh [row] rough

raus! [rowss] get out!

Rechner m [reshner] calculator; computer

Rechnung f [reshnoong] bill, (US) check

rechts [reshts] right

Rechtsabbieger right filter lane

Rechtsanwalt m [reshts-anvalt] lawyer

Rechtsanwältin f [reshts-anveltin] lawyer

rechts fahren keep to the right

rechts halten keep right

rechtshändig [reshts-hendish] right-handed

rechts (von) [reshts (fon)] on the right (of)

rechtzeitig [resht-tsytish] on time

reduziert reduced

Reformhaus n [reform-howss] health food shop

Reformkost f health food

Regen m [raygen] rain

Regenmantel m [raygen-mantel] raincoat

Regenschirm m [raygen-sheerm] umbrella

Regierung f [regeeroong] government

regnen [**rayk**nen] to rain
  es regnet [ess **rayk**-net] it's raining

regnerisch [**rayk**nerish] rainy

Reh n [ray] roe deer

Reibe f [**ribe**-uh] grater

reich [rysh] rich

reichen: das reicht [rysht] that's enough

reif [rife] ripe

Reifen m [**ryfen**] tyre

Reifendruck m [**ryfen**droock] tyre pressure

Reifenpanne f [**ryfen**pann-uh] puncture

Reihe f [**ry**-uh] row; series

reine Baumwolle pure cotton

reine Schurwolle pure wool

reine Seide pure silk

reine Wolle pure wool

reinigen [**ry**nigen] to clean

Reinigung f [**ry**nigoong] laundry

Reinigungscreme f [**ry**nigoongs-kraym] cleansing cream

Reise f [**rize**-uh] journey

Reiseandenken souvenirs

Reiseapotheke f [**rize**-uh-apo**tayk**-uh] first aid kit

Reiseauskunft f [**rize**-uh-owsskoonft] travel information

Reisebedarf m [**rize**-uh-bedarf] travel requisites

Reisebüro n [**rize**-uh-bOOro] travel agency

Reiseführer m [**rize**-uh-fOOrer] guide; guidebook

reisen [**rize**-en] to travel

Reisende [**ry**zend-uh] passengers

Reisepaß m [**rize**-uh-pas] passport

Reiseproviant m [**rize**-uh-prohvee-**ant**] food for the journey

Reisescheck m [**rize**-uh-sheck] travellers' cheque

Reißverschluß m [**rice**-fairshlooss] zip

Reitsport m [**rite**-shport] horse riding

Reitweg m [**rite**-vayk] bridle path

Reklamationen complaints

Reklame f [rek**lahm**-uh] advertising; advertisement

Rennbahn f race track

Rentner m, Rentnerin f old-age pensioner

Reparaturen repairs

Reparaturwerkstatt f [repa**toor**-vairkshtatt] garage, repairs

reparieren [repa**reer**en] to mend, to repair

Reportage f [report**ahJ**-uh] report

reservieren [rezair**veer**en] to reserve

reserviert [rezer**veer**t] reserved

Reservierung f [rezair**veer**oong] reservation

Restgeld wird zurückgegeben change will be given

Rettungsring m [**rett**oongs-ring] lifebelt

Rezept n [ret**sept**] recipe; prescription

rezeptpflichtig sold on

prescription only

Rhein m [rine] Rhine

Rheuma n [roymah] rheumatism

Richter m [rishter] judge

Richterin f [rishterin] judge

richtig [rishtish] right; correct

Richtung f [rishtoong] direction

riechen [reeshen] to smell

Riegel m [reegel] bolt

Risiko n [reezeeko] risk

Rock m skirt; rock music

Rodelbahn f [rohdelbahn] toboggan run

Rohr n [rohr] pipe

Rolle f [rol-uh] role; part

Rollsplitt loose chippings

Rollstuhl m [rol-shtool] wheelchair

Rolltreppe f [rol-trepp-uh] escalator

Roman m [romahn] novel

Röntgenaufnahme f [rurntgen-owfnahm-uh] X-ray

rosa [rohza] pink

Rosenmontagszug m [rohzen-mohntaks-tsook] carnival procession held on the Monday before Ash Wednesday (public holiday)

rot [roht] red

Röteln [rurteln] German measles

rothaarig [roht-hahrish] red-headed

Rubin m [roobeen] ruby

Rücken m [r@cken] back

Rückenschmerzen mpl [r@ckenshmairtsen] backache

Rückfahrkarte f [r@ckfahrkart-uh] return/round trip ticket

Rücklichter npl [r@cklishter] rear lights

Rückseite f [r@ckzite-uh] back; reverse

rücksichtslos [r@ckzishts-lohss] reckless

Rücksitz m [r@ckzits] back seat

Rückspiegel m [r@ck-shpeegel] rearview mirror

rückwärts [r@ckvairts] backwards

Rückwärtsgang m [r@ckvairts-gang] reverse gear

Ruderboot n [r00derboht] rowing boat

Ruf m [r00f] call

ruf doch mal an somebody somewhere wants a phonecall from you

rufen [r00fen] to call; to shout

Rufnummer f [r00fnoommer] telephone number

Rufsäule f [r00fzoyl-uh] emergency telephone

Ruhe f [r00-uh] quiet; rest

ruhestörender Lärm disturbance of the peace

Ruhetag closed all day

ruhig [r00-ish] quiet

ruhige Lage peaceful, secluded spot

rund [r00nt] round

Rundfahrt f [r00ntfahrt] guided tour

Rundgang m guided tour (on foot)

Rundreise f [r00nt-rize-uh]

Ru

guided tour
russisch [**roo**ssish] Russian
Rußland n [**roo**sslant] Russia

S

Sache f [za**KH**-uh] thing;
matter; affair
Sachsen n [za**k**zen] Saxony
Sackgasse f [za**ck**-gass-uh] cul-
de-sac, dead end
sagen [**zah**gen] to say
man sagt, daß ... [**zah**kt dass]
they say that ...
sagenhaft [**zah**genhaft] terrific
sah [zah], **sahen, sahst** saw
Salbe f [**zalb**-uh] ointment
Salon m [za**long**] lounge
salzig [**zalt**sish] salty
Sammelkarte f [**zamm**el-kart-uh]
multi-journey ticket
sammeln [**zamm**eln] to collect
Sammlung f [**zam**loong]
collection
Samstag m [**zam**stahk]
Saturday
samstags [**zam**stahks] on
Saturdays
Sandstrand m [**zant**-shtrant]
sandy beach
Sanitäter m [zanee-**tay**ter]
ambulanceman
Sanitätsdienst m [zani**tayts**-
deenst] ambulance service
Sanitätsstelle f [zani**tayts**-shtell-
uh] first aid centre
Satz m [zats] sentence; rate
sauber [**zow**ber] clean

säubern [**zoy**bern] to clean
sauer [**zow**er] sour; pissed off
Sauerstoff m [**zow**ershtoff]
oxygen
SB (Selbstbedienung) self
service
S-Bahn f [**ess**-bahn] local
urban railway
SB-Tankstelle f [ess-**bay**-
tankshtell-uh] self-service
petrol/gas station
Schachtel f [sha**KH**tel] box;
packet
schade: das ist schade [shahd-
uh] it's a pity
Schädel m [**shay**del] skull
Schaden m [**shah**den] damage
Schaf n [shahf] sheep
Schaffner m [**shaff**ner]
conductor
schal [shahl] stale
Schal m [shahl] scarf
Schallplatte f [**shall**platt-uh]
record
Schalter m [**shal**ter] counter;
switch
Schalterstunden hours of
business
Schaltknüppel m [**shalt**k-
n∞ppel] gear lever
schämen: sich schämen [zish
shaymen] to be ashamed
scharf [sharf] sharp; hot
Schatten m [**shat**ten] shade
Schauer m [**show**er] shower
Schaufenster n [**show**-fenster]
shop window
Scheck m [sheck] cheque, (US)
check

Scheckheft n [sheck-heft] cheque book

Scheckkarte f [sheck-kart-uh] cheque card

Scheibe f [shibe-uh] slice

Scheibenwischer m [shyben-visher] windscreen wiper

Schein m [shine] note, bill; appearance

Scheineingabe insert banknote

scheinen [shynen] to shine; to seem

Scheinwerfer mpl [shine-vairfer] headlights

Scheiße! [shice-uh] shit!

Scheißkerl m [shice-kairl] bastard

Schenkel m [shenkel] thigh

Schere f [shair-uh] scissors

scheu [shoy] shy

Schiedsrichter m [sheets-rishter] referee

Schiff n [shiff] ship; boat

Schild n [shilt] sign

Schirm m [sheerm] umbrella; screen

Schlafanzug m [shlahf-antsook] pyjamas

schlafen [shlahfen] to sleep

Schlaflosigkeit f [shlahflohzish-kite] insomnia

Schlafmittel n [shlahfmittel] sleeping drug

Schlafraum m [shlahfrowm] dormitory

Schlafsaal m [shlahfzahl] dormitory

Schlafsack m [shlahfzack] sleeping bag

Schlaftablette f [shlahf-tablett-uh] sleeping pill

Schlafwagen m [shlahfvahgen] sleeper, sleeping car

Schlafzimmer n [shlahf-tsimmer] bedroom

Schlafzimmerbedarf for the bedroom

schlagen [shlahgen] to hit

Schläger m [shlayger] racket; hooligan

Schlange f [shlang-uh] snake; queue

Schlange stehen [shtay-en] to queue

schlank [shlank] slim

Schlauch m [shlowKH] inner tube

schlecht [shlesht] bad; badly; unwell

Schlechte Fahrbahn bad road surface

schlechter [shleshter] worse

schlechteste [shleshtest-uh] worst

Schleudergefahr danger of skidding

schleudern [shloydern] to skid

Schleuderpreise prices slashed

schließen [shleessen] to close

Schließfach n [shleessfaKH] left luggage locker

Schließfächer luggage lockers

schloß [shloss] shut

Schloß n castle; lock

Schluckauf m [shloock-owf] hiccups

schlucken [shl**oo**cken] to swallow

Schluß m [shl**oo**ss] end

Schlüssel m [shl**oo**ssel] key; spanner; wrench

schmackhaft [shm**ack**-haft] tasty

schmecken [shm**ecken**] to taste; to taste good

Schmerz m [shm**airts**] pain

schmerzen [shm**airtsen**] to hurt

schmerzhaft [shm**airts**-haft] painful

Schmerzmittel n [shm**airts**-mittel] painkiller

schminken: sich schminken [zish shm**inken**] to do one's make-up

Schmuck m [shm**oock**] jewellery

schmutzig [shm**oot**sish] dirty

schnarchen [shn**arshen**] to snore

Schnauze! [shn**owts**-uh] shut your mouth!

Schnee m [shn**ay**] snow

schneebedeckt snow-covered

Schneeketten fpl snow chains

Schneeverhältnisse fpl [shn**ay**-fair-heltniss-uh] snow conditions

Schneeverwehung f [shn**ay**-fairvayoong] snow drift

schneiden [shn**yden**] to cut
  sich schneiden to cut oneself

Schneiderei f [shn**yder-i**] tailor's

schneien [shn**y**-en] to snow

schnell [shn**ell**] fast

Schnellimbiß m [shn**ell**-imbiss] snackbar

Schnellzug m [shn**ell**-ts**oo**k] express train

Schnupfen m [shn**oo**pfen] cold

Schnurrbart m [shn**oo**rrbart] moustache

schön [sh**urn**] beautiful; fine; nice

schon [sh**ohn**] already

Schönheitspflege f [sh**urn**hites-pflayg-uh] beauty care

Schönheitssalon m [sh**urn**hites-zalong] beauty salon

Schornstein m [sh**orn**-shtine] chimney

Schotte m [sh**ott**-uh] Scotsman

Schottin f [sh**ott**in] Scotswoman

Schrank m [shr**ank**] cupboard

Schranke f [shr**ank**-uh] barrier

Schraube f [shr**owb**-uh] screw

Schraubenschlüssel m [shr**owb**en-shl**oo**ssel] spanner, wrench

Schraubenzieher m [shr**owb**en-tsee-er] screwdriver

schreiben [shr**yben**] to write

Schreibmaschine f [shr**ipe**-masheen-uh] typewriter

Schreibpapier n [shr**ipe**-papeer] writing paper

Schreibtisch m [shr**ipe**-tish] desk

Schreibwaren pl [shr**ipe**-vahren] stationery

Schreibwarenladen m [shr**ipe**-vahren-lahden] stationer's

schreien [shr**y**-en] to scream

schrieb [shr**eep**], schriebst,

210

schrieben wrote

Schriftsteller m [shrift-shteller], Schriftstellerin f writer

Schritt m [shritt] step

Schritt fahren drive at walking speed

schüchtern [sh**oo**shtern] shy

Schuhcreme f [sh**oo**-kraym] shoe polish

Schuhe mpl [sh**oo**-uh] shoes

Schuhmacher m [sh**oo**maкHer] shoe repairer

Schuhreparaturen shoe repairs, heelbar

Schulbedarf school items

Schulden fpl [sh**oo**lden] debts

schuld: er ist schuld [air ist shoolt] it's his fault

schuldig [sh**oo**ldish] guilty

Schule f [sh**oo**l-uh] school

Schüler und Studenten school children and students

Schulhof m [sh**oo**l-hohf] school playground

Schulter f [sh**oo**lter] shoulder

Schüssel f [sh**oo**ssel] bowl

Schutt abladen verboten no tipping

schützen [sh**oo**tsen] to protect

Schützenfest n [sh**oo**tsenfest] local carnival

Schwaben n [shv**ah**ben] Swabia

schwach [shvaкH] weak

Schwachkopf m [shvaкH-kopf] idiot, wally

Schwachsinn m [shvaкH-zin] rubbish

Schwager m [shv**ah**ger] brother-in-law

Schwägerin f [shv**ay**gerin] sister-in-law

Schwamm m [shvamm] sponge

schwanger [shv**ang**-er] pregnant

Schwanz m [shvants] tail

schwarz [shvartz] black

Schwarzes Brett n [shvartsess] noticeboard

Schwarzwald m [shvartsvalt] Black Forest

schwarz-weiß [shvarts-**vice**] black and white

Schwein n [shvine] pig

Schweiz f [shvites] Switzerland

Schweizer m [shv**y**tser] Swiss

Schweizerin f [shv**y**tserin] Swiss woman

schwer [shvair] heavy; difficult

Schwerlastverkehr heavy vehicles

Schwester f [shvester] sister

Schwiegermutter f [shv**ee**ger-mooter] mother-in-law

Schwiegersohn m [shv**ee**gerzohn] son-in-law

Schwiegertochter f [shv**ee**ger-toкHter] daughter-in-law

Schwiegervater m [shv**ee**gerfahter] father-in-law

schwierig [shv**ee**rish] difficult

Schwimmbad n [shv**i**mmbaht] swimming pool

Schwimmen n [shv**i**mmen] swimming

schwimmen to swim

schwimmen gehen [g**ay**-en] to go swimming

Schwimmen verboten no

swimming

Schwimmer m [shvimmer], **Schwimmerin** f swimmer

Schwimmweste f [shvimmvest-uh] life jacket

schwindlig [shvintlish] dizzy

schwitzen [shvitsen] to sweat

schwul [shv00l] gay

sechs [zeks] six

sechzehn [zesh-tsayn] sixteen

sechzig [zesh-tsish] sixty

See m [zay] lake

See f sea

seekrank [zaykrank] seasick

Segelboot n [zaygelboht] sailing boat

Segeln n [zaygeln] sailing

Segler m [zaygler] yachtsman

Seglerin f [zayglerin] yachtswoman

sehen [zay-en] to see

Sehenswürdigkeit f [zay-ens-vOOrdishkite] sight

sehr [zair] very

sei [zy] be

seid [zite] are

seien Sie [zy-en zee] be

Seide f [zide-uh] silk

Seife f [zife-uh] soap

Seil n [zile] rope

sein [zine] to be; his; its

seine [zine-uh] his; its

seit [zite] since

seitdem [zite-daym] since

Seite f [zite-uh] side; page

Seitenstreifen nicht befahrbar soft verges, keep off

Sekunde f [zekoond-uh] second

selbe [zelb-uh] same

selbst [zelpst] even

er/sie selbst himself/herself

Selbstbedienung f [zelpst-bedeenoong] self-service

selbstverständlich [zelpst-fairshtentlish] of course

Selbstwählferndienst direct long-distance dialling

seltsam [zeltzahm] strange

senden [zenden] to send

Sender m [zender] (radio/TV) station

Sendung f [zendoong] programme

sensibel [zenzeebel] sensitive

Serviervorschlag serving suggestion

Sessellift m [zessel-lift] chairlift

setzen [zetsen] to put

sich setzen to sit down

sexistisch [seksistish] sexist

sicher [zisher] sure; safe

Sicherheitsgurt m [zisherhites-goort] seat belt

Sicherheitsnadel f [zisherhites-nahdel] safety pin

Sicherung f [zisheroong] fuse

Sicht f [zisht] visibility

sie [zee] she; her; they; them

Sie you

sieben [zeeben] seven

siebzehn [zeep-tsayn] seventeen

siebzig [zeep-tsish] seventy

Sieg m [zeek] victory

siehe ... see ...

siehst [zeest] see

sieht [zeet] sees

siezen [zeetsen] to use the

Silber n [zilber] silver

silbern [zilbern] silver

Silvester n [zilvester] New Year's Eve

sind [zint] are

singen [zing-en] to sing

sinken [zinken] to sink

Sitz m [zits] seat

Sitz für Schwerbehinderte seat for handicapped

Sitzplätze seats

skifahren [sheefahren] to ski

Skifahren n skiing

Skigebiet n [shee-gebeet] skiing area

Skihose f [shee-hohzuh] ski pants

Skilehrer m [shee-lairer], Skilehrerin f ski instructor

Skipiste f [sheepist-uh] ski slope

Skistiefel mpl [shee-shteefel] ski boots

Skistock m [shee-shtock] ski pole

Smoking m dinner jacket

so [zo] so; this way

so ... wie [vee] as ... as

sobald [zohbalt] as soon as

Socke f [zock-uh] sock

Sodbrennen n [zohtbrennen] heartburn

sofort [zofort] immediately

Sohn m [zohn] son

solange [zohlang-uh] as long as

Sommer m [zommer] summer

Sommerfahrplan m [zommerfahrplahn] summer timetable/schedule

Sommerferien fpl [zommer-fairee-en] summer holidays/vacation

Sommerschlußverkauf summer sale

Sonderangebot n [zonder-angeboht] special offer

Sonderflug m [zonderflook] special flight

sondern [zondern] but

Sonderpreis m [zonder-price] special price

Sondervorstellung f [zonderforshtelloong] special performance

Sonnabend m [zonnahbent] Saturday

Sonne f [zonn-uh] sun

sonnenbaden [zonnenbahden] to sunbathe

Sonnenbrand m [zonnenbrant] sunburn

Sonnenbrille f [zonnenbrill-uh] sunglasses

Sonnenöl n [zonnen-url] suntan lotion; suntan oil

Sonnenschein m [zonnen-shine] sunshine

Sonnenstich m [zonnen-shtish] sunstroke

Sonnenuntergang m [zonnen-oontergang] sunset

sonnig [zonnish] sunny

Sonntag m [zonntahk] Sunday

Sonntagsfahrer m [zonntahks-fahrer] roadhog, Sunday driver

sonn- und feiertags on

Sundays and public holidays
sonst [zonst] otherwise
Sorge f [zorg-uh] worry
sich Sorgen machen (um) [zish zorgen maKHen (oom)] to worry (about)
Sorte f [zort-uh] kind; sort
Souterrain n [zootereng] basement
soweit [zovite] as far as
sowieso [zoveezoh] anyway
sowohl ... als auch ... [zovohl alss owKH] both ... and ...
Spanien n [shpahnee-en] Spain
sparen [shpahren] to save
Sparguthaben n [shpahrgoot-hahben] savings account
Sparkasse f [shpahrkass-uh] savings bank
Spaß m [shpahss] fun; joke
spät [shpayt] late
wie spät ist es? [vee] what time is it?
Spaten m [shpahten] spade
Spätschalter m [shpayt-shalter] night counter
Spätvorstellung f [shpaytforshtelloong] late performance
spazieren gehen [shpatseeren gay-en] to go for a walk
Spaziergang m [shpatseergang] walk
Speiche f [shpysh-uh] spoke
Speisegaststätte f [shpize-uh-gast-shtett-uh] restaurant
Speiseraum m [shpize-uh-rowm] dining room
Speisesaal m [shpize-uh-zahl]

restaurant, dining room
Speisewagen m [shpize-uh-vahgen] restaurant car
Speisezimmer n [shpize-uh-tsimmer] dining room
Sperrgebiet prohibited area
Spiegel m [shpeegel] mirror
Spiel n [shpeel] game; match
spielen [shpeelen] to play
Spielende Kinder children at play
Spieler m [shpeeler], **Spielerin f** player; gambler
Spielkasino n [shpeel-kazeeno] casino
Spielplatz m [shpeelplats] playground
Spielwaren fpl [shpeel-vahren] toys
Spielzeug n [shpeeltsoyk] toy
Spinne f [shpinn-uh] spider
spinnen: du spinnst wohl! [doo shpinnst wohl] you've got to be joking!, you're out of your mind!
Spion m [shpee-ohn] spy
Spirale f [shpeerahl-uh] spiral; IUD
Spitze [shpits-uh] fantastic, magic
Spitzenqualität top quality
Spitzname m [shpitsnahm-uh] nickname
Sportartikel sports goods
Sportplatz m [shport-plats] sports ground
Sporttauchen n [shport-towKHen] skin-diving
Sportverein m [shport-fair-ine]

sports club

Sportwagen m [shport-vahgen] sports car; buggy

Sportzentrum n [shport-tsentroom] sports centre

Sprache f [shprahKH-uh] language

Sprachenschule f [shprahKHen-shool-uh] language school

Sprachführer m [shprahKH-fOOrer] phrasebook

sprechen [shpreshen] to speak; to talk

Sprechstunde f [shpresh-shtoond-uh] surgery

Sprechzimmer n [shpresh-tsimmer] surgery (room)

spricht [shprisht] speaks
wer spricht, bitte? [vair – bitt-uh] who's calling please?

springen [shpringen] to jump

Spritze f [shprits-uh] injection

Sprungschanze f [shproong-shants-uh] ski jump

Spüle f [shpOOl-uh] sink

spülen [shpOOlen] to do the dishes; to rinse

Spülmittel n [shpOOl-mittel] washing-up liquid

Staat m [shtaht] state

Staatsangehörigkeit f [shtahts-an-gehur-rish-kite] nationality

Staatsanwalt m [shtahts-anvalt] public prosecutor

Stadion n [shtahdee-on] stadium

Stadt f [shtatt] town; city

Stadthalle f [shtatt-hal-uh] city hall

Stadtmitte f [shtatt-mitt-uh] city centre

Stadtplan m [shtatt-plahn] map

Stadtzentrum n [shtatt-tsentroom] city centre

Stammgast m [shtammgast] regular customer

Stammtisch m [shtammtish] table for regulars

stand [shtant], **standen** [shtanden] stood

Standesamt n [shtandess-amt] registry office

Standlicht n [shtantlisht] sidelights

starb [shtarp], **starben** [shtarben] died

stark [shtark] strong; great

Starkes Gefälle steep gradient

Start m [shtart] start; take-off

Station f [shtats-yohn] (hospital) ward; stop

statt [shtatt] instead of

Stau m [shtow] tailback, traffic jam

Staub m [shtowp] dust

Staubsauger m [shtowp-zowger] vacuum cleaner

Std. (Stunde) hour

stechen [shteshen] to sting

Stechmücke f [shtesh-mOOck-uh] mosquito

Steckdose f [shteck-dohz-uh] socket

Stecker m [shtecker] plug

stehen [shtay-en] to stand
das steht mir [shtayt meer] it suits me

stehlen [shtaylen] to steal

Stehplätze mpl [shtayplets-uh] standing room

steil [shtile] steep

Stein m [shtine] stone

Steinschlag falling rocks

Steinschlaggefahr danger of falling rocks

Stelle f [shtell-uh] place

stellen [shtellen] to put

Steppdecke f [shteppdeck-uh] continental quilt

sterben [shtairben] to die

Stereoanlage f [shtayray-oh-anlahg-uh] stereo system

Stern m [shtairn] star

Steuer f [shtoyer] tax

Steuer n steering wheel

Stiefel m [shteefel] boot

Stift m [shtift] pen

Stil m [shteel] style

Stille f [shtill-uh] silence

stillen [shtillen] to breastfeed

Stimme f [shtimm-uh] voice; vote

stimmt [shtimmt] that's right

Stimmung f [shtimmoong] mood

Stirn f [shteern] forehead

Stock m [shtock] floor, storey; stick

Stockwerk n [shtockvairk] floor, storey

Stoff m [shtoff] material; fabric

stolz [shtolts] proud

Stöpsel m [shturpsel] plug

stören [shtur-ren] to disturb

stört es Sie, wenn ich ...? [shturt ess zee venn ish] do you mind if I ...?

Störungsstelle f [shtur-roongs-shtell-uh] faults service

Stoßdämpfer m [shtohss-dempfer] shock-absorber

Stoßstange f [shtohss-shtang-uh] bumper, fender

Str. (Straße) street

Straßenbauarbeiten roadworks

Straßenkilometer kilometres by road

Strafe f [shtrahf-uh] penalty; punishment

Strand m [shtrant] beach

Strandgut n [shtrant-goot] flotsam and jetsam

Strandkorb m [shtrantkorp] wicker beach chair

Strandpromenade f [shtrant-promenahd-uh] promenade

Straße f [shtrahss-uh] street; road

Straßenbahn f [shtrahssenbahn] tram

Straßenbauarbeiten fpl [shtrahssenbow-arbyten] roadworks

Straßenschild n [shtrahssen-shilt] road sign

Straßenverkehrsordnung f [shtrahssen-fairkairs-ortnoong] highway code

Strecke f [shtreck-uh] route; stretch

streichen [shtryshen] to paint; to cancel

Streichholz n [shtrysh-holts] match

strengstens untersagt strictly

prohibited

Streugut grit

stricken [shtricken] to knit

Strickwaren knitwear

Strom m [shtrohm] electricity; stream

Stromausfall m [shtrohm-owss-fal] power cut

Stromkosten [shtrohm-kosten] electricity costs

Strömung f [shtrurmoong] current

Strümpfe mpl [shtroompf-uh] stockings

Strumpfhose f [shtroompf-hohz-uh] tights, pantyhose

Stück n [shtOOck] piece; play

Student m [shtOOdent], **Studentin f** student

Stuhl m [shtOOl] chair

Stunde f [shtOOnd-uh] hour; lesson

Stundenplan m [shtOOnden-plahn] timetable, (US) schedule

stündlich [shtOOntlish] hourly

Sturm m [shtoorm] storm

stürmisch [shtOOrmish] stormy

Sturz m [shtoorts] fall

suchen [zOOKHen] to look for

Sucher m [zOOKHer] viewfinder

Süden m [zOOden] south

südliche Stadtteile city south

südlich von [zOOtlish fon] south of

Summe f [zOOmm-uh] sum

Super n [zOOper] four-star petrol, premium (gas)

super [zOOper] great

Suppenteller m [zOOppenteller] soup plate

süß [zOOss] sweet

T

Tabak m [tahbak] tobacco

Tabakwaren tobacconist's

Tabelle f [tabell-uh] (league) table

Tablett n tray

Tablette f [tablett-uh] pill, tablet

Tacho m [taKHo] speedometer

Tafel f [tahfel] plate; blackboard

Tag m [tahk] day

Tag der Deutschen Einheit Day of German Unity, 3rd October, a public holiday

Tagebuch n [tahg-uh-bOOKH] diary

Tagesdecke f [tahgess-deck-uh] bedspread

Tageskarte f [tahgess-kart-uh] day ticket; menu of the day

Tageszeitung f [tahgess-tsytoong] daily newspaper

täglich [tayklish] daily

täglich frisch fresh every day

Taille f [tal-yuh] waist

Taillenweite f [tal-yen-vite-uh] waist measurement

Tal n [tahl] valley

Talsperre f [tahlshpair-uh] dam

Tankstelle f [tankshtell-uh] petrol/gas station

Tankwart m [tankvart] petrol/gas pump attendant

Tanne f [tann-uh] fir tree
Tante f [tant-uh] aunt
Tanz m [tants] dance
Tanzcafé n [tants-kaffay] café with dancing
tanzen [tantsen] to dance
Tapete f [tapayt-uh] wallpaper
tapezieren [tapaytseeren] to wallpaper
tapfer brave
Tasche f [tash-uh] pocket; bag
Taschendieb m [tashen-deep] pickpocket
Taschenlampe f [tashen-lamp-uh] torch
Taschenmesser n [tashen-messer] penknife
Taschenrechner m [tashen-reshner] calculator
Taschentuch n [tashentOOKH] handkerchief
Tasse f [tass-uh] cup
tat [taht], tatst, taten did
taub [towp] deaf
tauchen [towKHen] to dive
Tauchen verboten no diving
tauschen [towshen] to exchange
tausend [towzent] thousand
Tauwetter n [tow-vetter] thaw
Taxistand m [taksi-shtant] taxi rank
TEE m [tay-ay-ay] Trans–Europe Express
Teekanne f [taykann-uh] teapot
Teelöffel m [tay-lurfel] teaspoon
Teestube f [tayshtOOb-uh] tea room
Teich m [tysh] pond

Teil m [tile] part
teilen [tylen] to share
teils ... teils ... [tiles] partly ... partly ...
Teilzahlung möglich credit available
Telefax n fax
Telefonbuch n [telefohn-bOOKH] phone book
Telefonieren ohne Münzen cardphone
Telefonkarte f [telefohnkart-uh] phonecard
Telefonnummer f [telefohn-noommer] phone number
Telefonzelle f [telefohn-tsell-uh] phone box
Teller m plate
Teppich m [teppish] carpet
Teppichboden fitted carpet
Termin m [tairmeen] appointment
Terrasse f [tairass-uh] patio
Tesafilm® m [tayzah-film] Sellotape®, Scotch tape®
teuer [toyer] dear; expensive
Theaterstück n [tay-ahtershtÜck] play
tief [teef] deep; low
Tiefe f [teef-uh] depth
Tiefgeschoß lower floor, basement
Tiefkühlkost frozen food
Tier n [teer] animal
Tierarzt m [teer-artst] vet
Tiergarten m [teergarten] zoo
Tierpark m [teerpark] zoo
Tinte f [tint-uh] ink
Tisch m [tish] table

Tischdecke f [tishdeck-uh] tablecloth

Tischtennis n [tish-tennis] table tennis

Tochter f [tokHter] daughter

Tod m [toht] death

Todesgefahr! danger of death!

Toilettenpapier n [twaletten-papeer] toilet paper

toll! tremendous!, brilliant!

Tollwutgefahr danger of rabies

Ton m [tohn] sound; clay

Topfpflanzen fpl [topf-pflantsen] pot plants

Tor n goal; gate

tot [toht] dead

Tote m/f [toht-uh] dead man/woman

töten [turten] to kill

Trage f [trahg-uh] stretcher

tragen [trahgen] to carry

Tragödie f [tragurdee-uh] tragedy

Trainingsanzug m [traynings-antsook] tracksuit

trampen [trempen] to hitchhike

Trampen n [trempen] hitchhiking

trank, trankst, tranken drank

Trauer f [trower] sorrow

Traum m [trowm] dream

träumen [troymen] to dream

traurig [trowrish] sad

Trauring m [trowring] wedding ring

treffen to meet

Treffen n meeting

Treffpunkt m [treffpoonkt] meeting place

Treibstoff m [tripe-shtoff] fuel

Treppe f [trepp-uh] stairs

Treppenhaus n [treppen-howss] stairs; staircase; stairwell

treu [troy] faithful

Trikot n [treekoh] jersey

Trimm-dich-Pfad jogging track; keep-fit track

trinken to drink

Trinkgeld n [trink-gelt] tip

trocken dry

trocknen to dry

Tropfen m drop

trotz [trots] in spite of

trotzdem [trots-daym] in spite of that; all the same; nonetheless

tschüs [chooss] cheerio

Tuch n [tookH] cloth

tun [toon] to do; to put

Tür f [toor] door

Türkei f [toor-ky] Turkey

Turm m [toorm] tower

Turnschuhe mpl [toornshoo-uh] trainers

TÜV m [tooff] (Technischer Überwachungs-Verein) MOT

Typ m [toop] guy, bloke

U

U-Bahn f [oo-bahn] underground, (US) subway

U-Bahnhof m [oo-bahnhohf] underground/subway station

über [ober] over; above

überall [**ober-al**] everywhere
überfahren [ooberf**ahr**en] to run over
Überfall m [**ober**-fal] attack
übergeben [oober-g**ay**ben] to hand over
  sich übergeben to be sick
Übergewicht n [**ober**gevisht] overweight; excess baggage
überholen [ooberh**ohl**en] to overtake
Überholen verboten no overtaking
Überholverbot no overtaking
Überlebende m/f [ooberl**ay**bend-uh] survivor
übermorgen [**oo**bermorgen] the day after tomorrow
Übernachtung f [oobernaкнtoong] night
Übernachtung mit Frühstück f [mit fr**oo**shtock] bed and breakfast
überqueren [oober-k**vair**en] to cross
überraschend [oober-r**a**shent] surprising
Überraschung f [oober-r**a**shoong] surprise
überreden [oober-r**ay**den] to persuade
Überschwemmung f [oobershv**em**moong] flood
übersetzen [ooberz**et**sen] to translate
Übersetzer m [ooberz**et**ser], **Übersetzerin** f translator
übertreiben [oobertr**y**ben] to exaggerate

Überweisung f [oober-v**y**zoong] transfer
überzeugen [oober-ts**oy**gen] to convince
üblich [**oo**plish] usual
Ufer n [**oo**fer] shore
Uhr f [oor] clock; o'clock
Uhrmacher m [**oor**makHer] watchmaker
UKW (Ultrakurzwelle) [oo-kah-**vay**] FM
um [oom] around; at
  um ... Uhr at ... o'clock
  um zu in order to
umbringen [**oom**bring-en] to kill
Umgebung f [oomg**ay**boong] surroundings; environment
Umgehungsstraße f detour; by-pass
Umkleidekabine f [**oom**klide-uh-kab**ee**n-uh] changing room
Umleitung f [**oom**-lytoong] diversion
Umschlag m [**oom**shlahk] envelope
Umstandskleid n [**oom**shtants-klite] maternity dress
umsteigen [**oom**-shtygen] to change (trains etc)
umstoßen [**oom**-shtohssen] to knock over
umtauschen [**oom**-towshen] to exchange
Umtausch gegen bar ist nicht möglich goods cannot be exchanged for cash
Umtausch nur gegen Quittung goods may not be exchanged without a receipt

umziehen: sich umziehen [zish **oo**mtsee-en] to change (clothes)

unabhängig [**oo**nap-heng-ish] independent

unangenehm [**oo**n-angenaym] unpleasant

unbedeutend [**oo**n-bedoytent] unimportant

unbefugt unauthorized

unbekannt [**oo**n-bekannt] unknown

und [oont] and

Unebenheiten uneven surface

Unentschieden n [**oo**n-entsheeden] draw

Unfall m [**oo**nfal] accident

Unfallgefahr accident black spot

Unfallrettung f [**oo**nfal-rettoong] ambulance, emergency service

Unfallstation f [**oo**nfal-shtats-yohn] casualty department

ungefähr [**oo**n-gefair] approximately

ungeschickt [**oo**n-geshickt] clumsy

unglaublich [oon-gl**ow**plish] incredible

Unglück n [**oo**n-gl**oo**ck] disaster; accident; unhappiness

unglücklich [**oo**n-gl**oo**cklish] unhappy; unfortunate

ungültig [**oo**n-g**oo**ltish] invalid

unhöflich [**oo**n-hurflish] impolite, rude

Unkosten pl [**oo**n-kosten] overheads

unmöbliert [**oo**n-mur-bleert] unfurnished

unmöglich [**oo**n-m**ur**klish] impossible

uns [oonss] us

unschuldig [**oo**n-shooldish] innocent

unser [**oo**nzer], **unsere** [**oo**nzer-uh] our

unsicher [**oo**n-zisher] unsafe; unsure

Unsinn m [**oo**nzinn] nonsense

unten [**oo**nten] down; at the bottom; downstairs

unter [**oo**nter] below, under; underneath; among

Unterbodenwäsche f [oonterb**oh**den-vesh-uh] underbody cleaning

unterbrechen [**oo**nterbreshen] to interrupt

Unterführung f [oonterf**oo**roong] underpass

Untergeschoß n [**oo**nter-geshoss] basement

Unterhaltung f [oonterhaltoong] entertainment; conversation

Unterhemd n [**oo**nter-hemt] vest, (US) undershirt

Unterkunft f [**oo**nterkoonft] accommodation

Unternehmen n [oontern**ay**men] company; undertaking

Unterricht m [**oo**nter-risht] lessons

untersagt prohibited

Unterschied m [**oo**ntersheet] difference

unterschreiben [oontershr**y**ben]

to sign

Unterschrift f [**oo**ntershrift]
signature

untersuchen [oonter-z**oo**KHen] to
examine

Untersuchung f [oonter-
z**oo**KHoong] examination;
check-up

Untertasse f [**oo**nter-tass-uh]
saucer

Untertitel m [**oo**nterteetel]
subtitle

Unterwäsche f [**oo**nter-vesh-uh]
underwear

untreu [**oo**ntroy] unfaithful

unverbleit [**oo**nfairblite]
unleaded

unverkäufliches Muster not
for sale, sample only

unverschämt [**oo**nfairshaymt]
outrageous

Unverschämtheit f [**oo**n-
fairshaymt-hite] cheek, nerve

unwichtig [**oo**nvishtish]
unimportant

uralt [**oo**r-alt] ancient

Urlaub m [**oo**rlowp] holiday,
vacation

Urlauber m [**oo**r-lowber],
Urlauberin f holidaymaker

Urteil n [**oo**rtile] sentence;
judgement

usw. (und so weiter) etc

V

vakuumverpackt vacuum-
packed

Vater m [**fah**ter] father

Vati m [**vah**tee] dad

Ventil n [vent**ee**l] valve

Ventilator m [ventil**ah**tor] fan

Verabredung f [fair-ap-raydoong]
appointment

verantwortlich [fair-antvortlish]
responsible

verärgert [fair-**air**gert] angry

Verband m [fairbant] bandage;
association

verbergen [fairb**air**gen] to hide

verbessern [fairb**e**ssern] to
improve

Verbindung f [fairb**i**ndoong]
connection

verbleit [fairbl**ite**] leaded

verboten [fairb**oh**ten]
forbidden, prohibited

Verbrauch m [fairbrowKH] use;
consumption

**zum baldigen Verbrauch
bestimmt** will not keep

Verbraucher m [fairbr**ow**KHer],
Verbraucherin f consumer

Verbrecher m [fairbr**e**sher],
Verbrecherin f criminal

verbrennen: sich verbrennen
[zish fairbr**e**nnen] to burn
oneself

Verbrennung f [fairbr**e**nnoong]
burn

verdammt (noch mal)!
[faird**a**mmt (noKH mahl)] bloody
hell!

verdienen [faird**ee**nen] to earn;
to deserve

Verein m [fair-**ine**] club

Vereinigte Staaten f [fair-**ine**-

isht-uh sht**ah**ten] United States
Vereinigtes Königreich n [fair-
ine-ishtess k**u**rnish-rysh] United
Kingdom
Verengte Fahrbahn road
narrows
Verengte Fahrstreifen road
narrows
Verfallsdatum n [fairfals-
dahtoom] best before date
Vergaser m [fairg**ah**zer]
carburettor
vergessen [fairg**e**ssen] to
forget
Vergewaltigung f [fairgeval-
tigoong] rape
vergleichen [fair-gl**y**shen] to
compare
Vergnügen n [fairg-n**œ**gen]
pleasure
vergriffen unavailable, out of
stock
Vergrößerung f [fair-
gr**u**rsseroong] enlargement
verhaften [fairh**a**ften] to arrest
verheiratet [fair-h**y**rahtet]
married
verhindern [fairh**i**ndern] to
prevent
Verhütungsmittel n [fair-
h**œ**toongs-mittel] contraceptive
Verkauf m [fairk**ow**f] sale
verkaufen [fairk**ow**fen] to sell
zu verkaufen [ts00] for sale
Verkauf nur gegen bar cash
sales only
verkaufsoffener Samstag
open on Saturday; Saturday
opening

Verkehr m [fairk**air**] traffic
verkehren [fairk**air**en] to run
verkehrt alle ... Minuten runs
every ... minutes
Verkehrspolizei f [fairkairs-
poleetsi] traffic police
Verkehrspolizist m [fairkairs-
polits**i**st] traffic policeman
Verkehrsunfall m [fairkairs-
oonfal] traffic accident
Verkehrszeichen n [fairkairs-
tsyshen] roadsign
verlangen [fairl**a**ngen] to ask
for
Verlängerungsschnur f
[fairl**e**ngeroongs-shn00r]
extension lead
verlassen [fairl**a**ssen] to leave
verleihen: zu verleihen [ts00
fair-l**i**-en] for hire, to rent
verletzt [fairl**e**tst] injured
verliebt [fairl**ee**pt] in love
verlieren [fairl**ee**ren] to lose
verlobt [fairl**oh**pt] engaged
Verlobte m/f [fairl**oh**pt-uh]
fiancé; fiancée
Verlobung f [fairl**oh**boong]
engagement
Verlust m [fairl**oo**st] loss
vermeiden [fairm**y**den] to avoid
vermieten: zu vermieten [ts00
fairm**ee**ten] for hire/to rent; to
let
Vermieter m [fairm**ee**ter]
landlord
Vermieterin f [fairm**ee**terin]
landlady
vermissen [fairm**i**ssen] to miss
Vermittlung f [fairm**i**ttloong]

operator

vernünftig [fairnœnftish] sensible

verpassen [fairpassen] to miss

verriegeln [fair-reegeln] to bolt

verrückt [fair-rœckt] mad

verschieden [fairsheeden] different

verschlafen [fairshlahfen] to oversleep

verschlucken [fairshloocken] to swallow

Verschluß m [fairshlooss] shutter

verschmutzt [fairshmootst] polluted

verschwinden [fairshvinden] to disappear

verschwinden Sie! go away!

Versicherung f [fairzisheroong] insurance

Versicherungspolice f [fairzisheroongs-poleess-uh] insurance policy

verspätet [fairshpaytet] late, delayed

Verspätung f [fairshpaytoong] delay

versprechen [fairshpreshen] to promise

verstauchen [fairshtowKHen] to sprain

verstehen [fairshtay-en] to understand

ich verstehe nicht [fairshtay-uh nisht] I don't understand

verstopft [fairshtopft] blocked; constipated

Versuch m [fairzooKH] attempt

versuchen [fairzooKHen] to try

Verteiler m [fairtyler] distributor

Vertrag m [fairtrahk] contract; treaty

Vertreter m [fairtrayter], **Vertreterin f** representative; agent; sales rep

verwählen: sich verwählen [zish fairvaylen] to dial the wrong number

verwitwet [fairvitvet] widowed

Verzeihung! [fair-tsī-oong] I'm sorry; excuse me

Verzogen nach ... moved to ...

Verzögerung f [fairtsurgeroong] delay

verzollen [fairtsollen] to declare

Vetter m [fetter] cousin

viel [feel] much, a lot (of)

viele [feel-uh] many

vielen Dank [feelen] thanks a lot

viel Glück! [feel glœck] good luck!

viel Glück zum Geburtstag! [tsoom geboortstahk] happy birthday!

vielleicht [feelysht] maybe

vier [feer] four

Viertel n [feertel] quarter; district

Vierwaldstätter See m [veervalt-shtetter zay] Lake Lucerne

vierzehn [feer-tsayn] fourteen

vierzig [feertsish] forty

Visitenkarte f [veezeeten-kart-uh] card; business card

Visum n [veezoom] visa

Vogel m [fohgel] bird

Volk: das Volk [follk] the people

voll [fol] full; crowded

voll belegt full, no vacancies

vollklimatisiert fully air-conditioned

Vollnarkose f [fol-narkohz-uh] general anaesthetic

Vollpension f [fol-pangz-yohn] full board

volltanken [foltanken] to fill up

vom Umtausch ausgeschlossen cannot be exchanged

von [fon] of; by

von ... bis ... from ... to ...

von ... nach ... from ... to ...

vor [for] before; in front of

vor ... Tagen ... days ago

vor dem Frühstück before breakfast

vor Kindern schützen keep out of reach of children

vor dem Schlafengehen before going to bed

Vorausbuchung unbedingt erforderlich reserved seats only

voraus: im voraus [vorowss] in advance

vorbei [forby] over

vorbei an ... past ...

Vorderrad n [forder-raht] front wheel

Vorderseite f [forder-zite-uh] front

Vorfahr m [forfahr] ancestor

Vorfahrt f [forfahrt] right of way

Vorfahrt beachten give way

Vorfahrt gewähren give way

Vorfahrtsstraße f [forfahrts-shtrahss-uh] major road (vehicles having right of way)

vorgestern [forgestern] the day before yesterday

Vorhang m [forhang] curtain

vorher [forhair] before

Vorhersage f [forhairzahg-uh] forecast

Vorliebe f [forleeb-uh] liking

Vormittag m [formittahk] (late) morning

vorn [forn] at the front

Vorname m [fornahm-uh] Christian name, first name

Vorprogramm n [for-programm] supporting programme

Vorschlag m [forshlahk] proposal, suggestion

vorschlagen [forshlahgen] to propose

Vorsicht f [forzisht] caution; take care

Vorsicht bissiger Hund beware of the dog

vorsichtig [forzishtish] careful

vorsichtig fahren drive carefully

Vorsicht Stufe! mind the step!

Vorstadt f [forshtatt] suburbs

vorstellen [forshtellen] to introduce

Vorstellung f [forshtelloong] performance

nächste Vorstellung um ... next performance at ...

Vorteil m [fortile] advantage

Vorurteil n [for-oortile] prejudice

Vorwahl f [forvahl] dialling code

Vorwahlnummer f [forvahl-noommer] dialling code

vorziehen [fortsee-en] to prefer

W

wach [vaKH] awake

wachsen [vaksen] to grow

wagen [vahgen] to dare

Wagen m car; coach; carriage

Wagenheber m [vahgen-hayber] jack

Wagenstandanzeiger order of carriages

Wahl f [vahl] choice; election

wählen [vaylen] to choose; to elect; to dial

Wahlkampf m [vahlkampf] election campaign

Wahnsinn m [vahnzinn] madness

Wahnsinn! fantastic!

wahr [vahr] true

während [vairent] during; while

Wahrheit f [vahr-hite] truth

wahrscheinlich [varshinelish] probable; probably

Währung f [vairoong] currency

Wald m [valt] forest

Waliser m [valeezer] Welshman

Waliserin f [valeezerin] Welshwoman

walisisch [valeezish] Welsh

Wand f [vant] wall

wandern [vandern] to hike, to walk

Wanderweg m [vandervayk] walk, route; trail

wann [van] when

war [var] was

waren [vahren] were

Waren fpl goods

Warenaufzug m [vahren-owftsook] service lift

Warenhaus n [vahren-howss] department store

warm [varm] warm; hot

warst [varst], **wart** [vart] were

warten [varten] to wait

Wartesaal m [vart-uh-zahl] waiting room

Wartezimmer n [vart-uh-tsimmer] waiting room

warum? [varoom] why?

was? [vass] what?

Waschbecken n [vashbecken] washbasin

Wäsche f [vesh-uh] washing; laundry

waschen [vashen] to wash **sich waschen** to wash (oneself)

Wäscherei f [vesher-ī] laundry

Waschlappen m [vashlappen] flannel; coward

Waschmaschine f [vashmasheen-uh] washing mashine

Waschpulver n [vashpoolver] washing powder

Waschraum m [vashrowm] wash room

Waschsalon m [vash-zalong] launderette, laundromat

Waschstraße f [vash-shtrahss-uh] car wash

Waschzeit washing time

Wasser n [vasser] water

wasserdicht [vasserdisht] waterproof

Wasserfall m [vasser-fal] waterfall

Wasserhahn m [vasser-hahn] tap, faucet

Wasserkessel m [vasser-kessel] kettle

wasserlöslich soluble in water

Wasserski n [vassershee] waterskiing

Wassersport m [vasser-shport] water sports

Waterkant f [vahterkant] North German name for the North German coastal area

Watte f [vatt-uh] cotton wool, absorbent cotton

wechselhaft [vekselhaft] changeable

Wechselkurs m [veksel-koors] exchange rate

wechseln [vekseln] to change

Wechselstube f [veksel-shtoob-uh] bureau de change

wecken [vecken] to wake up

Wecker m [vecker] alarm clock

weder ... noch [vayder – noKH] neither ... nor ...

Weg m [vayk] path

wegen [vaygen] because of

Wegen Krankheit vorübergehend geschlossen temporarily closed due to illness

Wegen Umbauarbeiten geschlossen closed for alterations

weggehen [vek-gay-en] to go away

wegnehmen [vek-naymen] to take away

Wegweiser m [vayk-vyzer] signpost

wegwerfen [vek-vairfen] to throw away

weh tun: es tut weh [ess toot vay] it hurts

weiblich [vipe-lish] female

weich [vysh] soft

Weihnachten n [vynaKHten] Christmas

weil [vile] because

Weile f [vile-uh] while

weinen [vynen] to cry

Weinhandlung f [vine-hantloong] wine shop

Weinprobe f [vine-prohb-uh] wine-tasting

Weinstraße f [vine-shtrahss-uh] route through wine-growing areas

Weinstube f [vine-shtoob-uh] wine bar (traditional style)

weiß [vice] know; knows; white

weißt [vysst] know

weit [vite] far; wide

weit entfernt far away

weiter [vyter] further

Weitzone f [vite-tsohn-uh] long-distance zone

welche? [velsh-uh] which?
Welle f [vell-uh] wave
Welt f [velt] world
wenden [venden] to turn
  sich wenden an to contact
wenig [vaynish] little; few
weniger [vayniger] less
wenn [venn] if
wenn vom Arzt nicht anders
  verordnet unless otherwise
  prescribed by your doctor
wer? [vair] who?
Werbung f [vairboong]
  advertising; publicity
werde [waird-uh] will; become
werden [wairden] to become;
  will
werdet [wairdet] will; become
werfen [wairfen] to throw
Werkstatt f [wairkshtatt] auto
  repairs
Werktag m [wairktahk] weekday
Werkzeug n [wairk-tsoyk] tool
wert [wairt] worth
Wert m [wairt] value
Wertmünzen tokens
Wertsachen fpl [wairtzaкнen]
  valuables
Wespe f [vesp-uh] wasp
Wessi m [vessee] West
  German
Weste f [vest-uh] waistcoat
Westen m [vesten] west
westliche Stadtteile city west
westlich von [vestlish fon] west
  of
Wette f [vett-uh] bet
wetten [vetten] to bet
Wetter n [vetter] weather

Wetterbericht m [vetter-berisht]
  weather forecast
Wettervorhersage f [vetter-
  forhair-zahg-uh] weather
  forecast
wichtig [vishtish] important
wider [veeder] against
widerlich [veederlish]
  disgusting
Widerrechtlich abgestellte
  Fahrzeuge werden
  kostenpflichtig abgeschleppt
  illegally parked vehicles will
  be removed at the owner's
  expense
widersprechen [veeder-
  shpreshen] to contradict
widerwärtig [veeder-vairtish]
  obnoxious
wie? [vee] how?
wie [vee] like
  wie bitte? pardon (me)?,
  what did you say?
  wie geht es Ihnen? [gayt ess
  eenen] how are you?
  wie geht's? how are things?
wieder [veeder] again
wiederholen [veeder-hohlen] to
  repeat
Wiederhören: auf Wiederhören
  [owf veeder-hur-ren] goodbye
  (said on the phone)
wiegen [veegen] to weigh
Wien [veen] Vienna
wieviel? [veefeel] how much?
wie viele? [vee feel-uh] how
  many?
Wildleder n [viltlayder] suede
will [vill] want to; wants to

willkommen! [villkommen]
welcome!

willst [villst] want to

Wimperntusche f [vimpern-toosh-uh] mascara

Windel f [vindel] nappy, diaper

windig [vindish] windy

Windschutzscheibe f
[vintshoots-shibe-uh]
windscreen

Winterfahrplan m
[vinterfahrplahn] winter
timetable/schedule

Winterschlußverkauf m winter
sales

wir [veer] we

wir müssen draußen bleiben
sorry, no dogs

wir sind umgezogen we have
moved

wird [veert] will; becomes

wirklich [veerklish] really

wirst [veerst] will; become

Wirt m [veert] landlord; host

Wirtin f [veertin] landlady;
hostess

Wirtschaft f [veert-shafft] pub;
economy

Wirtshaus n [veerts-howss] inn;
pub

wissen [vissen] to know

wißt [vist] know

Witwe f [vitv-uh] widow

Witwer m [vitver] widower

Witz m [vits] joke

wo? [vo] where?

woanders [vo-anderss]
elsewhere

Woche f [voKH-uh] week

Wochenende n [voKHen-end-uh]
weekend

Wochenkarte f [voKHenkart-uh]
weekly ticket

Woge f [vohg-uh] wave

woher? [vo-hair] where from?

wohin? [vo-hin] where to?

Wohnblock m [vohnblock]
block of flats, apartment
block

wohnen [vohnen] to live; to
stay

Wohnmobil n [vohn-mobeel]
caravan, (US) trailer

Wohnort m [vohn-ort] place of
residence

Wohnung f [vohnoong] flat,
apartment

Wohnwagen m [vohnvahgen]
caravan, (US) trailer

Wohnzimmer n [vohn-tsimmer]
living room

Wolke f [volk-uh] cloud

Wolle f [voll-uh] wool

wollen [vollen] to want

wollen Sie ...? do you
want ...?

womit [vo-mit] with which;
with what

worauf [vo-rowf] (up)on
which

worden [vorden] been

worin [vo-rin] in which

Wort n [vort] word

Wörterbuch n [vurterbooKH]
dictionary

wovon [vo-fon] from which;
from what

wozu? [vo-tsoo] what for?

Wunde f [voond-uh] wound
wunderbar [voonderbar] wonderful
Wunsch m [voonsh] wish
wünschen [voonshen] to wish
wurde [voord-uh] was; became
würde [voord-uh] would
wurden [voorden], wurdest, wurdet were; became
würzen [voortsen] to season
würzig [voortsish] spicy
wußte [voosst-uh], wußten, wußtest knew
Wut f [voot] fury
wütend [vootent] furious

Z

zäh [tsay] tough
Zahl f [tsahl] number
zahlbar [tsahlbar] payable
zahlen [tsahlen] to pay
Zahlung f [tsahloong] payment
Zahn m [tsahn] tooth
Zahnarzt m [tsahn-artst], Zahnärztin f [tsahn-airtstin] dentist
Zahnbelag m [tsahn-belahk] plaque
Zahnersatz m [tsahn-airzats] dentures
Zahnklinik f [tsahn-kleenik] dental clinic
Zahnpasta f [tsahn-pastah] toothpaste
Zahnschmerzen mpl [tsahn-shmairtsen] toothache
Zange f [tsang-uh] pliers

Zapfsäule f [tsapf-zoyl-uh] petrol/gas pump
Zaun m [tsown] fence
z.B. (zum Beispiel) eg
ZDF (Zweites Deutsches Fernsehen) [tset-day-eff] Second German Television Channel
Zebrastreifen m [tsaybrah-shtryfen] zebra crossing
Zehe f [tsay-uh] toe
zehn [tsayn] ten
Zehnmarkschein m [tsayn-mark-shine] ten-mark note/bill
Zeichen n [tsyshen] sign
zeichnen [tsyshnen] to draw
zeigen [tsygen] to show; to point
Zeit f [tsite] time
Zeitansage f [tsite-anzahg-uh] speaking clock
Zeitschrift f [tsite-shrift] magazine
Zeitung f [tsytoong] newspaper
Zelt n [tselt] tent
Zelten verboten no camping
Zeltplatz m [tseltplats] campsite
Zentimeter m [tsentimayter] centimetre
Zentner m [tsentner] 50 kilos
Zentralheizung f [tsentrahl-hytsoong] central heating
Zentrum n [tsentroom] centre
zerbrechen [tsairbreshen] to break
zerstören [tsairshtur-ren] to destroy
Zettel m [tsettel] piece of paper

Zeuge m [tsoyg-uh], **Zeugin** f witness

Ziege f [tseeg-uh] goat

ziehen [tsee-en] to pull

Ziel n [tseel] aim; destination

ziemlich [tseemlish] rather

Zigarre f [tsigarr-uh] cigar

Zimmer n [tsimmer] room

Zimmer frei room(s) to let/rent, vacancies

Zimmermädchen n [tsimmer-maytshen] chambermaid

Zimmernachweis m [tsimmer-naкнvice] accommodation service

Zimmerservice m [tsimmer-'service'] room service

Zimmer zu vermieten rooms to let/rent

Zinsen pl [tsinzen] interest

Zinssatz m [tsinss-zats] interest rate

Zoll m [tsol] Customs

Zollbeamte m [tsoll-buh-amt-uh], **Zollbeamtin** f customs officer

zollfrei [tsolfry] duty-free

zollfreie Waren fpl [tsolfry-uh vahren] duty-free goods

Zone 30 zone with 30 km/h speed limit

zu [tsoo] to; too; shut

zubereiten [tsoo-beryten] to prepare

Zuckergehalt sugar content

zufrieden [tsoofreeden] pleased

Zug m [tsook] train; draught

zu den Zügen to the trains

Zugabe f [tsoogahb-uh] encore

zugelassen für ... Personen carries ... persons

zuhören [tsoo-hur-ren] to listen

Zukunft f [tsookoonft] future

zum [tsoom] to the

zum Ochsen The Ox (pub etc name)

zunächst [tsoonaykst] first, firstly

Zunahme f [tsoonahm-uh] increase

Zuname m [tsoonahm-uh] surname

Zündkerze f [tsoont-kairts-uh] spark plug

Zündung f [tsoondoong] ignition

zunehmen [tsoonaymen] to increase; to put on weight

Zunge f [tsoong-uh] tongue

zur [tsoor] to the

zurück [tsoorook] back

zurückgeben [tsoorook-gayben] to give back

zurückkehren [tsoorook-kairen] to go back, to return

zurückkommen [tsoorook-kommen] to come back

zusammen [tsoozammen] together

Zusammenstoß m [tsoozammen-shtohss] crash

Zuschauer m [tsooshower], **Zuschauerin** f spectator

Zuschlag m [tsooshlahk] supplement

zuschlagpflichtig [tsooshlahk-pflishtish] supplement payable

zustimmen [tsooshtimmen] to agree

Zutaten fpl [ts00tahten] ingredients

Zutreffendes ankreuzen cross where applicable

Zutritt für Unbefugte verboten no admission to unauthorized persons

zuviel [ts00feel] too much

Zuwiderhandlung wird strafrechtlich verfolgt we will prosecute

zwanzig [tsvantsish] twenty

Zwanzigmarkschein m [tsvantsish-mark-shine] twenty-mark note/bill

Zweck m [tsveck] purpose

zwei [tsvy] two

Zweibettzimmer n [tsvybett-tsimmer] twin room

Zweig m [tsvike] branch

Zweigstelle f [tsvike-shtell-uh] branch

Zweimal täglich einzunehmen to be taken twice a day

zweite(r,s) [tsvite-uh, -er, -ess] second

zweite Klasse f [tsvite-uh klass-uh] second class

zweiter Stock m [tsvyter shtock] second floor, (US) third floor

zweite Wahl seconds

Zwillinge mpl [tsvilling-uh] twins

zwischen [tsvishen] between

Zwischenlandung f [tsvishen-landoong] intermediate stop; stopover

Zwischenmahlzeit f [tsvishen-mahltsite] snack between meals

zwölf [tsvurlf] twelve

z.Zt. (zur Zeit) at the moment

Menu Reader: Food

Essential Terms

bread das Brot [broht]
butter die Butter [bootter]
cup die Tasse [tass-uh]
dessert der Nachtisch [naKHtish]
fish der Fisch [fish]
fork die Gabel [gahbel]
glass: a glass of ... ein Glas ... [ine glahss]
knife das Messer
main course das Hauptgericht [howpt-gerisht]
meat das Fleisch [flysh]
menu die Speisekarte [shpize-uh-kart-uh]
pepper der Pfeffer
plate der Teller
salad der Salat [zalaht]
salt das Salz [zalts]
set menu die Tageskarte [tahgess-kart-uh]
soup die Suppe [zoop-uh]
spoon der Löffel [lurfel]
starter die Vorspeise [for-shpize-uh]
table der Tisch [tish]

another ..., please noch ein ..., bitte [noKH ine bitt-uh]
excuse me! Entschuldigung! [ent-shooldigoong]
could I have the bill, please? kann ich bitte bezahlen? [kan ish
  bitt-uh betsahlen]

Aal [ahl] eel

Aalsuppe [ahlzoop-uh] eel soup

Ananas [ananass] pineapple

angemacht mit prepared with

Äpfel [epfel] apples

Äpfel im Schlafrock [shlahfrock] baked apples in puff pastry

Apfelkompott stewed apples

Apfelkuchen [-kooKHen] apple pie

Apfelmeerrettich [-mayr-rettish] horseradish with apple

Apfelmus [-mooss] apple purée

Apfelrotkohl red cabbage cooked with apples

Apfelsinen [apfelzeenen] oranges

Apfelstrudel apple strudel

Apfeltasche [-tash-uh] apple turnover

Aprikosen [aprikohzen] apricots

Arme Ritter [arm-uh] bread soaked in milk and egg then fried

aromatisiert aromatic

Artischocken artichokes

Artischockenherz [-hairts] artichoke heart

Aspik [aspeek] aspic

Auberginen [ohbairJeenen] aubergines, eggplants

Auflauf [owf-lowf] (baked) pudding or omelette

Aufschnitt [owf-shnitt] sliced cold meats, cold cuts

Austern [owstern] oysters

Bachforelle [baKH-forell-uh] river trout

backen to bake

Backobst [backohpst] dried fruit

Backofen oven

Backpflaumen [-pflowmen] prunes

Baiser [bezzay] meringue

Balkansalat [balkahn-zalaht] cabbage and pepper salad

Bananen [banahnen] bananas

Bandnudeln [bantnoodeln] ribbon noodles

Basilikum basil

Bauernauflauf [bowern-owflowf] bacon and potato omelette

Bauernfrühstück [-frooshtook] bacon and potato omelette

Bauernomelett [-omlet] bacon and potato omelette

Baumkuchen [bowmkooKHen] cylindrical, layered cake

Béchamelkartoffeln sliced potatoes in creamy sauce

Béchamelsoße [-zohss-uh] creamy sauce with onions and ham

Beilagen [bylahgen] side dishes; side salads, vegetables

belegtes Brot [belayktess broht] sandwich

Berliner (Ballen) [bairleener (bal-en)] jam doughnut with icing

bestreut mit sprinkled with

Bienenstich [beenen-shtish] honey and almond tart

Bierschinken [beer-shinken] ham sausage

Biersuppe [beerzoop-uh] beer soup

Birnen [**bee**rnen] pears

Biskuit [biskw**ee**t] sponge

Biskuitrolle [biskw**ee**t-rol-uh] Swiss roll

Bismarckheringe [-hairing-uh] filleted pickled herrings

Blätterteig [bl**e**ttertike] puff pastry

Blattsalat [-zal**ah**t] green salad

Blattspinat [-shpinaht] leaf spinach

blau [blow] boiled, au bleu

Blaufelchen [bl**ow**-faylshen] blue Lake Constance trout

Blaukraut [bl**ow**krowt] red cabbage

Blumenkohl [bl**oo**menkohl] cauliflower

Blumenkohlsuppe [-zoop-uh] cauliflower soup

blutig [bl**oo**tish] rare

Blutwurst [bl**oo**t-voorst] black pudding, blood sausage

Bockwurst large frankfurter

Bohnen beans

Bohneneintopf [-ine-topf] bean stew

Bohnensalat [-zal**ah**t] bean salad

Bohnensuppe [-zoop-uh] bean soup

Bonbon [bongb**o**ng] sweet

Bouillon [booly**o**ng] clear soup

Bouletten meat balls

Braten [br**ah**ten] roast meat

braten to fry

Bratensoße [-zohss-uh] gravy

Brathähnchen [br**ah**t-haynshen] roast chicken

Bratheringe [-hairing-uh] (pickled) fried herrings (served cold)

Bratkartoffeln fried potatoes

Bratwurst [-**voo**rst] grilled pork sausage

Brezel [br**ay**tsel] pretzel

Brombeeren [br**o**mbairen] blackberries

Brot [broht] bread

Brötchen [br**u**rtshen] roll

Brotsuppe [br**oh**tzoop-uh] bread soup

Brühwurst [br**oo**voorst] large frankfurter

Brunnenkresse [br**oo**nnen-kress-uh] watercress

Bückling [b**oo**kling] smoked red herring

bunte Platte [b**oo**nt-uh pl**a**t-uh] mixed platter

Burgundersoße [boorg**oo**nder-zohss-uh] Burgundy wine sauce

Butterbrezel [b**oo**tter-braytsel] butter pretzel

Buttercremetorte [b**oo**tterkraym-tort-uh] cream cake

Champignoncremesuppe [-kraym-zoop-uh] cream of mushroom soup

Champignons [sh**a**mpinyongs] mushrooms

Champignonsoße [-zohss-uh] mushroom sauce

Chicorée [sh**i**koray] chicory

Chinakohl [sh**ee**na-kohl] Chinese leaf

Chips crisps, potato chips
Cordon bleu veal cordon bleu
Curryreis [-rice] curried rice
Currywurst [-voorst] curried pork sausage

Dampfnudeln [-nOOdeln] sweet yeast dumpling
dazu reichen wir ... served with ...
deutsches Beefsteak [doytshess] mince patty
dicke Bohnen [dick-uh] broad beans
Dillsoße [-zohss-uh] dill sauce
durchgebraten [doorsh-gebrahten] well-done
durchwachsen [doorsh-vacksen] with fat
durchwachsener Speck [shpeck] streaky bacon

Edelpilzkäse [aydelpilts-kayz-uh] blue cheese
Ei [ī] egg
Eier [ī-er] eggs
Eierauflauf [-owf-lowf] omelette
Eierkuchen [-kOOKHen] pancake
Eierpfannkuchen pancake
Eierspeise [-shpize-uh] egg dish
eingelegt [ine-gelaykt] pickled
eingelegte Bratheringe pickled herrings
eingemacht [ine-gemaKHt] preserved
ein paar ... some ...
Eintopf [ine-topf] stew
Eintopfgericht [-gerisht] stew
Eis [ice] ice; ice cream

Eis am Stiel [shteel] ice lolly
Eisbecher [-besher] sundae
Eisbein [-bine] knuckles of pork
Eisbergsalat [-bairk-zalaht] iceberg lettuce
Eisschokolade [-shockolahd-uh] iced chocolate
Eissplittertorte [-shplitter-tort-uh] ice chip cake
Endiviensalat [endeev-yen-zalaht] endive salad
englisch [eng-lish] rare
Ente [ent-uh] duck
Entenbraten [entenbrahten] roast duck
entgrätet boned
Entrecote sirloin steak
Erbsen [airpsen] peas
Erbsensuppe [-zoop-uh] pea soup
Erdäpfel [airt-epfel] potatoes
Erdbeeren [airtbairen] strawberries
Erdbeertorte [-tort-uh] strawberry gâteau
Erdnüsse [airtnOOss-uh] peanuts
Essig vinegar

falscher Hase [fal-sher hahz-uh] meat loaf
Fasan [fazahn] pheasant
Faschierte Laibchen [fasheert-uh lipe-shen] rissoles
Faschiertes [fasheertess] minced meat
Feldsalat [feltzalaht] lamb's lettuce
Fenchel fennel
Filet [fillay] fillet (steak)

Fisch [fish] fish
Fischfilet fish fillet
Fischfrikadellen fishcakes
Fischgerichte fish dishes
Fischstäbchen [-shtaypshen] fish fingers
Flädlesuppe [flaydl-uh-zoop-uh] soup with strips of pasta
flambiert flambé
Fleisch [flysh] meat
Fleischbrühe [-br00-uh] bouillon
Fleischkäse [-kayz-uh] meat loaf
Fleischklößchen [-klurss-shen] meat ball(s)
Fleischpastete [-pastayt-uh] meat vol-au-vent
Fleischsalat [-zalaht] diced meat salad with mayonnaise
Fleischtomate [-tomaht-uh] beef tomato
Fleisch- und Wurstwaren meats and sausages
Fleischwurst [-voorst] pork sausage
Flugente [flook-ent-uh] wild duck
Folienkartoffel [fohl-yen-] baked potato
Fond [font] meat juices
Forelle [forell-uh] trout
Forelle blau [blow] trout au bleu
Forelle Müllerin (Art) [m00llerin] trout coated with breadcrumbs and served with butter and lemon
Frikadelle [frickadell-uh] rissole
frisch gepreßt freshly squeezed

Frischwurst [-voorst] fresh sausage
fritiert [friteert] (deep-)fried
Froschschenkel [frosh-shenkel] frogs' legs
Frühlingsgemüse [fr00lings-gem00z-uh] spring vegetables
Frühlingsrolle [-rol-uh] spring roll

Gabelrollmops [gahbel-] rolled pickled herring, rollmops
Gans [ganss] goose
Gänsebraten [genz-uh-brahten] roast goose
Gänseleber [-layber] goose liver
Gänseleberpastete [-pastayt-uh] goose liver pâté
gar cooked
garniert [garneert] garnished
Gebäck [gebeck] pastries, cakes
gebacken fried
gebeizt [gebytst] marinaded
gebraten [gebrahten] roast
gebunden [geb00nden] thickened
gedämpft [gedempft] steamed
Gedeck set meal
gedünstet [ged00nstet] steamed
Geflügel [gefl00gel] poultry
Geflügelleber [-layber] chicken liver
Geflügelleberragout [-rag00] chicken liver ragout
Geflügelsalat [-zalaht] chicken/poultry salad
gefüllt [gef00lt] stuffed
gefüllte Kalbsbrust [kalpsbroost] veal roll

gegart cooked
gegrillt grilled
gehackt minced; chopped
Gehacktes [gekokнt] minced meat
gekocht [gekokнt] boiled
gekochtes Ei [ī] boiled egg
Gelee [Jellay] jelly
gemischter Salat [gemishter zalaht] mixed salad
gemischtes Eis [ice] assorted ice creams
Gemüse [gemooz-uh] vegetable(s)
Gemüseplatte [plat-uh] assorted vegetables
Gemüsereis [-rice] rice with vegetables
Gemüsesalat [-zalaht] vegetable salad
Gemüsesuppe [-zoop-uh] vegetable soup
gepökelt [gepurkelt] salted, pickled
geräuchert [geroyshert] smoked
gerieben [gereeben] grated
Germknödel [gairm-k-nurdel] yeast dumplings
geschlagen [geshlahgen] whipped
geschmort [geshmohrt] braised, stewed
geschnetzelt [geshnetselt] chopped
Geschnetzeltes strips of meat in thick sauce
Geselchtes [gezelshtess] salted and smoked meat
gespickt mit ... larded with ...
geschwenkt [geshvenkt] sautéd

Gewürze [gevoorts-uh] spices
Gewürzgurken [-goorken] gherkins
Goldbarsch [goltbarsh] type of perch
Götterspeise [gurttershpize-uh] jelly
gratiniert [gratineert] au gratin
Grießklößchen [greessklurs-shen] semolina dumplings
Grießsuppe [-zoop-uh] semolina soup
grüne Bohnen [groon-uh] French beans
grüne Nudeln [noodeln] green pasta
grüner Aal [ahl] fresh eel
Grünkohl (curly) kale
Gugelhupf [googel-hoopf] ring-shaped cake
Gulasch goulash
Gulaschsuppe [-zoop-uh] goulash soup
Gurke [goork-uh] cucumber; gherkin
Gurkensalat [-zalaht] cucumber salad

Hackepeter [hack-uh-payter] minced meat
Hackfleisch [-flysh] minced meat
Hähnchen [haynshen] chicken
Hähnchenkeule [-koyl-uh] chicken leg
Haifischflossensuppe [hyfishflossen-zoop-uh] shark-fin soup
halbes Hähnchen [haynshen]

half chicken

Hammelbraten [-brahten] roast mutton

Hammelfleisch [-flysh] mutton

Hammelkeule [-koyl-uh] leg of mutton

Hammelrücken [-rōōcken] saddle of mutton

Handkäse [hant-kayz-uh] very strong-smelling cheese

hartgekochtes Ei [hartgekoKHtess ī] hard-boiled egg

Hartkäse [-kayz-uh] hard cheese

Haschee [hashay] hash

Haselnüsse [hahzelnōōss-uh] hazelnuts

Hasenbraten [hahzenbrahten] roast hare

Hasenkeule [-koyl-uh] haunch of hare

Hasenpfeffer jugged hare

Hauptgerichte main dishes

Hauptspeisen main courses

Hausfrauenart [howssfrowenart] home-made style

hausgemacht [howss-gemaKHt] homemade

Hausmacher (Art) [howssmaKHer] home-made style

Hausmarke [howss-mark-uh] own brand

Hecht [hesht] pike

Hechtsuppe [-zoop-uh] pike soup

Heidelbeeren [hydelbairen] bilberries

Heilbutt [hile-boott] halibut

Heringssalat [hairings-zalaht] herring salad

Heringsstipp [-shtip] herring salad

Heringstopf pickled herrings

Herz [hairts] heart

Himbeeren [himbairen] raspberries

Himmel und Erde [oont aird-uh] potato and apple purée with liver sausage

Hirn [heern] brains

Hirschbraten [heershbrahten] roast venison

Hirschmedaillons [-medah-yongs] small venison fillets

Holsteiner Schnitzel [holshtyner shnitsel] breaded veal cutlet with vegetables, topped with a fried egg

Honig [hohnish] honey

Honigkuchen [-kōōKHen] honeycake

Honigmelone [-melohn-uh] honeydew melon

Hoppelpoppel bacon and potato omelette

Hüfte [hōōft-uh] haunch

Huhn [hōōn] chicken

Hühnerbrühe [hōōner-brōō-uh] chicken broth

Hühnersuppe [-zoop-uh] chicken soup

Hülsenfrüchte [hōōlzenfrōōsht-uh] peas and beans, pulses

Hummer [hoommer] lobster

Imbiß [imbiss] snack

inbegriffen included

Inklusivpreis all-inclusive price

Jagdwurst [yahkt-voorst] ham sausage with garlic

Jägerschnitzel [yaygershnitsel] pork with mushrooms

junge Erbsen [yoong-uh airpzen] spring peas

Kabeljau [kahbelyow] cod

Kaiserschmarren [kyzershmarren] sugared pancakes with raisins

Kalbfleisch [kalpflysh] veal

Kalbsbraten [-brahten] roast veal

Kalbsbries [-breess] sweetbread

Kalbsfrikassee veal fricassee

Kalbshaxe leg of veal

Kalbsmedaillons [-medah-yongs] small veal fillets

Kalbsnierenbraten [-neeren-brahten] roast veal with kidney

Kalbsschnitzel [-shnitsel] veal cutlet

kalte Platte cold meal

kalter Braten [brahten] cold meat

kaltes Bufett cold buffet

kalte Speisen cold dishes

Kaltschale [kaltshahl-uh] cold sweet fruit soup

kalt servieren serve cold

Kaninchen [kaneenshen] rabbit

Kaninchenbraten [-brahten] roast rabbit

Kapern [kahpern] capers

Karbonade [karbonahd-uh] carbonade, beef and onion stew cooked in beer

Karfiol [karf-yohl] cauliflower

Karotten carrots

Karpfen carp

Karpfen blau [blow] carp au bleu

Kartoffel potato

Kartoffelbrei [-bry] potato purée

Kartoffelklöße [-klurss-uh] potato dumplings

Kartoffelknödel [-k-nurdel] potato dumplings

Kartoffeln potatoes

Kartoffelpuffer [-pooffer] potato fritters

Kartoffelpüree [-pɷray] potato purée

Kartoffelsalat [-zalaht] potato salad

Kartoffelsuppe [-zoop-uh] potato soup

Käse [kayz-uh] cheese

Käsebrötchen [-brurtshen] cheese roll

Käsegebäck [-gebeck] cheese savouries

Käsekuchen [-kookhen] cheesecake

Käseplatte [-plat-uh] selection of cheeses, cheeseboard

Käse-Sahne-Torte [-zahn-uh-tort-uh] cream cheesecake

Käsesalat [-zalaht] cheese salad

Käseschnitzel [-shnitsel] escalopes with cheese

Käsesoße [-zohss-uh] cheese sauce

Käsespätzle [-shpetz-luh] home-made noodles with cheese

Kasseler Rippenspeer [rippen-

241

shpair] salted ribs of pork

Kasserolle [kasserol-uh] casserole

Kassler smoked and braised pork chops

Kastanien [kastahn-yen] chestnuts

Katenleberwurst [kahtenlayber-voorst] smoked liver sausage

Katenrauchwurst [-rowKH-voorst] smoked sausage

Keule [koyl-uh] leg, haunch

Kieler Sprotten [keeler shprotten] smoked sprats

Kinderteller children's portion

Kirschen [keershen] cherries

klare Brühe [klahr-uh broo-uh] clear soup

Klößchensuppe [klurss-shen-zoop-uh] clear soup with dumplings

Klöße [klurss-uh] dumplings

Knäckebrot [k-neck-uh-broht] crispbread

Knacker frankfurter(s)

Knackwurst [-voorst] frankfurter

Knoblauch [k-nohb-lowKH] garlic

Knoblauchbrot [-broht] garlic bread

Knochen [k-noKHen] bone

Knochenschinken [-shinken] ham on the bone

Knödel [k-nurdel] dumplings

kochen [koKHen] to cook; to boil

Kohl cabbage

Kohlrabi [-rahbee] kohlrabi (type of cabbage)

Kohlrouladen [-roolahden] stuffed cabbage leaves

Kohl und Pinkel cabbage, potatoes, sausage and smoked meat

Kompott stewed fruit

Konfitüre [konfitoor-uh] jam

Königinpastete [kurnigin-pastayt-uh] chicken vol-au-vent

Königsberger Klopse [kurniksbairger klops-uh] meatballs in caper sauce

Königskuchen [kurniks-kooKHen] type of fruit cake

Kopfsalat [kopfzalaht] lettuce

Kotelett [kotlet] chop

Krabben shrimps, prawns

Krabbencocktail prawn cocktail

Kraftbrühe [kraftbroo-uh] beef consommé, beef tea

Krapfen jam doughnut with icing

Kräuter [kroyter] herbs

Kräuterbutter [-bootter] herb butter

Kräuterkäse [-kayz-uh] cheese flavoured with herbs

Kräutersoße [-zohss-uh] herb sauce

Krautsalat [krowtzalaht] coleslaw

Krautwickel [-vickel] stuffed cabbage leaves

Krebs [krayps] crayfish

Kren [krayn] horseradish

Kresse [kress-uh] cress

Kroketten croquettes

Kruste crust

Küche [kOOsh-uh] cooking; cuisine; kitchen

Kuchen [kOOKHen] cake; pie

Kümmel [kOOmel] caraway

Kümmelbraten [-brahten] roast with caraway seeds

Kürbis [kOOrbiss] pumpkin

Labskaus [lapskowss] meat, fish and potato stew

Lachs [lacks] salmon

Lachsersatz [-airzats] sliced and salted pollack

Lachsforelle [-forell-uh] sea trout

Lachsschinken [-shinken] smoked rolled fillet of ham

Lakritz liquorice

Lamm Lamb

Lammrücken [-rOOken] saddle of lamb

Languste [langoost-uh] crayfish

Lauch [lowKH] leek

Lauchsuppe [-zoop-uh] leek soup

Leber [layber] liver

Leberkäse [-kayz-uh] baked pork and beef loaf

Leberklöße [-klurss-uh] liver dumplings

Leberknödel [-k-nurdel] liver dumplings

Leberknödelsuppe [-zoop-uh] liver dumpling soup

Leberpastete [-pastayt-uh] liver pâté

Leberwurst [-voorst] liver sausage

Lebkuchen [layp-kOOKHen] type

of gingerbread biscuit

legiert thickened

Leipziger Allerlei [lipe-tsiger al-er-ly] mixed vegetables

Lendensteak loin steak

Linseneintopf [linzen-inetopf] lentil stew

Linsensuppe [-zoop-uh] lentil soup

Lutscher [lootsher] lollipop

mager [mahger] lean

Majoran [mahyo-rahn] marjoram

Makrele [makrayl-uh] mackerel

Makronen [makrohnen] macaroons

Mandarine [mandareen-uh] tangerine

Mandeln almonds

Margarine [margareen-uh] margarine

Marille [marill-uh] apricot

Marinade [mareenahd-uh] marinade

mariniert marinaded, pickled

Markklößchen [-klurss-shen] marrow dumplings

Marmelade [marmelahd-uh] jam

Marmorkuchen [marmor-kOOKHen] marble cake

Maronen [marohnen] sweet chestnuts

Matjesfilet [matyess-fillay] fillet of herring

Matjes(hering) [-hairing] young herring

Maultaschen [mowl-tashen] pasta filled with meat,

vegetables or cheese
Medaillons [**may**dah-yongs]
small fillets
Meeresfische [**mai**ress-fish-uh]
seafish
Meeresfrüchte [-frœsht-uh]
seafood
Meerrettich [**mai**r-rettish]
horseradish
Meerrettichsoße [-zohss-uh]
horseradish sauce
Mehl [mayl] flour
Mehlspeise [-shpize-uh] sweet
dish, flummery
Melone [mel**oh**n-uh] melon
Menü set menu
Miesmuscheln [**mee**ss-moosheln]
mussels
Milch [milsh] milk
Milchreis [-rice] rice pudding
Mirabelle [meerab**e**ll-uh] small
yellow plum
Mischbrot [**mi**shbroht] rye and
wheat bread
Mohnkuchen [**moh**nkooKHen]
poppyseed cake
Mohnstrudel poppy-seed
strudel
Möhren [**mur**-ren] carrots
Mohrrüben [**moh**r-rœben]
carrots
Mus [**moo**ss] purée
Muscheln [**moo**sheln] mussels
Muskat(nuß) [**moo**sk**ah**t(nooss)]
nutmeg

nach Art des Hauses [**how**zess]
à la maison
nach Hausfrauenart [**how**ss-

frowenart] home-made
nach Jahreszeit depending on
season
Nachspeisen [**na**KH-shpyzen]
desserts
Nachtisch [**na**KHtish] dessert
Napfkuchen [**na**pf-k**oo**KHen]
ring-shaped pound cake
natur [nat**oo**r] plain
nicht gar underdone
Nierenragout [**nee**ren-rag**oo**]
kidney ragout
Nudeln [**noo**deln] pasta
Nudelsalat [-zal**ah**t] noodle
salad
Nudelsuppe [-z**oo**p-uh] noodle
soup
Nuß [nooss] nut
Nüsse [n**œ**ss-uh] nuts

Obst [ohpst] fruit
Obstsalat [-zal**ah**t] fruit salad
Ochsenschwanzsuppe [**o**ksen-
shvants-z**oo**p-uh] oxtail soup
ohne Knochen filleted
Öl [url] oil
Oliven [ol**ee**ven] olives
Olivenöl olive oil
Omelett [**o**mlet] omelette
Orangen [**o**ron-Jen] oranges
Originalrezept original recipe

Palatschinken [**pa**llatshinken]
stuffed pancakes
Pampelmuse [pampel-m**oo**z-uh]
grapefruit
paniert [pan**ee**rt] with
breadcrumbs
Paprikarahmschnitzel

[papreekah-**rah**mshnitsel] cutlet in creamy sauce with paprika

Paprikasalat [-zal**ah**t] pepper salad

Paprikaschote [-**shoht**-uh] pepper

Paradeiser [parad**y**zer] tomatoes

Parmesankäse [parmez**ah**nkayz-uh] Parmesan cheese

Pastete [past**ay**t-uh] vol-au-vent; pâté

Pellkartoffeln potatoes boiled in their jackets

Petersilie [payterz**ee**l-yuh] parsley

Petersilienkartoffeln potatoes with parsley

Pfannengerichte fried dishes

Pfannkuchen [-k**oo**kнen] pancake

Pfeffer pepper

Pfefferminz peppermint

Pfeffernüsse [-n**oo**ss-uh] gingerbread biscuits

Pfefferrahmsoße [-**rah**mzohss-uh] peppered creamy sauce

Pfifferlinge [pf**i**fferling-uh] chanterelles

Pfirsiche [pf**ee**rzish-uh] peaches

Pflaumen [pf**low**men] plums

Pflaumenkuchen [-k**oo**kнen] plum tart

Pflaumenmus [-m**oo**ss] plum jam

Pichelsteiner Topf [p**i**shelshtyner] vegetable stew with diced beef

Pilze [p**i**lts-uh] mushrooms

Pilzsoße [p**i**lts-zohss-uh] mushroom sauce

Pilzsuppe [-z**oo**p-uh] mushroom soup

Platte [pl**at**-uh] selection

Plätzchen [pl**e**ts-shen] biscuit

pochiert [posh**eert**] poached

Pökelfleisch [p**ur**kelflysh] salted meat

Pommes frites [pom fr**it**] chips, French fries

Porree [p**o**rray] leek

Potthast [p**o**t-hast] braised beef with sauce

Poularde [poоll**ard**-uh] young chicken

Preiselbeeren [pr**y**zel-bairen] cranberries

Preßkopf [pr**e**sskopf] brawn

Prinzeßbohnen [printse**ss**-] unsliced runner beans

Pumpernickel black rye bread

Püree [pоо**ray**] (potato) purée

püriert [pоо**reert**] puréed

Putenschenkel [p**oo**tenshenkel] turkey leg

Putenschnitzel [-**shnitsel**] turkey escalope

Puter [p**oo**ter] turkey

Quark [kv**ark**] type of low-fat cream cheese, quark

Quarkspeise [-sh**pize**-uh] dish made with low-fat cream cheese

Radieschen [rad**ee**ss-shen] radishes

Rahm (sour) cream

Rahmschnitzel [-**shnitsel**] cutlet

in creamy sauce

Räucheraal [**roy**sher-ahl] smoked eel

Räucherhering [-hairing] kipper, smoked herring

Räucherlachs [-lacks] smoked salmon

Räucherspeck smoked bacon

Rauchfleisch [**row**KH-flysh] smoked meat

Rehbraten [**ray**-brahten] roast venison

Rehkeule [-**koyl**-uh] haunch of venison

Rehrücken [-**rœ**ken] saddle of venison

Reibekuchen [**ribe**-uh-k00KHen] potato waffles

Reis [rice] rice

Reisauflauf [-owf-lowf] rice pudding

Reisbrei [**rice**-bry] creamed rice

Reisfleisch [-flysh] meat with rice and tomatoes

Reisrand [-rant] with rice

Reissalat [-zalaht] rice salad

Reissuppe [-zoop-uh] rice soup

Remoulade [rem00lahd-uh] remoulade (mayonnaise and herb dressing)

Renke [**renk**-uh] whitefish

Rettich [**rettish**] radish

Rhabarber [**rabarber**] rhubarb

rheinischer Sauerbraten [**ry**nisher **zow**erbrahten] braised beef

Rinderbraten [**rinder**-brahten] pot roast

Rinderfilet [-fillay] fillet steak

Rinderleber [-layber] ox liver

Rinderlende [-lend-uh] beef tenderloin

Rinderrouladen [-r00lahden] stuffed beef rolls

Rinderschmorbraten [-shmohr-brahten] pot roast

Rinderzunge [-tsoong-uh] ox tongue

Rindfleisch [**rint**flysh] beef

Rindfleischsalat [-zalaht] beef salad

Rindfleischsuppe [-zoop-uh] beef broth

Rippchen [**rip**shen] spareribs

Rippe [**ripp**-uh] rib

Risi-Pisi [reezee-**pee**zee] rice and peas

roh raw

Rohkostplatte [-plat-uh] selection of salads

Rollmops rolled-up pickled herring, rollmops

rosa rare to medium

Rosenkohl Brussels sprouts

Rosinen [rohz**ee**nen] raisins

Rostbraten [-brahten] roast

Rostbratwurst [-braht-voorst] barbecued sausage

Rösti [**rur**shtee] fried potatoes and onions

Röstkartoffeln [**rurst**-] fried potatoes

Rotbarsch [**roht**barsh] type of perch

rote Bete [**roht**-uh **bayt**-uh] beetroot, red beet

rote Grütze [**roht**-uh gr**œ**ts-uh] red fruit jelly

Rotkohl [roht-] red cabbage

Rotkraut [-krowt] red cabbage

Roulade [roolahd-uh] beef olive

Rühreier [rΦr-i-er] scrambled eggs

Russische Eier [roossish-uh i-er] egg mayonnaise

Sachertorte [zaKHertort-uh] rich chocolate cake

Sahne [zahn-uh] cream

Sahnesoße [-zohss-uh] cream sauce

Sahnetorte [-tort-uh] cream gateau

Salat [zalaht] salad; lettuce

Salate salads

Salatplatte [-plat-uh] selection of salads

Salatsoße [-zohss-uh] salad dressing

Salatteller side salad; selection of salads

Salz [zalts] salt

Salzburger Nockerln [zaltsboorger] sweet soufflés

Salzheringe [-hairing-uh] salted herrings

Salzkartoffeln boiled potatoes

Sandkuchen [zantkooKHen] type of Madeira cake

Sauerbraten [zowerbrahten] marinaded potroast

Sauerkraut [zowerkrowt] white cabbage, finely chopped and pickled

Sauerrahm [-rahm] sour cream

Schafskäse [shahfs-kayz-uh] sheep's milk cheese

Schaschlik [shashlik] (shish-) kebab

Schattenmorellen morello cherries

Schellfisch haddock

Schildkrötensuppe [shiltkrurten-zoop-uh] real turtle soup

Schillerlocken [shiller-] smoked haddock rolls

Schinken [shinken] ham

Schinkenbrötchen [-brurtshen] ham roll

Schinkenröllchen [-rurlshen] rolled ham

Schinkenspeck [-shpeck] bacon

Schinkenwurst [-voorst] ham sausage

Schlachtplatte [shlaKHtplat-uh] selection of fresh sausages

Schlagobers [shlahk-obers] whipped cream

Schlagsahne [-zahn-uh] whipped cream

Schlei [shly] tench

Schmorbraten [shmohrbrahten] pot roast

Schnecken [shnecken] snails

Schnittlauch [shnitt-lowKH] chives

Schnitzel [shnitsel] cutlet

Schokolade [shokolahd-uh] chocolate

Scholle [sholl-uh] plaice

Schollenfilet [-fillay] fillet of plaice

Schulterstück [shoolter-shtOOck] slice of shoulder

Schwarzbrot [shvartsbroht] dark rye bread

Schwarzwälder Kirschtorte [shv**a**rtsvelder k**ee**rshtort-uh] Black Forest gateau

Schwarzwurzeln [-voortseln] salsifies

Schweinebauch [shv**ine**-uh-bowкн] belly of pork

Schweinebraten [-brahten] roast pork

Schweinefilet [-fill**ay**] fillet of pork

Schweinefleisch [-flysh] pork

Schweinekotelett [-kotlet] pork chop

Schweineleber [-layber] pig's liver

Schweinerippe [-ripp-uh] cured pork chop

Schweinerollbraten [-rolbrahten] rolled roast of pork

Schweineschmorbraten [-shmohr-brahten] roast pork

Schweineschnitzel [-shnitsel] pork fillet

Schweinshaxe [shv**ine**-ss-hacks-uh] knuckle of pork

Seelachs [z**ay**lacks] pollack

Seezunge [-tsoong-uh] sole

Sellerie [z**e**lleree] celery

Semmel [z**e**mmel] bread roll

Semmelknödel [-k-nurdel] bread dumplings

Senf [zenf] mustard

Senfsahnesoße [-zahn-uh-zohss-uh] mustard and cream sauce

Senfsoße mustard sauce

serbisches Reisfleisch [z**a**irbishess r**i**ce-flysh] diced pork, onions, tomatoes and rice

Sohle [z**oh**l-uh] sole

Soleier [z**oh**l-ī-er] pickled eggs

Soße [z**oh**ss-uh] sauce; gravy

Spanferkel [shp**ah**n-fairkel] suckling pig

Spargel [shp**a**rgel] asparagus

Spargelcremesuppe [-kraym-zoop-uh] cream of asparagus soup

Spätzle [shp**e**ts-luh] home-made noodles

Speckkartoffeln [shp**e**ck-] potatoes with bacon

Speckknödel [-k-nurdel] bacon dumplings

Speckstreifen [-shrtyfen] strips of bacon

Speisekarte [shp**ize**-uh-kart-uh] menu

Spezialität des Hauses our speciality

Spiegeleier [shp**ee**gel-ī-er] fried eggs

Spieß: am Spieß [shp**ee**ss] on the spit

Spießbraten [shp**ee**ss-brahten] joint roasted on a spit

Spinat [shpin**ah**t] spinach

Spitzkohl [shp**i**ts-] white cabbage

Sprotten [shpr**o**tten] sprats

Stachelbeeren [shtaкнel-bairen] gooseberries

Stangenspargel [sht**a**ngen-shpargel] asparagus spears

Stangen(weiß)brot [sht**a**ngen-(vice-)broht] French bread

Steinbutt [sht**ine**-boott] turbot

Steinpilze [-pilts-uh] type of mushroom
Stollen [shtollen] fruit loaf
Strammer Max [shtrammer] ham and fried egg on bread
Streuselkuchen [shtroyzel-kOOkнen] sponge cake with crumble topping
Sülze [zOOlts-uh] brawn
Suppe [zoop-uh] soup
Suppen soups
Suppengrün [zoopengrOОn] mixed herbs and vegetables (in soup)
Süßigkeiten [zOOssish-kyten] sweets
Süßspeisen [zOOss-shpyzen] sweet dishes
Süßwasserfische [zOOss-vasser-fish-uh] freshwater fish
Szegediner Gulasch [shegaydeener] goulash with pickled cabbage

Tafelspitz [tahfel-shpits] soured boiled rump
Tagesgericht [tahgess-gerisht] dish of the day
Tageskarte [-kart-uh] menu of the day; set menu
Tagessuppe [-zoop-uh] soup of the day
Tatar [tatahr] raw mince with spices
Taube [towb-uh] pigeon
Teigmantel [tike-mantel] pastry covering
Teigwaren [-vahren] pasta
Thunfisch [tOOnfish] tuna

Tintenfisch [-fish] squid
Tomate [tomahtuh] tomato
Tomatensalat [-zalaht] tomato salad
Tomatensuppe [-zoop-uh] tomato soup
Topfen quark
Törtchen [turtshen] tart(s)
Torte [tort-uh] gateau
Trauben [trowben] grapes
Truthahn [trOOt-] turkey

überbacken [OОberbacken] au gratin
Ungarisches Gulasch [oongahrishess] Hungarian goulash

Vanilleeis [vanill-uh-ice] vanilla ice cream
Vanillesoße [-zohss-uh] vanilla sauce
vegetarisch [vegaytahrish] vegetarian
verlorene Eier [fairlohren-uh ī-er] poached eggs
Vollkornbrot [follkornbroht] dark rye bread
vom Grill grilled
vom Kalb veal
vom Lamm lamb
vom Rind beef
vom Rost grilled
vom Schwein pork
vorbereiten to prepare
Vorspeisen [forshpyzen] hors d'œuvres, starters

Waffeln [vaffeln] waffles

Waldmeister [**va**ltmyster] woodruff

Waldorfsalat [**va**ldorf-zal**aht**] salad with celery, apples and walnuts

Wassermelone [**va**sser-mel**ohn**-uh] water melon

Weichkäse [**vy**sh-kayz-uh] soft cheese

Weinbergschnecken [**vine**-bairk-shnecken] snails

Weincreme [**vine**-kraym] pudding with wine

Weinkraut [-krowt] sauerkraut

Weinschaumcreme [-**showm**-kraym] creamed pudding with wine

Weinsoße [-zohss-uh] wine sauce

Weintrauben [-trowben] grapes

Weißbrot [**vice**-broht] white bread

Weißkohl white cabbage

Weißkraut [-krowt] white cabbage

Weißwurst [-voorst] veal sausage

Wiener Schnitzel [**vee**ner shn**itsel**] veal in breadcrumbs

Wiener Würstchen [**vo̅o̅**rstshen] frankfurter(s)

Wild [vilt] game

Wildbret [-brayt] venison

Wildgerichte venison dishes

Wildschweinkeule [**vi**ltshvine-koyl-uh] haunch of wild boar

Wildschweinsteak wild boar steak

Windbeutel [**vi**ntboytel] cream puff

Wirsing [**vee**rzing] savoy cabbage

Wurst [voorst] sausage

Wurstbrötchen [-brurtshen] roll with sausage meat

Würstchen [**vo̅o̅**rstshen] frankfurter(s)

Wurstplatte [**vo̅o̅**rst-plat-uh] selection of sausages

Wurstsülze [-zo̅o̅lts-uh] sausage brawn

Würzfleisch [-flysh] spicy meat

Zander [tsander] pike-perch, zander

Zartbitterschokolade [tsartbitter-shokol**ahd**-uh] plain chocolate

Ziegenkäse [ts**ee**gen-kayz-uh] goat's cheese

Zigeunerschnitzel [tsig**oy**ner-shnitsel] veal or pork with peppers and relishes

Zitrone [tsitr**ohn**-uh] lemon

Zucchini [tsook**ee**nee] courgettes, zucchini

Zucker [ts**oo**cker] sugar

Zuckererbsen [-airpsen] mangetout peas

Zunge [ts**oo**ng-uh] tongue

Zwiebel [tsv**ee**bel] onion

Zwiebelringe [-ring-uh] onion rings

Zwiebelrostbraten [-rostbrahten] steak with fried onions

Zwiebelsuppe [-zoop-uh] onion soup

Zwiebeltorte [-tort-uh] onion tart

Zwischengerichte entrées

Menu Reader: Drink

Essential Terms

beer das Bier

bottle die Flasche [fla**sh**-uh]

brandy der Weinbrand [**vine**-brant]

coffee der Kaffee [**kaff**ay]

cup: a cup of ... eine Tasse ... [**ine**-uh ta**ss**-uh]

fruit juice der Fruchtsaft [fro**oKH**tzaft]

gin der Gin

 a gin and tonic einen Gin Tonic [**ine**-en]

glass: a glass of ... ein Glas ... [ine glahss]

milk die Milch [milsh]

mineral water das Mineralwasser [miner**ahl**vasser]

orange juice der Orangensaft [o**ronj**en-zaft]

red wine der Rotwein [**roh**tvine]

rosé der Roséwein [rohz**ay**-vine]

soda (water) das Sodawasser [**zoh**da-vasser]

soft drink das alkoholfreie Getränk [alkoh**ohl**fry-uh get**renk**], der
 Soft drink

sugar der Zucker [ts**oo**cker]

tea der Tee [tay]

tonic (water) das Tonic

vodka der Wodka [**vo**dka]

water das Wasser [**va**sser]

whisky der Whisky

white wine der Weißwein [**vice**-vine]

wine der Wein [vine]

wine list die Weinkarte [**vine**-kart-uh]

another ..., please noch ein ..., bitte [noKH ine ... **bitt**-uh]

alkoholfreies Bier [alkoh**ohl**fry-ess beer] alcohol-free beer

Alsterwasser [-vasser] shandy

Alt(bier) [alt(beer)] light brown beer, not sweet

Apfelsaft [**a**pfelzaft] apple juice

Apfelschorle [-shorl-uh] sparkling apple juice

Apfelwein [-vine] cider

Äppelwoi [**e**ppelvoy] cider

Auslese [**ow**sslayz-uh] wine selected from ripest bunches of grapes in top wine category

Ausschankwein [**ow**ss-shank-vine] wine by the glass

Bananenmilch [ban**ah**nen-milsh] banana milk shake

Beerenauslese [**bai**ren-owsslayz-uh] wine from specially selected single grapes in top wine category

Berliner Weiße [bairl**ee**ner vice-uh] fizzy beer

Bier [beer] beer

Bockbier [**bock**beer] strong beer

Bowle [**bohl**-uh] punch

Buttermilch [**boo**ttermilsh] buttermilk

Cidre [**seed**-ruh] cider

Doppelkorn grain schnapps

Eierlikör [**ier**-likur] advocaat

Eiswein [**ice**-vine] wine made from grapes picked after frost

entkoffeiniert [entkoffay-een**eert**] decaffeinated

Erdbeermilch [**airt**bair-milsh] strawberry milk shake

Erzeugerabfüllung estate bottled

Federweißer [**fay**der-vysser] new wine

Feuerzangenbowle [**foy**er-tsangen-bohl-uh] red wine punch with rum which has been flamed off

Flasche [**flash**-uh] bottle

Flaschenwein [**flash**en-vine] bottled wine

fruchtig [froo**KH**tish] fruity

Fruchtsaft [froo**KH**tzaft] fruit juice

Gespritzter [geshpr**it**ster] wine and soda, spritzer

Getränke beverages

Glühwein [gl**oo**-vine] mulled wine

Grog hot water with rum and sugar

halbsüß [**halp**-z**oo**ss] semi-sweet

halbtrocken [**halp**-] medium dry

Hefeweizen [**hayf**-uh-vytsen] fizzy beer made with yeast and wheat

Heidelbeergeist [**hy**delbair-gyst] blueberry brandy

heiße Zitrone [**hice**-uh tsitr**ohn**-uh] hot lemon

heiße Milch [**hice**-uh milsh] hot milk

Helles [**hell**ess] lager
herb [hairp] very dry
Himbeergeist [**h**imbair-gyst]
raspberry brandy

Jahrgang [**yah**rgang] vintage

Kabinett light, usually dry,
wine in top wine category
Kaffee [kaff**ay**] coffee
Kaffee mit Milch [milsh] white
coffee
Kakao [kak**ow**] cocoa; hot
chocolate
Kännchen (Kaffee) [**k**ennshen
(kaff**ay**)] pot (of coffee)
Kellerei [**k**eller-**ī**] (wine)
producer's
Kir [keer] white wine with a
dash of blackcurrant liqueur
Kir Royal [roy**ahl**] champagne
with a dash of blackcurrant
liqueur
koffeinfrei [koffay-**ee**n-fry]
decaffeinated
Kognak [**k**onyak] brandy
Korn type of schnapps
Kräuterlikör [**k**royterlikur] herbal
liqueur
Kräutertee [-tay] herbal tea
Krimsekt [**k**rimzekt] Crimean
champagne

Landwein [**l**antvine] country
wine
Likör [lik**ur**] liqueur
Limo [**lee**mo] lemonade
Limonade [limon**ah**d-uh]
lemonade

Liter [**lee**ter] litre

Malzbier [**m**altsbeer] sweet
stout
Maß [mahss] litre of beer
(Bavaria)
Milchmixgetränk [milshmix-
getrenk] milkshake
Mineralwasser [miner**ah**l-vasser]
sparkling mineral water
mischen [**m**ishen] to mix
Mokka mocha
Most [mosst] fruit wine

Nektar fruit squash
neuer Wein [**n**oyer vine] new
wine

Obstler [**oh**pstler] fruit
schnapps
offener Wein [vine] wine by
the glass
Orangensaft [or**o**nJenzaft]
orange juice

Pikkolo quarter bottle of
champagne
Portwein [-vine] port
Pulverkaffee [**p**oolver-kaffay]
instant coffee

Qualitätswein b.A. quality
wine from a special wine-
growing area
Qualitätswein m.P. top quality
German wine

Radler(maß) [**rah**tler-mahss]
shandy

Rosé(wein) [rohzay(vine)] rosé wine

Rotwein [rohtvine] red wine

Saft [zaft] juice

Schokolade [shokolahd-uh] chocolate

Schokomilch [shoko-milsh] chocolate milk shake

schwarzer Tee [shvartser tay] tea

Sekt [zekt] sparkling wine, champagne

Spezi [shpaytsee] cola and lemonade

Spirituosen spirits

Sprudel(wasser) [shprool (-vasser)] mineral water

Steinhäger® [shtine-hayger] type of schnapps

Sturm [shtoorm] new wine

Tafelwasser [tahfel-vasser] still mineral water

Tafelwein [tahfelvine] table wine

Tee [tay] tea

Trinkwasser [-vasser] drinking water

trocken dry

vollmundig [fol-moondish] full-bodied

vom Faß [fom fass] draught

Wasser [vasser] water

Wein [vine] wine

Weinberg [vinebairk] vineyard

Weinbrand [vine-brant] brandy

Weingut [-goot] wine-growing estate

Weinkarte [-kart-uh] wine list

Weinkeller [-keller] wine cellar

Weinkellerei [-keller-ī] wine producer's

weiß [vice] white

Weißbier [vicebeer] fizzy, light-coloured beer made with wheat

Weißherbst [-hairpst] type of rosé wine

Weißwein [-vine] white wine

Weizenbier [vytsenbeer] wheat beer

Zitronentee [tsitrohnen-tay] lemon tea

Zwetschenwasser [tsvetshen-vasser] plum brandy